Managing Magic: The Government's UFO Disclosure Project

Grant Cameron
with
Katarina Castillo

Copyright © 2017 by Grant Cameron

Cover Produced by Matt Lacasse. Girl pictured on front cover is Natalie Castillo Urrego.

All rights reserved.

No part of this publication may be reproduced, distributed, or transmitted in any form or by any means, including photocopying, recording, or other electronic or mechanical methods, without the prior written permission of the publisher, except in the case of brief quotations embodied in critical reviews and certain other noncommercial uses permitted by copyright law. For permission requests, write to the publisher, addressed "Attention: Permissions Coordinator," at the address below.

Printed in the United States of America

First Printing, February 2017

ISBN-13: 978-1542857697

ISBN-10: 1542857694

Itsallconnected Publishing
445 Hudson Street
Winnipeg, Manitoba
Canada R3T OR1

whitehouseufo@gmail.com

Table of Contents
Page

Note on Terminology 1
Note on Classification 4
Introduction 7
The Disclosure Story 15
The 64 Reasons 17
Disclosure Efforts 1940-1950 45
Disclosure Efforts 1950-1960 50
Disclosure Efforts 1960-1970 63
Disclosure Efforts 1970-1980 64
Disclosure Efforts 1980-1990 92
Disclosure Efforts 1990-2000 126
Disclosure Efforts 2000-2015 144
The Wiki-Leaks UFO Story 162
    John Podesta 163
    John Podesta - The UFO Queries 170
The Tom DeLonge Disclosure Story 194
    The Greer DeLonge Quandary 202
    DeLonge and Disinformation 203
    The Cargo Cult Theory 207
    Alien False Flag 211
Evil Aliens 215
The Three Kings 227
    The Big Meeting 228
    Podesta Makes a Supporting Statement 230
    And so, what happened? 232
Additional Tales 233
    Has the President Been Abducted? 233
    The MJ-12 Group 236

A Plan for Accelerated Acclimatization 247
The Future of Disclosure 266
Conclusion 273
Final Word 287
Appendix 1 - The Illusion of Deaths by Religion........................290
Appendix 2 - MJ-12 Document Leaks..292
Appendix 3 - The Five Messiahs 293
Appendix 4 - The Fourteen Magicians 297
Appendix 5 - The Defense Intelligence Agency Connection 310
Appendix 6 - Revision of "True" Article on Flying Saucers.......314
Appendix 7 - Donald Trump and the ETs 318
Index 332
Endnotes 337

Note on Terminology

Words mean a lot in the UFO community. This attitude of using the correct terminology is stressed a lot in the community, and it is safe to say there is a bit of an anal attitude surrounding this, and many people are adamant about using the right terminology when discussing UFOs.

That, however, does not mean that there is any agreement on which terms to use. There isn't. There is a constant chatter by opposing sides that the opposing side is using the wrong words.

This is especially true in 2017 as the latest gradual disclosure unfolds. I predict that there will be a battle of words and definitions that will rival the divisiveness of the 2016 American election.

The biggest fight seems to be over the term UFO (unidentified flying object) itself. It was a term developed by the USAF in 1952, in an attempt to stop the public from using the more commonly used terms flying saucers and flying discs. Those two words, it was felt, implied the objects were of an extraterrestrial origin, and in a situation requiring secrecy and deception, such use was unacceptable.

The term UFO implies something unknown and unidentifiable, and that is exactly the way the Air Force wanted it. Press people confronting the Air Force with UFO sightings could now believe the phenomena was unknown and unidentified, but not extraterrestrial.

The Air Force likes the term, but many in the UFO community hate it. They think that the term is one of derision, and that science and the media will never take us seriously as long as we continue to employ it.

Now, researchers use new terms such as UAP (unidentified aerial phenomena). In this way, people fool themselves into believing that by using the term UAP scientists' study of the phenomena commands more respect. On the other side of the coin, you find researchers who hate the term UFO and prefer the term extraterrestrial. They claim there is nothing "unidentified" about it at all.

In this book, I will use the word UFO. I use it not to imply what the phenomenon is or isn't. I simply use it because when you use the word UFO, there is no question by the man on the street as to what you mean. One hundred years from now when we know what the origin of the phenomena is, and people accept it, it will be time to change the term. In 2017 it remains a UFO in the public's mind.

This position is even backed up by the top military advisor in touch with rock musician Tom DeLonge, whose story appears in the last section of this book. One of the key things this military official pointed out to DeLonge in four pages of notes on how to talk with the public about the subject was "stop calling it the phenomena. Call it UFOs, so people will know what you are talking about."

The second term that causes political turmoil in the UFO community is the term alien. It is hated almost as much as UFO. Everyone in the community has some sort slant to what they think the intelligence is and they insist that everyone reflect their personal take on it.

Many insist on the term ET or extraterrestrial. Some in the love and light crowd insist on using the words "benevolent visitors" or some such variations.

The other terms people argue about are abduction versus visitation. Abduction implies something being done against your will, whereas visitation involves a more respectful encounter.

I have my personal take on what the intelligence is, but I will not push it in this book. I will use the word alien, because on the street when you say "aliens are flying around in a UFO" everyone knows what you are saying.

The most significant term now seems to be disclosure. Most everyone in the UFO community envisions disclosure as the president having a special news conference to announce we are not alone in the universe, and that there is nothing to fear. Others envision an alternate scenario where perhaps a UFO crashes in New York and the public captures the images on their iPhones and thus the secret can no longer be kept, or else aliens land on the White House lawn to announce they come in peace or are taking over the country. That I would define as full disclosure, where the milk is spilled, and cannot be put back in the glass.

Disclosure by definition simply means to reveal, or to disclose something that is secret.

This book will discuss disclosure and how politicians have attempted to address it. For example, when Hillary Clinton said, "They may already be here," or when her husband Bill said, "If we were visited someday, I wouldn't be surprised," that is a type of disclosure.

Those comments can be considered as disclosure because the Clintons are the first high level politicians to hint that aliens can come here or that they may already be here, as opposed to saying "I believe there is life out there but we will never see it."

In this sense, every leak by the government, every movie in Hollywood that has an alien theme, and every UFO joke by the president is a type of disclosure. Disclosure is happening all the time. The things revealed may be small and inconspicuous, but I believe they are part of a plan that was discussed in a think tank years ago and is in the best interests of the people.

Finally, I have used the word paranormal to describe what the UFO phenomenon is because the word paranormal just means beyond what we consider to be normal. Anything beyond the little box of what we believe is real will by definition be unknown and appear as mysterious, and even magical until we know how it works.

Some may disagree with my approach to these terms. I understand their concerns and where they stand on the issue.

Note on Classification

For the reader to keep the accounts in this book in perspective, security classification has to be understood and carefully considered every time there is an apparent leak in government regarding the UFO secret.

One of the key reasons Hillary Clinton lost the 2016 election was because of the private email server that she had while serving as Secretary of State for the United States government. Every time she tried to put the issue to bed it was revived by Wiki-Leaks and then the FBI.

The general impression among voters was that it was the private email server that initiated the calls at Trump rallies to "Lock her Up...Lock Her Up." During one of the presidential debates, Trump stated that if he won, he would initiate an investigation to put Hillary in jail over the email server issue. Even after Trump won, he and his top surrogates declared they still might charge Hillary and send her to jail.

Having private email accounts and servers are not the issue. Former secretaries of state had used private email accounts before. Everyone, except maybe Donald Trump, has a private email account.

The issue rather was the claim, as supported in part by the FBI, that classified material was being *sent* to a private server, thereby breaking the laws that govern the handling of classified material. According to 18 U.S. Code § 798 – "Disclosure of classified information,"

> *Whoever knowingly and wilfully communicates, furnishes, transmits, or otherwise makes available to an unauthorized person, or publishes, or uses in any manner prejudicial to the safety or interest of the United States or for the benefit of any foreign government to the detriment of the United States any classified information...Shall be fined under this title or imprisoned not more than ten years, or both.*

The "lock her up" chants had to do with Hillary leaking classified material, not the email server itself. Security is taken very seriously by the United States government.

To understand what happens when classified material is leaked, all one has to do is look back to the case of Stephen Jin-Woo Kim. He was a former State Department contractor who after a four-year court battle pleaded guilty in 2014 to a felony count of disclosing classified information to Fox News reporter James Rosen. The "disclosing of information" was really a 12-minute conversation outside the state department, where Kim told the reporter what was already common knowledge and a consensus on the street that the North Koreans were planning a nuclear test. Kim leaked no documents.

He received a sentence of 13 months which would have been 15 years if he had not taken the plea bargain. Kim and his parents ended up financially destroyed. Kim described that after his arrest, he thought of killing himself every day. That is what happens when someone leaks classified material.

Therefore, of the many explanations that might account for the revelations in this book, *the least likely explanation* is that someone has violated their security oath and is wandering around leaking classified information, with the government is doing nothing to stop it.

In 2013, a man appeared on tape at the Citizen's Hearing in Washington claiming to be a former CIA officer who had had a meeting with Eisenhower. In that meeting, Eisenhower complained that he couldn't get inside Area 51 and he wanted the man and his boss to go in and deliver a message that the president would invade with the army if they continued to obstruct him.

When asked if he was now talking about classified information, he replied that there were 40 and 50-year rules on classification and that now that over 50 years had elapsed, he could talk about it.

The problem with that testimony is that there is no such thing as a 40 or 50-year rule. Things remain classified until they are no longer a threat to national security.

If the 50-year rule existed, we would have declassified Roswell documents along with the knowledge of how to build an atomic bomb. There will never be a declassification of the papers on building an atom bomb, and no one who worked on it will ever be allowed to talk about it openly.

In a small attempt to verify this, I contacted the Truman Library and found out that after 64 years, the library still has 20,000 pages of documents which remain *classified*. A similar request to the Eisenhower Library, with a collection that is at least 56 years old, showed that 250,000 documents remain *classified*.

There are scores of people who have claimed they have received classified information on UFOs, despite the fact that they are not authorized to see them. They claim they are getting the material without any repercussions.

Why would that be? In light of people prosecuted for espionage offences, it does not seem possible. I believe it is happening because it is a purposeful dissemination of true/false information disguised as "classified information." I detail many such accounts in this book.

In this book, I mention some CIA officials and officers who were involved in the gradual disclosure of the UFO story. They are not exempt from the rules dealing with classification.

Everyone attached to the agency must sign a CIA Secrecy Agreement, Form 368. It states that before releasing anything while working for the agency, or after they leave, that the material must be reviewed by the agency:

> *I contemplate disclosing publicly or that I have actually prepared for public disclosure, either during my employment...or at any time thereafter, prior to discussing it or showing it to anyone who is not authorized to have access.... I further agree that I will not take any steps toward public disclosure until I have received written permission to do so from the Central Intelligence Agency.*

The rule applies even when no classified material is involved "if the material is unnecessarily close to or draws undue attention to sensitive material."

Courts have held that this signed agreement is a lifetime enforceable contract and that the secrecy agreement is a prior restraint of First Amendment freedom.

This rule means that the chances of officers running around telling everything they know, without having cleared it with the CIA, are slim to none.

It also means that all leaked UFO documents are not real. They have probably modified versions of the originals or documents composed partly of real information. This scheme provides plausible deniability.

All classification is controlled by the President, so all direction is from the White House.

Introduction

"*If we wanted you dead, you would have been dead ten years ago. We don't do that kind of thing anymore...*" **A High-level intelligence official talking to a key person and friend of mine in the UFO community.**

Compiling the "facts" is complicated by the participation of so many criminally minded individuals and the inability of honest people to sort between fact, fantasy, and criminality as well as the tendency of the mentally ill to distort or invent to fill in detail or bend to their delusions. False information was injected into just about every source of information. You can collect a large assortment of documents, but compiling the "facts" is another matter. **Ron Pandolfi posting on Open Minds Forum**.

For those who are new to the UFO research world or those who have followed the rumors, hopes, and discussions about UFO disclosure, let me point out that UFO disclosure, like the UFO story itself, has a long history.

I recall this like it was yesterday - it was late 1988, and I was having snail mail discussions with Florida reporter Billy Cox about rumors of possible imminent disclosure by Ronald Reagan of the ET presence.

On October 18, 1988, just weeks before the election, a TV documentary called "UFO Cover-up?... Live" had been broadcast. The rumor in the UFO community was that the documentary would contain revelations about actual UFO knowledge held by the government regarding the UFO question.

Later the website Alien Zoo described the build-up:

> *Anticipation ran high. Promotions for the show were everywhere as we waited to see the live [broadcast television] connection they promised with a prominent Soviet ufologist, who would announce on U.S. TV that Soviet scientists accepted the ET presence and that many UFOs are ETs interstellar vehicles. Mike Farrell was the master of ceremonies of the show that was produced by Tracy Torme. The*

cast was a showcase of many of the best-known faces in Ufology at that time.[1]

The documentary did introduce some new ideas such as the idea of Area 51, a live alien being a guest of the US government, and a flow chart of the departments that make up the government UFO program. The biggest rumor I recall, however, was the story about the final day of Reagan's presidency.

Reagan had a reputation of being a bit obsessed with paranormal things like UFOs, ghosts, and astrology. In fact, it was revealed while he was in office that a psychic astrologer hired by Nancy Reagan was setting the president's schedule.

The story that I and others waited for would occur on the last day before Reagan left office. The rumor was that Reagan would appear on TV with a live alien held in a secure compound near the Washington Mall.

In the end, Reagan did not appear with the alien and UFO research went on unperturbed by the failure of the prediction. That is how ufology works. It moves from one disclosure rumor to the next. Slowly, through leaks and rumors, knowledge of the ET presence grows. Meanwhile, the classified aspects of the UFO story remain safe.

When viewed moment to moment, UFO research appears as a total failure by researchers to separate the wheat from the chaff. However, seen over the span of 70 years in the modern era, it is evident our understanding has come a long way from 1947, the year of Roswell.

The belief systems we now have about UFO reality result not just from the work of UFO researchers, but one 'government leak' after another. Ideas in society grow, but with no official confirmations by governments.

The best example of this is Area 51. Accounts surfaced of UFOs being back-engineered at Area 51 in October 1988 in the documentary mentioned above, but the government did not even acknowledge Area 51 existed until decades later.

Then, in November of 1988, as George H.W. Bush was preparing to take over the White House, they set up a physicist by the name of Bob Lazar so he could disseminate the idea of flying saucers at Area 51.

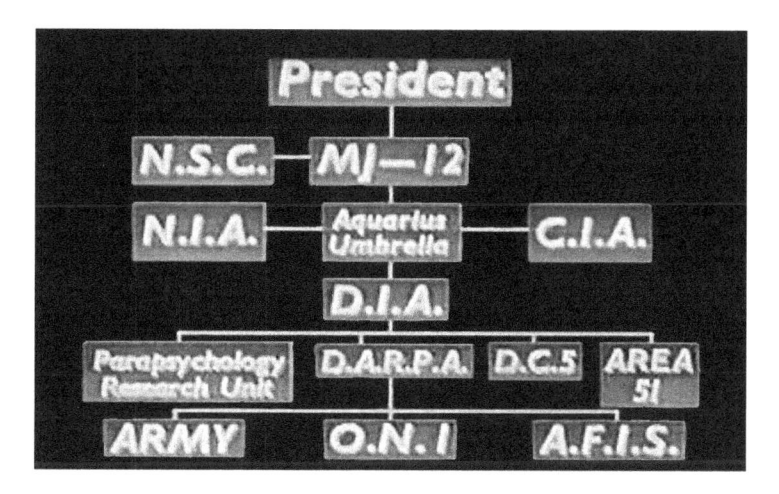

Figure 1- UFO organizational flow chart that appeared on 1988 documentary called *UFO Cover-up? Live.*

Lazar was friends with UFO researcher and famous pilot John Lear. Lear had gotten interested in UFOs and had heard UFO work was going on at the base. Earlier, Lear had revealed that the base had a Soviet MIG concealed there and provided the lead to KLAS-TV in Las Vegas, who broke the story.

In early 1989, Lear returned to KLAS to get them to cover the UFO story, but the news producer wanted nothing to do with it and said if something like that were going on, he would have heard about it. George Knapp, a reporter there, overheard the conversation and talked to Lear.

Not only was Lear saying there were UFOs at Groom Lake, but he was also promoting much more controversial theories about underground bases and firefights with aliens, which made people view Lear as a gullible researcher. The stage was ready.

When Lazar went for a job interview at Area 51, the first question in the second interview was "What is your relationship to John Lear and what do you think of him?" It was immediately apparent that Area 51 officials knew that Lazar and Lear were friends.

Logically, their prevailing friendship should have eliminated Lazar from being placed in the area where UFO research/back-engineering was taking place, but that is right where they placed him. Not only that. On his second day at work, Lazar was provided with around 125 documents, and the documents contained several accounts of the U.S. government's Top-Secret UFO program.

The idea was that Lazar would take the story to Lear and Lear would reveal what he knew to the world, and the public would ignore it thinking, "That's just another of John Lear's crazy stories."

The story, however, would circulate quickly, and become part of the modern UFO myth, while the UFO back-engineering work at Area 51 would continue unaffected.

Most stories leaked into the UFO community go well, but this one got out of control.

What the government didn't anticipate was that George Knapp, a respected Emmy Award-winning investigative reporter, would invite Lazar as a guest on his show in March 1989. Indeed, Knapp had an open spot and asked Lear if his buddy, who used to work at the base, could come on.

That back-lit interview Knapp did with Lazar went viral. The next thing the government knew, tour buses were going up into the mountains. The people on the tours were now looking down over the most secret base in the world, hoping to see the government testing a UFO. Now everything done at the base became the interest of the public, thanks to Knapp's interview with Lazar.

Bill Clinton was forced to issue a Presidential Determination which kept the curious citizens back and tried to prevent them from seeing anything close up.

Eventually, the story died down. The UFO community became convinced there were UFOs at the base. The media had a good unproven story, and the government continued with their secret work unaffected.

The skeptical side of the UFO community saw the Area 51 story in a different light. To them, it did not mean that there were aliens or alien technology at Area 51 but viewed the UFO accounts as a way the U.S. government was trying to throw the Soviet Union off track, keeping them from knowing what the black ops people were really up to at the base.

The immediate question to that argument is: How did the skeptic's argument work out?

It didn't work out because it was a stupid argument. The Soviets were not idiots, and American intelligence was not trying to throw them off. The Soviets had spy satellites that flew over Area 51 every day, and they had a much better idea of what was going on there than the American people did.

It was the American people's consciousness the government was trying to influence, and it's a plan that they have been executing for years.

Those who are in charge of the UFO cover-up are not corrupt government intelligence officials who get up every morning and spend all day trying to screw around with UFO researchers. They, in reality, don't spend five minutes a year thinking about UFO researchers.

The people who are running the cover-up are themselves engaged in the mystery and trying to make a difference.

After Roswell in 1947, they discovered the biggest scientific mystery and public relations nightmare one could imagine. The problem was one which they would have to figure out in secret. The technology involved in the flying saucers was so advanced that it provided the ultimate mystery to unravel. It also created the challenge of keeping the technology out of the hands of enemies who in their opinion would use it to kill Americans.

The UFO research community, on the contrary, realized that there was sufficient evidence to conclude that there was some non-human intelligence visiting the Earth and that military and government officials knew it.

Significant numbers of researchers made calls to the United States government to disclose what they knew, and I supported the researchers in their demands for transparency on the UFO issue.

My mind was changed significantly when for the first time, I met with Robert Emenegger. In the early 1970s, while working as a Vice President of Grey Advertising in Los Angeles, Emenegger, and his partner Allan Sandler, were officially approached by the Department of Defense and were asked to do a documentary on UFOs.

Representatives informed them that they could do interviews with government officials, and use film of UFOs taken by NASA and the military. More importantly, they got access to video footage of an alien craft landing at Holloman Air Force Base, where beings left the ship and interacted with base officials.

The two men proceeded with their documentary and had no problem talking to anyone they wanted to talk to, including one high-level CIA official. They entered the Pentagon without signing in and were allowed to drive around the highly-secured Holloman base looking at whatever they wished.

Emenegger maintained and still contends that there is no cover-up because the government held back nothing from him.

His story, which he has told me many times, in the same way, raised a new hypothesis in my mind as to what was going on. It seemed clear that those in charge of the cover-up were allowing pieces of the story to leak.

Why else would Emenegger be told seemingly classified things starting in 1973, when in 1969 the United States government had shut down USAF Project Blue Book after two decades of UFO research stating that nothing was going on?

The Air Force Blue Book report concluded:

1. No UFO reported, investigated and evaluated by the Air Force was ever an indication of threat to our national security;
2. There was no evidence submitted to or discovered by the Air Force that sightings categorized as "unidentified" represented technological developments or principles beyond the range of modern scientific knowledge; and
3. There was no evidence indicating that sightings categorized as "unidentified" were extraterrestrial vehicles.

The report successfully killed the UFO questions and released the government from the public affairs problem that came with it. This process is a procedure that every other western country has now followed.

The government never had to talk about UFOs again. The public relations nightmare was over. The research on UFOs could now continue in black unacknowledged special access programs, in the same way that the remote viewing program would be shut down in 1995, killing the paper trail, and allowing highly classified work to continue outside the gaze of the public.

Why then would Emenegger and Sandler be dragged to Norton Air Force Base in 1973, where the military stored all of its film, to be asked to do a UFO documentary with $250,000 that would be "given" to them by the MacArthur Foundation?

The event effectively threw gasoline on the almost dead embers of the 1969 Air Force UFO report, written three years earlier. The offer to support a documentary with government films and photos, cooperation with administration officials, and hundreds of thousands of dollars, showed that something had changed from 1969 to 1972.

The Emenegger account was evidence that something new was happening. The question is – what was the government doing?

There are three possible options for what the government was doing in 1972 and still appears to be doing in 2017.

Plan 1: A Government Cover-up - The government plan might be to cover-up and bury the UFO story. If that were the case, their actions would be to simply shut up about the subject and never talk about it again.

Canada, as an example, released all their UFO sighting files in 1967, announced they would no longer investigate UFOs, and then completely shut up.

Unlike the United States, in Canada, there have been no whistleblowers, government rumors about underground bases, or leaked documents. Government UFO researchers in Canada have nothing to research or research. The lack of any discussion on the part of the Canadian government makes it look like they might, in fact, not be involved anymore.

If there is a cover-up, it is a cover-up of what the Canadians described in a 1950 Top Secret memo to be the "**most highly classified subject in the United States.**"

The release of that information is punishable by ten years in jail for every item leaked.

The amount of "seemingly" leaked material that I will point out in this book strongly indicates that there is no full cover-up going on. There have been no UFO related prosecutions, and it is very evident that officials are aware of the UFO leaks, and where they originate.

Plan 2: The Disclosure Plan - The second possibility is that the United States government is preparing for full disclosure. This theory is flawed from the start because they would not be leaking bits and pieces of unsupported stories into the public domain.

If the plan were to disclose, the president would just stand in front of the White House press corps and announce whatever the truth is behind the UFO mystery. If the government wanted full disclosure, they would take the editor of the *The New York Times* and *The Washington Post* to an underground base and show them a downed saucer and alien bodies. Then they would provide whatever statements, photos, and documents required to do a front-page article with the truth. What has been going on for 70 years does not fit this scenario.

Plan 3: An Acclimatization Plan - The third possibility is that over an extended period of time, they are preparing the population with the knowledge that we are not alone in the universe. When the evidence gets a fair review, it seems apparent that there is some long-term acclimatization plan going on, and that is the subject of this book.

This book is a review of what the U.S. government is doing to reveal the UFO story to the public, why it is being done the way that it is, and what was the final plan.

The United States government has not shut up and remained quiet as in Plan 1. They have not made a disclosure announcement as in Plan 2, so they are obviously doing something in between.

Once the actions of the United States government are seen as a possible gradual disclosure or acclimatization event, the things they have done, and continue to do, start to make sense.

Here is the story of what they did, and perhaps why they did it.

Section 1
The Plan to Manage Magic

The Disclosure Story

How are the American people ever going to know what the truth is? How are they going to know what the truth is about what we are doing and we have done over the years? We operate in secrecy, we deal in deception and disinformation, and then we burn our files. How will the historians ever be able to learn the complete truth about what we've done in these various operations, these operations that have had such a major impact on so many important events in history? **Senior officer talking to CIA officer Victor Marchetti in 1957.**

I couldn't answer him, then. And I can't answer him now. I don't know how the American people will ever really know the truth about the many things that the CIA has been involved in. Or how they will ever know the truth about the great historical events of our times. The government is continually writing and rewriting history -- often with the CIA's help -- to suit its own purposes. **Victor Marchetti**

President Roosevelt appears to be the first United States president to have faced the UFO mystery. By all accounts, the UFO technology discovered dwarfed anything that anyone had or could even imagine. The discovery must have been like finding magic. It was magic that could undoubtedly be employed for advances in technology, or to defeat the evil enemies of the United States. All that was needed was to keep it quiet until someone figured out how the magic worked.

The story of the controlled efforts by the United States government to reveal the ET presence on Earth has been told for many years, going back to even before the modern UFO era. Like other secrets held by the government, a process had been developed to keep the cat in the bag.

Victor Marchetti, a former special assistant to the Deputy Director of the Central Intelligence Agency, stated, "The government is continually writing and rewriting history -- often with the CIA's help --

to suit its own purposes." This book is an attempt to document the story the government and the CIA have written about UFOs.

What is certain is that the United States government is purposefully telling the story behind the UFO mystery, and they are the only country in the world doing it.

The story that the government has been telling is not what most UFO researchers want. What UFO disclosure advocates want is the president or someone in authority to stand up and say ETs are here, or UFOs are real. What they have gotten is a gradual storyline unraveling, where the skeptics and disbelievers can still walk away with their beliefs intact.

Rarely discussed are the fact that the aliens have done the same thing. They have contacted many people, usually one on one. They have shown their ships to many people and done some weird stuff, which has convinced the majority of society to believe that something paranormal is going on.

They have not landed on the White House lawn and announced their existence. They have rarely given an experiencer an instrument or photo they could use as proof. What they have done, in short, is the same thing the government has done.

They have dropped a trail of breadcrumbs that make it look more and more likely every day that we earthlings are not alone in the universe. It has been, like the government's 70+ year involvement - a gradual disclosure.

This action by the aliens leads to the possibility that the government and intelligent life forms are working together on the disclosure, or that the government is imitating what they see the aliens doing.

The only one who can disclose the truth behind the UFO mystery, as the government understands it, is the president of the United States. Anyone below the president, unless the disclosure is approved by the president, in in violation of leaking classified material, where they face the Hillary Clinton jail dilemma.

Thirteen presidents have dealt with the UFO problem, and all have done the same thing. That action appears to be secrecy with a gradual release of information to acclimatize the population to the fact we are not alone.

The 64 Reasons

The American government is taking the lead on this measured disclosure. When the facts get reviewed, this becomes very evident.

Many have written and stated that other countries have disclosed the truth about UFOs and that the American government has not. The argument is that they should follow suit. Neither statement is true.

First, all the governments that usually get named such as Canada, Brazil, Britain, Australia, New Zealand, Russia, Japan, Ireland, France, Chile, and Denmark have only released files regarding sightings. They have not made any official disclosure announcements. No Secret, Top Secret, and Above Top Secret files have been published by any country, except for one Top Secret document declassified by the Department of Transport in Canada.

All the governments in question have released their sighting files and letters to the government on UFOs from citizens. Releasing sighting data is not disclosure. It is, in fact, just the opposite. It is part of a plan to cover up the actual knowledge of what they know. Let me cite two examples.

The first example is the "disclosure" that some believe is going on in Britain. It is the latest country doing what is effectively a document dump.

For 70 years, the British government kept their sighting reports away from the eyes of the public. Then, in October 2008, they started to release thousands of pages of UFO documents. None of these were Top Secret. None of the documents were policy documents about how the UFO subject is to be investigated and controlled. There are no aircraft gun camera footage or crash reports.

It was interpreted as a government preparing to tell its surreptitious UFO story. In reality, it was the British government shutting down its UFO desk so that it can operate outside the view of the public.

The government statement was very clear, "Please note it is no longer MoD policy to record, respond to, or investigate UFO sightings. The MoD has no opinion on the existence or otherwise of extra-terrestrial life. However, in over 50 years, no UFO report has revealed any evidence of a potential threat to the United Kingdom."

Other governments made the same sort of statement as Britain. They stated that the UFO files they hold don't prove anything. The report then indicates that the government in question is no longer investigating UFOs.

The report put out by the Denmark military, for example, said, "We decided to publish the archives because frankly there is nothing really secret in them. The Air Force has no interest in keeping unusual sightings a secret. Our job is to maintain national security, not investigate UFOs."

The president or prime minister who makes the ET reality announcement will face numerous fallouts, such as having his entire political agenda overrun by the ET issue.

Finally, although the 64 reasons deal with the United States government, many of the reasons apply to all the countries of the world.

Often people will describe the cover-up as simply the evil American military industrial complex shutting down the truth. This irrational conspirational view seems almost foolish because 14 admnistrations have done the same thing and could not all be evil.

The focus on the Ameican military is a very American centric view of the world as if the United States is the only country in the world. There is a total of 196 countries, and they are all not controlled by the American military industrial complex.

They too have encountered the UFO phenomena, and they too are covering up. Therefore, many of the reasons listed have nothing to do with the American military industrial complex and illustrate the reasons behind the silence are very complex and wide ranging.

The Reasons and Excuses

....

The following are a list of 64 reasons/excuses that might be stopping the United States government from disclosing the full truth about the UFO mystery.

The list does not imply that this is why the cover-up is taking place. It is simply a list of considerations that briefers might have come up with for continuing the cover-up when presenting the UFO problem to a new president.

The fact is that 14 United States presidents (7 Democrat and 7 Republican) have dealt with the UFO mystery, and everyone has done the same thing – cover-up. There must be a reason they all believed secrecy was justified. The silence is especially visible because some of the presidents taking power such as Ford and Carter were very pro-UFO disclosure when taking office.

The list is just my speculation as to the possible reasons/excuses given to the president that caused people like Carter and Ford to go along with the cover-up.

1. **Mass shock and world-wide panic:** When I first put this list together in 2009, I put the idea of panic way down the list believing that, as John Podesta has stated, "People can handle the truth." I have now moved it back to the top of the list.

Despite the notion that society has matured, the government knows that shock and panic would be the order of the day. People did panic during 911 and during the 2003 Northeast blackout. Even President George W. Bush panicked in the hours following 911.

In both cases, the New York Stock Exchange had to be closed to stop a meltdown in stock prices. They were able to open it again after they showed the public that there was a plan to control the situation.

The difference with the UFO meltdown scenario is that unlike the 911 and blackout situations, there may be nothing they can do to show they have the situation under control. Therefore, once they open the stock market again, it would continue to melt down as nothing would have changed.

Once the government spills the milk, there is no turning back. What happens will happen, and there is nothing that can be done to stop it. Politicians are not the types of people who like to roll the dice. They poll every move they make, and if there is the slightest chance the issue will go south, they will choose to ignore it.

The argument is made that very few people will panic, and that is true, at least in the United States. HOWEVER, it doesn't take 100% of the people to become alarmed to cause the sheeple to start jumping off the cliff. It only takes 2% of people with a lot of oil shares to start selling in hopes of buying back in later for pennies on the dollar. There is a good chance this race for the bottom could occur.

Sellers might not even be panicked. They might start shorting the market as a perceived opportunity to make money. The media which makes money by selling fear would promote the uncertainty creating a self-fulfilling prophecy.

One of the other things that made me move this panic idea back to the top of the list was a conversation I had with film producer James Fox in 2016. He told me that he had done an interview with Bob Bigelow, and Bigelow had stated there had been more than one think tank study about how the people would react. The conclusion was that there would a total meltdown, and there consequently would never be full disclosure. Bob Dean mentioned a 1964 study done by NATO, and Edgar Mitchell also revealed that Battelle, Brookings, and RAND as having done studies.

We know of one of the studies that Bigelow may have been referencing. It was the $96,000 190-page 1960 report produced by the Brookings Institute for NASA entitled "Proposed Studies on the Implications of Peaceful Space Activities for Human Affairs." The report included a section entitled "Implications of a Discovery of Extraterrestrial Life."

> *Societies sure of their own place have disintegrated when confronted by a superior society," said the NASA report. "Others have survived even though changed. Clearly, the better we can come to understand the factors involved in responding to such crises the better prepared we may be.[2]*

2. **Classification:** There are many possible explanations for a cover-up or embargo of UFO information, but one of the most important is classification.

The American Civil Liberties Union's 'Secrecy Report,' issued in July 2011, stated that the U.S. classified 76,795,945 documents in 2010, the most in history and eight times as many as were classified in 2001.

This use of classification is the way the government with its military and intelligence operate. Classify and be safe. The obsession with classification goes across the board and does not just apply to the UFO subject.

A lot of material is classified every day and withheld from the taxpayers. Governments have learned that operating in secrecy is much more efficient than sharing the latest developments in weapons, black operations, treaty negotiations, and political strategies. It continues today despite Executive Order 13526 signed by President Obama which was intended to curtail excess secrecy.

> *In no case, shall information be classified...in order to: conceal violations of law, inefficiency, or administrative error; prevent embarrassment to a person, organization, or agency... or prevent or delay the release of information that does not*

require protection in the interest of the national security.

The Security Oversight Office (ISOO) found that 35% of the classified documents examined did not meet the classification criteria set out by the president. Therefore, the first rule becomes the protection of secrecy as opposed to an informed public.

In the famous November 1950, Canadian Top Secret document, it was stated that Canadian officials had been told by "American officials" that the subject of flying saucers was the most highly classified secret in the United States.

Following logic, it would mean that if the government is classifying almost 77 million pages of documents, and if UFOs are the most secret thing, there is no chance that the secret keepers will be volunteering anything to enlighten the average citizen.

It is highly likely that when US officials saw the Roswell wreckage and beings, they immediately concluded that this discovery would remain secret for a real long time.

Some deep throats have maintained that there is a 50-year rule that allows them to speak, but there is not. There is no agency declassifying documents as they reach their 50th birthday. If such a law existed, Roswell and the plans for the atomic bomb would be public records. They are not. A secret remains classified until it no longer poses a threat to national security, or when it is politically advantageous to release it.

The government, particularly the executive branch of the government, would like to deal with the issue in total secrecy. In the early years of government involvement, the government dealt with the UFO issue in part by the use of a public investigation via Project Blue Book. The whole project turned out to be a public relations nightmare where the government was forced to deal publicly with every UFO sighting, and other non-related items that people believed were related to the phenomena.

It is much easier to deal with an issue, especially one where there is no roadmap, in secrecy. All the dirty laundry and mistakes are handled outside the scrutiny of media and the public.

It is this classification issue that appears to handcuff the president who knows what is going on but who can't do anything about it. He can't do anything about it because he is the Wizard of Oz in charge of ending the cover-up. All secrecy is born through executive orders, and the president is the only one that can write them. As Pandolfi at the CIA said, "The president cannot be a player."

The president, therefore, has two options. 1) Out himself as the source of the UFO cover-up, or 2) continue the cover-up.

3. **Consciousness:** When officials recovered the Roswell wreckage they realized that the technology did not just involve the craft but also involved the beings who were flying the ship. This discovery came from one of the aliens that survived and was recovered in the crash, and described by various witnesses. The key thing mentioned about the live alien was that it was telepathic and witnesses described hearing the being talking in their head.

This telepathic ability to read other people's minds and talk in people heads must have been considered a highly-classified secret that would provide many military advantages if it could be understood and duplicated.

There is further related information collected from 3,000 people who have claimed contact with the beings in ET craft. From the Foundation for Research into Extraterrestrial Experiences (FREE) we see that "55% have received "telepathic" messages, or thought transferences from NHI. 14% believed they had flown the craft, in every case I checked out, experiencers said they used their mind to do it. There have been 48% who stated that the craft "was alive"- the craft was a living entity. If this is true, and if such a ship were involved the Roswell crash, it would have commanded a highly-classified secret.

4. **Poker Game:** This is the idea that the battle to understand the technology behind the UFO phenomena is not just an American effort. At least the Russians and the Chinese are also fighting to solve the UFO mystery and gain knowledge regarding the advanced technology. The major researcher of the 1950s and 1960s, Major Donald Keyhoe, talked about this saying, "I've gradually learned more, and I see now the hell of a spot they've been in. Because if they came out with – you see, one of the big factors is the fact that Russia and the United States have both been trying to get the technical secrets (of UFOs). And if either one gets them ahead of the other, that's it. They own the world."[3]

None of the three countries wants to be the first to put their cards on the table, because, in doing so, they may, in fact, provide the enemy the 20% of the data they require to unlock the technology. This hiding of one's cards would apply to President Trump giving China the pieces they might be missing, or China providing Trump the final pieces of the puzzle.

Once one of the countries gets 100% of the answers, they can change their position, not disclose, and start building weapons with technology that no one can stop. Now they have the upper hand in any future war or standoff because they effectively now have an unstoppable secret weapon.

5. **Complexity:** The ET presence is not a simple story such as "they are here." All collected evidence points to the fact that the final story will be very involved and possibly multi-dimensional. The more researchers study the phenomena, the more visiting races there appear to be, and the more complicated their technology looks. It seems to be far beyond what we know or can even comprehend.

Keyhoe stated that he had talked to insiders about what was known. "They have some parts of them, yeah. I was told by sources that I believed right along, "It's infuriating that we still do not have the technical answers. We know what the results are, like their control of gravity, and we've been spending millions on it. But we still don't have the answers to that."[4]

Recent UFO research has continued to show a phenomenon that is regularly starting things, stopping things, changing, and becoming more complex. In the U.K., for example, a series of "crop circles" began in the 1980s. It became more complicated and then died out.

In the same way, cattle mutilations started in 1967, evolved in number and complexity, and then died out in the United States, only to start up in Argentina.

The #1 reported being, according to the 3000 people who replied to a FREE survey of experiencers said, is not a flesh and blood being. The phenomena, therefore, may not even be extraterrestrial as most assume.

6. **Don't know what to do:** The cover-up may simply be a case of the government not knowing what to do about the ET situation. They might be only covering up their ignorance. Tom DeLonge claimed that a top military person he was dealing with told him, "I think what you might find is a bunch of men standing around an elephant."

Wilbert Smith, who headed up the Canadian government investigation into flying saucers from 1950-1954, said "The only reason that those in authority have said nothing about it is that they simply don't know what to do about it."[5]

This "not knowing what to do" led to a situation inside the Canadian government of helplessness. Wilbert B. Smith stated, "Fact is when certain government officials came face to face with the reality of the space people, and realized there was nothing they could do about it, they promptly closed their eyes and hoped the whole thing would go away."

7. **Fear:** The president and other high officials might be simply afraid. Afraid to deal with the issue.

When President Clinton and his executive branch people took over the government in 1993, Dr. Steven Greer obtained an inside opportunity to brief Congressman Dan Burton, the chairman of the powerful House Government Reform and Oversight Committee. Burton was very interested in the UFO case that was being made by Greer. He asked Greer for everything that he had on the subject.

One year later Burton had backed off his UFO quest after he and his chief aid experienced some strange surveillance indications. On an interview with Art Bell on the radio show "Coast to Coast AM," Greer stated that Burton had now become like everyone else in government - afraid of dealing with the issue. "The problem is no one wants to act," said Greer. "They're not acting because they are afraid."[6]

Edgar Mitchell, the Apollo 14 astronaut, commented on the reason for the secrecy, based on information shared with him by old timers familiar with the intelligence factors related to the UFO cover-up. Mitchell said there is a very simple reason why governments have been so secretive: fear.

8. **Alien Cover-up:** Some of the aliens are covering up as well. They appear to be using what some researchers call a "leaky embargo." They present themselves, but in a way that does not provide proof. Instead of landing and announcing they are here, they fly beside aircraft for some minutes or pass messages to lone individuals who take the message to the world.

The aliens could land anytime they want and make themselves known. The aliens have refused to directly announce their presence and this forces hesitation on the part of governments.

If the aliens won't announce, why should the government go first? The government is waiting to see what the ultimate goal of the aliens is and there are so many different types of aliens, they are not sure about all of the agendas.

9. **Alien Masters:** The aliens are in fact in charge. They directly control everything related to their presence and the future disclosure of their existence. This superiority is something the government could never admit publicly.

Government files illustrate some disturbing UFO sighting reports that could be read as "hostile actions" by some alien species. Does the government want to announce this to the public, especially if the government cannot control events?

10. **Government gridlock:** The announcement of an ET presence on earth would be front page news for months. It would stymie and dominate the government's every action and not allow it to carry out any of its planned business. It would exponentially be like the Monica Lewinski situation.

The president who makes the ET reality announcement will face numerous fallouts, such as having his entire presidential agenda overrun by the ET issue.

Agencies like NASA would become irrelevant overnight. The government would face the question of why they continued to fund NASA when they knew the prime space efforts were a waste of taxpayer money.

> *"The purpose of the international conspiracy is to maintain a workable stability among the nations of the world and for them, in turn, to retain institutional control over their respective populations. Thus, for these governments to admit there are beings from outer space attempting to contact us, beings with mentalities and technological capabilities obviously far superior to ours, could, once fully perceived by the average person, erode the foundations of the Earth's traditional power structure. Political and legal systems, religions, economic and social institutions could all soon become meaningless in the mind of the public. The national oligarchical establishments, even civilization as we know it, could collapse into anarchy."*[7]

11. **Population Resistance:** The government knows that the population is not ready to deal with aliens. It is conceivable that a certain percentage of citizens would not accept the alien presence and would in fact personally seek to attack the aliens. Also, certain political factions would immediately start painting the aliens as "poison skittles" as has been done with the Mexicans, Chinese, and Arabs.

This fear of outsiders is something that the government would have a hard time controlling as American citizens have a constitutional right to bear arms. People might view aliens as invaders or agents of the devil "in sheep's clothing."

Any attack against the aliens might result in a counterattack causing massive damage on the country. (This point, however, is good news, as it shows the aliens could never take over no matter what advanced technology they had. They would end up bogged down in a Vietnam style quagmire like the one facing the United States today in Iraq.)

12. **People Don't Care:** Before Obama, the president had only faced the UFO question twice. In the 2004 election, there was not a single UFO related question to one of the two major candidates. The people, therefore, do not see the UFO-ET presence as a critical issue. Why would the government risk all the potential fallouts for an issue that no one takes seriously?

13. **Past statements:** The government has lied for almost 70 years and thus must continue the lie. One falsehood has been used to cover another, and it is becoming impossible to come clean.

To come, clean the government would be required to find a way to explain why they have been misleading the public for almost 70 years. In 1977, Keyhoe described what his Pentagon contacts said about past behaviors, "they're sure they're going to catch holy hell if they come out and admit they've been misleading the public and being really harsh in some of their attacks on some of the witnesses for 30 years."

14. **The collapse in Belief systems:** This would be particularly evident among government scientists and engineers who would have to deal with the fact that their employer has been lying to them and feeding them false data, and more importantly the fact that most of their treasured scientific beliefs were wrong. The 1961 Brookings Institute study defined the problem:

> *It has been speculated that of all groups, scientists and engineers might be the most devastated by the discovery of relatively superior creatures since these professions are most clearly associated with the mastery of nature, rather than with the understanding and expression of man.*[8]

As the Newtonian science paradigm fuels the modern technological advances any upheaval would negatively affect the economy.

15. **Fear of Death:** One possibility is that the president faced threats of death by another group who controls the UFO problem.

Steven Greer told a story by a close friend of Bill Clinton that "If the President does what you say - he fears that he will end up like Jack Kennedy."

This theory of the president being threatened with death to keep him quiet is quite popular in the UFO community. There have even been controversial documents leaked into the UFO community that claim the assassination of Kennedy occured because he gave the order to declassify the ET presence to the Russians. Shortly after issuing the executive order, the story says he was dead.

16. **Old Style Conservatives:** Like in some religious settings the "conservatives" want to hang on to status quo as long as possible. The government would have to deal with this group which would not be willing to negotiate or make compromises. Some describe this as the reason major newspapers do not follow the UFO story. The editors are just simply old-style skeptic conservatives.

17. **Democratic Disclosure:** There is a vote that takes place within the group in control of the knowledge on UFOs whether or not to disclose. As there is no disclosure, it would appear that the Conservatives still hold the majority of the vote. Hillary Clinton hinted at this in one of the answers she gave to UFO questions she faced during the 2016 election campaign about disclosing information related to the UFO mystery. She stated "if I can get an agreement," as one of the conditions for releasing UFO information.

Because she and John Podesta came up with the plan to disclose, it is safe to assume they have some knowledge of how the system works. By talking about "getting an agreement," she implied she would require a vote within MJ-12, high-level national security officials, or whoever is tasked with the UFO problem.

Apparent government disclosure leaks suggest that the vote may have swung from cover-up to disclosure.

18. **Weapons Development:** There is a need to develop ET based technology into super-weapons in the case of alien attack (as portrayed in the movie Independence Day where they used one of the aliens' own ships to infiltrate them). There is also a great desire by the military weapons people to develop weapons that are more efficient at killing. The alien technology would be a dream come true for the weapon development people.

Researcher Gary Bekkum described the possible fields as "telepathy, psychic perception (remote viewing), precognition of future events for the war on terror, antigravity, gravity-like force beams, clusters of electrical charge for use as weapons, extracting energy from empty space, wormholes, and warps drives, to name but a few.

Developers who control such technology may want to keep things secret to solidify their control over the technology before the public finds out. "My friends," wrote Peter Gersten, "as long as the technology is the prize, no official disclosure will ever take place."[9]

Lead time is the gauge of the power of technology in war. Lead time is how long it will take the enemy to develop your secret weapon if you suddenly use it.

If the American military people have figured out 70% of the secrets behind the alien technology, it would be dangerous to release this. The piece published might be exactly the piece required by the enemy to complete their weapons system. The defense sector knows that in modern war lead time is critical, as many present-day wars only last days or months. Any advantage gained by alien technology would develop a weapons lead-time of years or decades. The enemy would have no time to build their own system.

This lead time problem would also apply to lead times that might have been gained by an enemy also working on the alien technology. Giving our adversaries an indication of what we know would allow the enemy to attack if the enemy knew we had no counter measure.

19. **Reverse Engineering** – The government is buying for time till they have completed back engineering crashed saucers. This delay is related to weapons lead time. The farther ahead the development is, the harder it is for the enemy to recover if the secret weapon gets deployed. There is absolutely no reason to tell the enemy how far along the technology has developed.

20. **Need to Know:** The population does not have the need to know. One Navy captain informed researcher Ray Stanford in 1964 "those dealing with the problem are capable of rational judgment in the face of the unexpected. They know the facts… people are not ready to know the facts."

Dr. Eric Walker said the following to one researcher who was trying to make the point that the people had the right to know:

> *As I say, it is none of your business. Just to satisfy your curiosity? It is not going to do any damn good except to make you happy. Is that not true? Are we going to change the plans and regulations just to make you happy? If you say you are looking for the truth, you will never get it anyway, so forget it…Why*

should we bother to spend the time and money just to make you happy? Answer me that.[10]

"Need-to-know" is a strong principle inside the military where they have special access to information that the population should not be given access to for various reasons. UFOs have always been described as a "need to know" item. Vice President Dick Cheney for example, when asked if he had been officially briefed on the subject of UFOs stated: "If I had been briefed on that subject, it probably would have been classified and I wouldn't be talking about it."

21. **Kickbacks and Profits:** He who has the gold makes the rules. If the cover-up is controlled by insiders, as many believe, they could be resisting disclosure because of astronomical profits and kickbacks being made from siphoning classified extraterrestrial ultra-technology into insider corporations. Once the secret is out, they would have to share.

22. **Dependence on Oil:** The entire economy is dependent on oil, and everyone addicted to it has become addicted to the technologies involved. It is part of the status quo, and people don't like change.

Oil also involves a lot of money and jobs. This would be a major factor in keeping the money flowing to the people who are benefiting now.

Retooling an economy from an oil economy to a zero-point energy economy would be very disruptive to society.

23. **Short Sightedness:** The government operates in the short term, and UFOs is a long-term issue. Steven Greer stated that a person attached to the National Security Advisor to President Reagan stated that long term in the government is five years.

The president only has a term of 4 years, and because he is always seeking votes, his key interests usually lie in things that are achievable within his period of four years. The case is significant if one measures the possible fallout of disclosure versus the votes gained.

24. **Nationalism:** Disclosure of the ET presence would transfer citizen allegiance from the United States to the world, otherwise known as the one world government. It has often been said, "Nationalism is the only game in town." Loss of power - power brokers who now control the situation would lose power. They would have less power in a world-style government because the U.S. population is tiny.

A future consideration is that if there is a one-world view, the military, weapons developers, and security services people would find it hard to sell arms and fear.

The ideas of separation/individuality and fear are used to sell and make money. Without nations, there is oneness, where everyone is a brother, and where division fades away. We would all realize as President Reagan mentioned when he talked about the threat of an alien invasion that we "would all come together" and "we'd realize we are all God's children."

25. **Government Black Operations** - Many UFOs are secret government experiments that get protected by disguising them as UFOs. The 1997 CIA study *A Die-Hard Issue: CIA's Role in the Study of UFOs, 1947-90*, written by CIA historian, Gerald K. Haines, made this case. Haines stated that most of the UFOs seen since 1947 were intelligence planes such as the U-2 and the SR-71.

26. **Abductions:** If the government would disclose that there is an ET presence here on Earth, one of the first questions that would be asked to the president is, "As President, you are constitutionally responsible for the protection of the American people. It has been estimated that 6-8 million people have been abducted by the extraterrestrials. In light of this Mr. President, what are you doing to stop it?" Based on the presently available evidence it appears that not only does the president not know how to stop it, he probably does not even know why the aliens are doing it.[11]

27. **Mutilations:** The confirmation by the government that 10,000 or more cattle have been mutilated would send panic throughout the American populous. The fact that the government knew and did nothing to stop it would lead to a rash of lawsuits from farmers all over the country. As the government can do nothing to stop the mutilations, they would face a losing situation. If the government itself is doing the mutilations, as some claim, this naturally could never be disclosed.

Some contend that there have been human mutilations, and if true it appears that the government cannot stop this either. The confirmation of a human element to the mutilation phenomena would be like a nuclear bomb going off in Washington, D.C.

28. **Viruses:** There is a crucial account that in January 1996, at least one alien was captured in Varginha, Brazil. One policeman, Marco Eli Chereze, was a key witness who rescued one of the injured aliens that he saw on the side of the road as he was driving, and held him in his car as he drove to the hospital. In a short span of time, Marco developed a respiratory infection and other strange physical

reactions, and died at the age of 33. This is one example raised by Tom DeLonge as a threat to the American population from what he calls "the others."

29. **Waived Special Access Programs ("SAPs"):** There are also levels of SAPs, the first being a division into acknowledged and unacknowledged SAPs. Black Program is slang for an unacknowledged SAP. An unacknowledged SAP is so sensitive that its very existence is a "core secret." Indeed, some unacknowledged SAPs are sensitive to the extent that they are "waived" (a technical term) from the normal management and oversight protocols. Even members of Congress on appropriations committees (the Senate and House committees that allocate budgets) and intelligence committees are not allowed to know anything about these programs. In the case of a waived SAP, only eight members of Congress (the chairs and ranking minority members of the four defense committees) are even notified that a given program has been waived (without being told anything about the nature of the program). Such a program is certainly deep black (though I am not sure if that designation is actually used in the business).[12]

30. **The Government Is Playing for Time:** There is a theory that the government might have many answers and is buying for time until they have the ability to deal with some of the more difficult UFO problems. The 1960 Brookings report stated, "The better we can come to understand the factors involved in responding to such crises the better prepared we may be."

Perhaps the control group has all the answers and the news is not good for the future of man. They may know that the alien agenda is bad and that they are helpless to stop it. The government certainly wouldn't want to release such an end-of-the-world scenario.

Perhaps the aliens are good but the group that has been in control (labeled by many as The Cabal) is afraid the aliens will tell everyone the truth of what has been going on since the 1940s and they would then lose control.

31. **Building a Defense System:** Those in control of the UFO data may be working on creating counter measures to defend or even attack the high technologies exhibited by UFOs. Bringing down UFOs "at will" would certainly be one technology that the military is busy trying to develop. This would be especially true if the military is taking the view that the UFOs represent the enemy.

32. **We Are Being Studied:** As portrayed in the movie *The Day the Earth Stood Still*, paranoid cultures who project to others their own

intentions, based on their own past actions, would state that it's a valid rule of thumb is that if "they" discover you, "they" are your technological superiors. They feel human history has shown us time and again the tragic results of a confrontation between a technologically superior civilization and a technologically inferior one. The "inferior" is usually subject to physical conquest. Again, this is based on the perception of an aggressor who can only speculate and see things in terms of fear and conquest. Poachers who kill often view wild animals as something to be feared - kill them before they kill you type of mentality.

This view holds that history has shown a technologically superior people are possessors of a virile and aggressive culture. In a confrontation between two peoples of significantly different cultural levels, those with a less virile culture often suffer absorption by the conquering culture, and tragically, also extinction.

The Brookings Study on the implications of the discovery of extraterrestrial life best described our fear that an encounter by our civilization with an advanced race might mean our destruction. "Anthropological files contain many examples of societies, sure of their place in the universe, which have disintegrated when they had to associate with previously unfamiliar societies espousing different ideas and ways of life; others that survived such an experience usually did so by paying the price of changes in values and attitudes and behavior."[13]

33. **Lobby groups:** The UFO community has only one lobbyist with very little money. Other interest groups such as the oil industry have scores of lobbyists. These lobbyists spend millions of dollars to influence congressional decisions. Since much of what happens in Washington is highly influenced by lobbyists and Ufology does not have the public support or money, it therefore cannot exert pressure on the political system and simply doesn't have the same influence.

34. **Money:** Ufology doesn't have much money, and it takes a certain amount of it to finance proper research. In order to get the UFO mystery seriously looked at, there would have to be a political movement forcing the government to take a look. The idea here is that we are no different than any other social or political movement and that the time will come when ufology becomes important enough and all other concerns will pale in comparison.

35. **Alien threat:** Perhaps the aliens have directly ordered the government (or government within the government) not to disclose the UFO secret until an appointed time. Or perhaps the aliens already know what the appointed time is and are actually directing the

disclosure timeline. President Obama actually joked in 2016 during an appearance on the Jimmy Kimmel show that the aliens were in control and had ordered the cover-up.

36. **The apprehension of invasion:** Concern of human slavery, especially by the upper-class elites, possible imprisonment at the hands of colonizing alien races, and God knows what else. It was recorded in the 1997 CIA UFO study that the UFO flap over the White House in July 1952 was a serious concern of President Truman's staff.

37. **Religious fallout.** Fears of how the knowledge of alien life would affect religion in American society.

In 1994, a study was conducted where 1,000 priests, ministers, and rabbis were questioned about the impact of an ET presence on religion. One question dealt specifically with how religion would react if ET were to "proclaim responsibility for producing human life." 28% of all respondents replied that the believed or believed strongly that it would create a religious crisis.[14] (28% of the American population would equal over 82 million people in crisis)

It could be argued that the number of people affected by fallout in their belief structure would be small in the 21st century, but even a small percentage would deserve some protection in a group that holds a lot of power and influence.

Moreover, religious beliefs sometimes influence those who control or gather the intelligence on the subject. Inside the CIA, it was said that fundamentalist Christian agents believed remote viewing was satanic and helped put an end to the research. Charlie Rose (D. North Carolina) of the House Select Committee on Intelligence stated that CIA officials "know this remote-viewing stuff works but... have been blocked by publicity-shy superiors."

Christians are waiting for the second coming of Jesus Christ. The Jews are waiting for the Messiah. Despite the fact that in 2008 Pope Benedict IVI said it was okay to believe in aliens, the appearance of aliens before the arrival of Jesus or the Messiah may not be handled well by fundamentalists.

Conservative religious leaders might declare aliens the agents of the devil and a religious war could break out between pro and anti-alien forces.

38. **Evolution:** This would have to rank as one of the key reasons a cover-up is being supported by the people in control of the cover-up. On many occasions, intelligence has leaked the idea that some of the aliens purport to be our creators and further that they had a hand in

Christianity. If true, these revelations would cause many problems for disclosure.

American society has a huge Christian base, and most believe that mankind was a special creation and follow a particular timeline for when Adam and Eve were created. To present the public with the idea that aliens have been involved in not only Adamic creation but other creations as well might make them feel they are part of an alien science project.

Add to this the complexity of the different species, some humanoid, some not, some who claim they know Jesus and acknowledge that he is Divine, some who claim they know of Jesus but that he was just a man, some who claim they don't know him at all, some who claim what is important is Jesus' message of love and practicing the Golden Rule. Perhaps all faiths would find something in common in contact with the wide variety of aliens reported and it would be up to each individual to pick and choose the message they best resonate with. Perhaps the most common message will be that God likes to create and has created not just us but others as well, and some of them are not humanoid in appearance.

39. **Dark Inner Secrets:** The cover-up of the ET reality might involve other secrets within the UFO cover-up. It is hard to image what these secrets might be, but one secret might for example be, what if 5,000 Americans were killed in the early years to protect the secret? It might be a short trip to jail for many if the cover-up ended. Secondly, the government would have to deal with the fallout from the revelation that both military and non-military people were ridiculed, harassed and threatened into keeping quiet, and those who didn't suffered an end to their careers or worse, their lives. Some never revealed what they knew, not even to their spouses.

40. **Who's in Charge:** Perhaps the government is not covering up. President Bill Clinton told Sarah McClendon there was a government inside the government that he did not control. Perhaps the government is trying but has no power to disclose. Many in fact believe that control over the UFO subject is compartmentalized away from the legal and constitutional chain-of-command. These people according to Steven Greer are "risk-averse, do not like significant change, and will not give up control and power easily."[15]

Elected public officials such as the president are transient faces that will be gone in 4,6, or 8 years.

The government's UFO role may have been run for the last 58 years by some unelected group and elected government officials may have no more power to disclose the UFO secrets than the average American citizen. They may be totally out of the loop as is illustrated by a story told about Clinton's Secretary of Defense, William Cohen. Dr. Steven Greer recounted this story.

An astronaut, Gordon Cooper, approached Cohen and gave him a piece of UFO evidence, along with the providence for the piece. Cohen spent much time and effort trying to track where this piece of evidence had gone and was unsuccessful.

41. **Status Quo:** Things aren't all that bad, and it's not worth the trouble that might arise from trying to get disclosure. Dr. Eric Walker was the former president at Penn State University and former Chairman of the Board at the Institute for Defense Analysis, which is the top military think tank to the U.S. Department of Defense. When asked to talk in 1987 about whether or not a certain set of crashed saucer documents were shredded, Walker shot back, "You know it's a ridiculous situation. What the hell difference does it make whether or not it is shredded? What's all, forty years have gone by, and nobody's blown up the world."

This philosophy is that everyone has a job and the people are satisfied. Don't rock the boat. The secret weapon should be brought out only in the most extreme situations. There are still oil options to exploit like the Alaska nature areas.

42. **Psi Warfare:** There is much to indicate that mental phenomena are a large part of how the aliens fly the craft and how they communicate with UFO abductees/experiencers. The intelligence community wants this technology and would be terrified of such technology falling into enemy hands.

The fact that "mental phenomena" is an essential part of the UFO phenomena is found as far back as a Canadian Top Secret UFO memo written by Wilbert Smith:

> *I was further informed that the United States authorities are investigating along quite a number of lines which might possibly be related to the saucers such as mental phenomena and I gather that they are not doing too well since they indicated that if Canada is doing anything in geo-magnetics, they would welcome a discussion with suitably accredited Canadians.*[16]

The idea that "mind control" technology is part of the reason for the cover-up was raised by Cecil B. Jones with President Clinton's science advisor in 1994. Jones was a partner with Laurance Rockefeller and part of the initiative to get President Clinton to declassify classified UFO files.

In a February 17, 1994, letter to Dr. Jack Gibbons, Jones wrote:

> *My mention of mind control at the February 4 meeting was quite deliberate. Please be careful about this. There are reasons to believe that some government group has interwoven research about this technology with alleged UFO phenomena. If that is correct, you can expect to run into early resistance when inquiring about UFOs, not because of the UFO subject, but because that has been used to cloak research and applications of mind-control activity.* [17]

43. Communism: It is very clear from what experiencers have said about the intelligence behind the phenomena that it will challenge many of the political and economic ideas that the western world holds near and dear.

This was pointed out in a May 28, 1952, FBI document on UFO contactee George Adamski where Adamski reported that the government had discovered the communist connection in communications with the aliens:

> *Adamski stated that in this interplanetary communication, the Federal Communications Commission asked the inhabitants of the other plane concerning the kind of government they had there and the reply indicated that it was very different from the democracy of the United States. Adamski stated that his answer was kept secret by the United States government, but he added, "If you were to ask me they probably have a Communist form of government and our American government wouldn't release that kind of information, naturally." That is a thing of the future – more advanced...The United States today is in a state of deterioration as was the Roman empire prior to its collapse and it will fall as the Roman empire did...the government in this country is corrupt form of government and capitalists are enslaving the poor.*

The Adamski statements about the link between aliens and communism were so direct that the FBI came to view Adamski and his declarations as a "security matter." His "murmuring" was described as the "spreading of Russian propaganda."

Adamski's description of the aliens and their social structure was not far off the mark. The UFO intelligence appears to be a hive society almost like theoretical communism where everyone only takes what they need in exchange for contributing what they have. It completely contradicts the American idea of capitalism that values material possession and money.

A close look at the UFO intelligence shows that they appear to have no interest in material possessions, and do not have money. This is not an idea that those who control the wealth and direct the commerce would want disseminated to the masses. It would affect people's ideas regarding consumerism.

44. **President as Goat:** Fear by the president of being the goat. Presidents have big egos and they want to be recorded in history as heroes. There is a good chance that many things would go wrong in disclosure and the president would go down in history as the president who ruined American ideology. It might be this need to protect his ego that stops the president from releasing.

45. **Alien Hidden Agenda:** The mission of visiting ETs is not clear. Until this is clear, it would be dangerous to release. The UFO element will get a lot of crazy media coverage without any concrete evidence to counter the wild claims.

The aliens are withholding the announcement of their presence for a reason. If the government announces and the aliens don't, the government would then be forced to explain the secrecy.

46. **No Answers:** The government has no answer, or few answers, to many aspects of the UFO phenomena, such as how consciousness fits in, cattle mutilations, human abduction or alien intent. Moreover, there is a good chance government not only does not know how to stop it – they don't even know why the aliens are doing it. It would be absolutely impossible to put the President of the United States in front of a news conference where he would appear as "the emperor with no clothes."

The problem may be much more complex than people think. When confronted about disclosing, Dr. Eric Walker hinted that the government may have few answers, "Only a couple people are capable of handling this issue," he said. "Unless your mind ability is like Einstein's or likewise, I do not think you can achieve anything."

Lastly, I heard a very reliable story of a high-level official with knowledge who was asked after a briefing "Who's in charge." He answered with two words, "They are."

47. **Counter-intelligence against the American People:** UFO disclosure might put the government into having to admit that they spent years spreading false stories to public media sources to cover up for the fact that they had no control of the situation. This counter-intelligence will have cost many people reputation and money.

48. **Alien airspace:** UFO disclosure might force the government to admit that aliens are allowed to fly around in U.S. airspace at will, which would mean that all NORAD officials are able to do is watch. It is hard to believe officials would want to make this revelation.

49. **Stock Market Collapse:** There would be a meltdown of the stock market. Those in control own stock. They would, therefore, hesitate to do things that would eliminate their holdings.

Oil stocks would lose most of their value within minutes of the confirmation of an extraterrestrial presence. This would lead to panic and traders selling other stocks to protect their positions. In the cases of 911 and the 2003 blackout, the stock market crashed and there was not much the government could do except to close the market before it reached zero. The government was able to open the market after a couple days after convincing the population that they had the situation under control and that the event would never happen again. In the case of UFOs there is no indication that the government has any control over the situation, so opening the stock market would lead to a continued meltdown.

A close associate of Wilbert Smith who did metallurgic analysis of UFO fragments for Smith told me clearly in an interview I did with him in the 1970s, "If you ever find out that they are going to release the UFO secret tomorrow, be sure you sell everything you have today, because tomorrow everything will be worth nothing."

50. **End of Nationalism:** Americans would transfer their allegiance from the United States to the world. There would no longer be a pledge of allegiance to the United States flag. There would be calls for a one world government.

The consequences for the American government and all its departments would be obvious. In the new system, whose rules would dominate? Would Americans still be allowed to control the vast majority of world resources with their small population?

Situations like the collapse of the former Soviet Union resulting in more than a dozen countries shows clearly that the tendency among humans has been to divide and retain a sense of nationalism based on race, religion, and political belief structures. How would disclosure fit into this with a multitude of alien species being introduced? Who would identify with whom and what would that mean?

51. **Free Energy Dilemma:** Free energy to countries like China and India who currently survive on one to three dollars an hour wages would devastate the American economy.

It would be important for the American government to retain control over the new free energy technology until it has fully assessed how the changeover to free energy would affect the current worldview.

Disclosure of free energy would also lead to disclosures of other ET technology, some of which could be used by terrorists against American interests at home and abroad. There have been many examples in UFO encounters which show that the alien technology has great potential for destruction.

52. **Procrastination:** The nature of government is to procrastinate on everything. Of all the issues being put off to another time, the ET presence is the biggest. Henry Kissinger, former Secretary of State for Richard Nixon and often rumored to be a member of the group controlling UFO secrets, was rumored to have stated, "UFOs are the biggest hot potato in Washington."

Rarely does a government take up a new idea and simply pass it. Government flows with the pressures exerted by lobby groups and polls. They are in power to carry out the will of the people, not introduce new ideas.

53. **The Shift in Credibility:** If the government were to disclose they would lose all their credibility on the subject after years of secrets and lies. This distrust would spill over into statements being made by government officials on other non-UFO related items. The power would shift from the government to the UFO community.

More importantly, the credibility on telling the UFO story would shift to the UFO community who will claim they were right all along. Many in the media and public will look to the UFO community for answers instead of the government they feel lied to them.

However, many in the UFO community know that the UFO community itself is not united, and that there are some fringe elements. These fringe elements will serve as more sensationalism for the media, such as humans are being served in an alien McDonald's on the back side of the moon (Soylent Green). Researchers with negative alien viewpoints could spin the abduction and animal mutilation stories into an uncontrollable public relations disaster. Talk shows and reality TV would be inundated with the UFO subject.

54. **Overpopulation**: New alien medical technologies would cut disease and increase life spans which would cause rapid overpopulation. Some estimated state 23,000 children needlessly die each day from disease and hunger. Most of these children, however, are in third-world countries, which because of low wages, have no recourse to import products to the U.S., thus affecting jobs for Americans. How would advance technologies affect population growth worldwide?

55. **An uncontrolled Release:** Any attempt to make a partial disclosure announcement (the ETs are here but we won't talk about areas of the subject that are still classified) would give the green light to people who are "read into" the program. These people might consider the partial disclosure as a green light to start talking about what they know. This might include material the government doesn't want to be released.

56. **Increased terrorist power:** Military people who were threatened into being silent but seek revenge by releasing information to other countries or terrorists, might see American leaders as being in a secret relationship with evil aliens who want to take over the world. In this scenario, continued complete control over the powerful UFO technologies would be seen as the only safe alternative. The technology must be controlled in the same way nuclear technology has been guarded for the past 60 years.

57. **Foreign Weapons:** Government may be concerned some UFOs may actually be other nations' weapons systems. In 1953 the U.S. Air Force had a project called "Blue Moon," involving photographing unidentified enemy aircraft. It was hoped the project would identify new enemy prototypes, modifications and installations being made on present enemy aircraft. The idea is to secretly study all unknown in hopes of identifying advanced technology which could be used by the U.S. military or might be a threat to U.S. military.

58. **No Public Support:** Ufology groups have been unable to marshal up the public support to create a massive demonstration. Therefore, disclosure is an issue people don't really want. The lack of support tells the people in control that they should continue the secrecy. In this view, if the secrecy situation was really serious and detrimental to the well-being of society, more people would speak up and demand disclosure.

59. **Sources & Methods:** Any disclosure announcement may lead to people who have kept their silence for too long to reveal the locations of where the back-engineering technologies have been taking place. This would be free intelligence to the enemy allowing them to point their spies and satellites in said directions.

60. **Dead pilots:** In the early days of the modern UFO era, the USAF made a number of attempts to shoot down UFOs. There were many reports of not only pilots dying but aliens too and the public knowing what those actual numbers are would be a source of embarrassment to people in control to say the least. People may demand that heads roll.

61. **Nuclear Weapons:** Encounters suggest the aliens are able to turn off nuclear weapons. Are they doing this because they want to invade us? Or are they doing this because they are trying to send us a message that we shouldn't have or use nuclear weapons? Or are they just showing us that they are in total control of the nuclear situation? Many people take one view or the other. At the present time, newly elected President Trump is promoting more nuclear weapons.

62. **The Alien:** The aliens or whoever is behind the UFO phenomena have many reasons for keeping the whole subject secret if we look carefully. They are undisputedly part of the cover-up.

They are not here to do our homework. In fact, many experiencers have been told that "Earth is a school." If you do your child's homework, he will get good marks, but he will learn nothing.

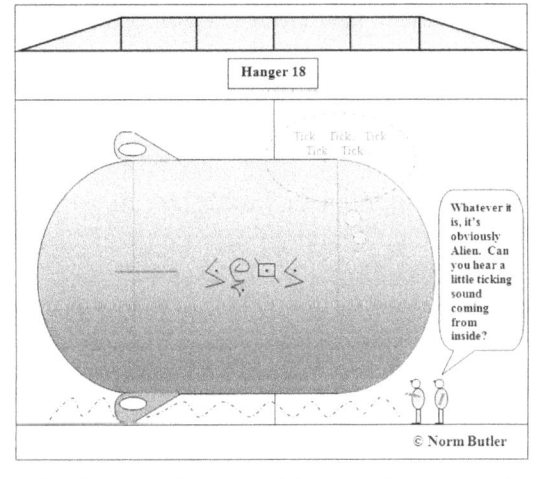

There appears to be a policy of non-intervention known in Star Trek as The Prime Directive. They are not supposed to interfere with our evolution. In the early 1950s the head of the Canadian flying saucer program was in contact with at least two aliens, Tyla and AFFA. In his conversations with AFFA, this idea of non-interference with the human race was brought up by AFFA. Smith was told that the only time the beings would step in is if there was a nuclear war. They assured Smith that they could stop such a war stating that if the world didn't believe it they could take the moon in front of the whole world, split it in half and put it back together in microseconds to prove their ability. Others than AFFA stated they will allow mankind to stew in their own juices.

However, aliens were supposed to have offered a warning to President Eisenhower regarding nuclear testing being conducted.

According to Charles L. Suggs, a retired Sgt. from the US Marine Corps, his father Charles L. Suggs, (1909-1987) was a former Commander with the U.S. Navy who attended the event. In a 1991 interview with a prominent UFO Suggs stated that according to his father, he had:

> *"Accompanied President Ike along with others on Feb. 20th. They met and spoke with 2 white-haired Nordics that had pale blue eyes and colorless lips. The spokesman stood a number of feet away from Ike and would not let him approach any closer.*
>
> *A second Nordic stood on the extended ramp of a bi-convex saucer that stood on tripod landing gear on the landing strip. According to Charlie, there were B-58 Hustlers on the field even though the first one did not fly officially till 1956. These visitors said they came from another solar system.*
>
> *They posed detailed questions about our nuclear testing."*

If true, it happened only days before one of the largest nuclear explosions conducted by the American government, resulting in one of the greatest nuclear contamination events ever caused by a weapons test.

The test was called Castle Bravo. It was part of a series of six Operation Castle atmospheric blasts testing thermonuclear weapons small enough to be carried and dropped by aircraft, as compared to the first thermonuclear bomb test in November 1952, which was 82 tons and which Oppenheimer comically stated could only be delivered by "oxcart or ship."

The test took place on February 28, 1954 at Bikini Atoll in the Marshall Islands. This was almost exactly a week after the reported Eisenhower alien meeting.

The test went totally out of control, being 250% more powerful than expected and resulting in a bomb 1,000 times the power of the bomb dropped in Hiroshima. The crew in charge of the detonation had to be rescued from a nearby island twenty miles away when radiation detectors told them something serious had gone wrong and their lives were now at risk. Like giant ghosts at Halloween they covered themselves with bed sheets, with holes cut out so they could see, to protect themselves from the radioactive fallout. They ran to a nearby landing pad where helicopters from the command ship rescued them.

The test ended up causing the most significant radiological contamination accident ever caused by the United States government. ($250 million has been paid to try and clean up the mess). The original projection of the size of the test was 4-6 megatons, but the calculations were completely off. The test ended up being 15 megatons.

A total of 5,000 square miles were contaminated and two islands had to be evacuated because the hundreds of residents were sick from the radioactive fallout. Those evacuated have never returned. There was suddenly a change in the world's view of nuclear tests, and there was an international call for the end of atmospheric nuclear testing.[18]

Garnet Schulhauser, a lawyer in Calgary, Canada, wrote two books based on what he claims he was told by his spirit guide who appeared to him as a homeless man one day on the street. At one point his guide takes him to see the Council of the Wise Ones consisting of different alien races. During that encounter he was told about the law of non-intervention that countless experiencers have been told about.

Often people will raise the question as to why don't the aliens come down and help us. We have wars, and starving people, and if they are here to help they aren't doing a very good job. This, however, confuses aliens with Santa Claus. The western world belief seems to be that they are here to bring us more stuff to make us happy. They will provide us with free energy so we can drive big cars again, and give us the technology to travel to the stars so we have a new place to go after we get tired of Puerto Vallarta. Instead of seeing aliens as Santa Claus coming to bring us "more stuff," it would be more accurate to see them as "teaching us to fish." A proper understanding of "help" is required.

They are here to preserve the planet, a more advanced sentient life form. In this view, the aliens see us in the same way that physicist David Bohm viewed the human race – like a swarm of locusts that have descended on the Earth. The aliens are here to save the planet and if that means removing humans to save the Earth, so be it (as Klaatu stated in *The Day The Earth Stood Still*, "I am a friend to the Earth"). Messages regarding a cataclysm on Earth due to the way humans behave are being imparted to experiencers who seem to be ignored except by a few researchers and a few high-level government officials. Visitations by varying species seemed to increase after humans detonated the first nuclear bomb.

63. **Hiding from Aliens:** This paranoid view is espoused by Tom DeLonge. It proposed that the government is not hiding the UFO truth from the public, but that rather military officials are hiding what they know from evil aliens in order to defend the people from these malevolent creatures from outer space. However, many experiencers who have been threatened with death or worse (harming of their loved ones) if they spoke to anyone about what they saw, interestingly found the individuals doing the threatening far more scarier than the ships or aliens they had seen during their encounters. After decades of government denial, would people (whether they be experiencers or non-experiencers), believe the government who has lied to them and threatened them or the aliens they have developed a relationship with? After all this time, will there be people who see the government/military as the people who were "trying to protect you this entire time" and/or will there be people who believe the messages coming from various forms of ET intelligence espousing love, brotherhood, unity and a galactic neighborhood?

64. **Military Re-Abduction of Abductees/Experiencers**: Reports exist of the abductees/experiencers recalling being abducted by government or military personnel either working in accordance with ETs or using ET technology to disguise their activities as ET activity. These events are known as **milabs** - short for military abductions.

If intelligence or military units are reabducting UFO experiencers, this would be very hard to justify in terms of people's civil rights. How does the president justify kidnapping American citizens? They would likely justify it by saying it was a matter of national security.

There is a possibility that there is some totally unknown factor that is causing the government to choose secrecy over disclosure. This could be something that is not wholly understood by current science, and considered knowledge that needs to be protected (like merging timelines that must be lived out until the very end, at which time they will merge). In the same vein, perhaps there is no cover-up. Perhaps they have released everything they have on the subject as their public statements claim.

Disclosure Efforts 1940-1950

In the UFO community, the Roswell UFO crash is considered the first major crash, but there is substantial evidence of one having occurred earlier, and it comes from two sisters who were in their 80s when they first contacted the Center for UFO Studies in December 1999.

The gradual leaking of the UFO story goes back to at least World War II. It goes back almost to the beginning of the official secrecy policy within the Executive Branch of the United States government.

The first Executive Order on Secrecy (EO8381) was signed in March 1940 by President Roosevelt with security levels labeled "confidential" and "secret."

Truman extended this secrecy believing that his executive power gave him the responsibility to classify anything he chose to protect as a matter of national security. In 1947, Truman created the Central Intelligence Agency and empowered its directors to protect "intelligence sources and methods from unauthorized disclosure." Then he signed two more executive orders adding Top Secret as a category and extending classification authority to any executive branch agency.

Eisenhower added, "Anything that might be seen as a threat to national security." Nixon extended the definition of national security to include any information in "The interest of the national defense or foreign relations of the United States." Reagan extended the document classification period and suspended automatic declassification.

Just after 911, the signing of the Patriot Act signaled that if you fought for openness, you fell into the category of treasonous activities. Attorney General for George W. Bush, John Ashcroft, who still maintains Hillary Clinton can be prosecuted for compromising classified material, even if President-elect Trump doesn't want her prosecuted, testified during his tenure as follows:

> *To those who scare peace-loving people with phantoms of lost liberty, my message is this: your tactics only aid terrorists for they erode our national unity and diminish our resolve. They give ammunition to America's enemies and pause to*

America's friends. They encourage people of good will to remain silent in the face of evil.[19]

People assume there has always been classified material and that is not true. As pointed out above, classified material began in 1940 when President Roosevelt signed an executive order to protect the technologies that were being developed in secret by the United States, such as the atomic bomb, radar, code breaking, homing torpedoes and a host of other inventions.

The fact that the secrecy is established under Executive Order is important because it means that all classification and all security clearances is run out of the Executive Branch, with the President of the United States as Commander-in-Chief of the armed forces.

The president is the beginning and end of all secrecy. He has no security clearance, can see whatever he wants, and determines what everyone else is allowed to see. There is no document held by the United States government that the president can't see for reasons of national security.

Figure 2 Allene Holt Gramley and Lucile Andrew

The story that these two sisters told clearly showed that during World War II people appeared to be violating national security to publicly talk with people about the most highly classified subject in the country. The other possibility is that permission was given to leak the story.

The two women involved were Lucile Andrew and Allene Holt Gramley. They were daughters of the late Reverend Turner Holt, who was the minister at the Shenandoah Christian Church in Greenwich, Ohio. He was also a community leader and the author of the book *Life's Convictions*.

I had seen the two sisters interviewed by their daughter and was so impressed that in April 2009, I traveled to Ashland, Ohio to interview them. They told me that in 1948 they were separately told an amazing story about creatures in Washington.

Lucille stated that she had been told the story as a teenager and was too young to realize the significance of what her father told her.

Allene knew that it was in 1948 when her father talked to her while she was with her two-year-old daughter Eloise who was playing in the back yard. Her father started the conversation by stating, "Now that the next generation is here, I have a story I would like to share with you. I think that someone in my family should know this besides me."

According to Allene, this conversation was unusual because she and her father did not talk often. He was usually busy working in his upstairs office. He insisted that the story not be told until he, and his cousin Cordell Hull, President Roosevelt's Secretary of State from 1933 to 1944 were dead. Although Reverend Holt did not give a date for the event, it had to have occurred no later than 1944, when Hull left office due to ill health, or three years before the Roswell crash.

The story told by Reverend Hull is that while attending a conference in Washington, his cousin Cordell took him to a sub-basement in the U.S. Capitol building, and showed him an unusual sight.

Figure 3 Cordell Hull with Roosevelt

According to what both daughters heard from their father, after being sworn to secrecy, their father reported four "creatures" inside fluid-filled large glass jars. Near the bodies was a wrecked round metallic object which Holt was asked to lift. He reported that it was very light compared to its size. Their father stated they looked like people, but they weren't. He figured they were about 4' tall. Cordell said that what Holt had seen had to remain secret as the public would panic if told.

Holt's daughters had nothing more to add to the story. Both were told the same story about some creatures that the United States government was holding secretly in Washington.

Later research showed that there is a sub-basement under the Capitol building. One researcher talked to U.S. Capitol building curator Barbara A. Wolamin who said she told the Ohio researchers, "She had never heard about these creatures stored at the Capitol, but she did confirm there was a sub-basement that was divided into storage rooms back then."

1947

On June 24, 1947, Kenneth Arnold, a private pilot, began the modern UFO era with the sighting of a string of nine, shiny flying objects flying past Mount Rainier at speeds that Arnold estimated to be a minimum of 1,200 miles an hour. After Arnold had stated that "they flew erratic, like a saucer if you skip it across the water," the craft were labeled "flying saucers" by the media and the term stuck.

That is the part of the story people know well, but what people don't know is that he was contacted by the military and was given two 8 x 11 photos of flying discs. They told Arnold that the photos were by the Fourth Air Force which was the primary air defense command for the West Coast. They also assured him that they were legitimate pictures. His daughter Kim stated:

> *The military intelligence, when they gave him these photographs – they told him in person that they believed these were authentic pictures. They were given to him by 4th Air Force. Military Intelligence at Hamilton Field, California.*[20]

The modern UFO era had begun, and with it came the efforts of the U.S. government to gradually leak the story and at the same time control the key players within the UFO arena.

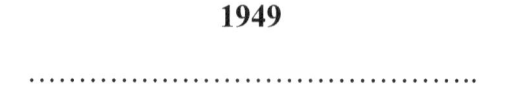

1949

It was 1949 when the first UFO movie, *The Flying Saucer* (1950), went into production. According to Robbie Graham, an expert on the Pentagon influence in UFO movies, the Air Force was busy controlling how the UFO subject got portrayed and, like they did in 1947 with Kenneth Arnold, the Air Force was handing out UFO footage with the claim to the producer that it was the real deal. The actions were classic partial disclosure. Graham wrote:

The film's director, Mikel Conrad, had claimed publicly whilst still in production that he had managed to secure genuine footage of a real flying saucer for use in his movie. In September 1949, Conrad told the Ohio Journal Herald, "I have scenes of the saucer landing, taking off, flying and doing tricks." Conrad further claimed that his remarkable footage was "locked in a bank vault" and would not be shown to anybody prior to his movie's release; shortly thereafter Conrad became the subject of a two-month official Air Force investigation. Documents released under the Freedom of Information Act reveal that an agent of the Air Force Office of Special Investigations was dispatched not only to grill Conrad about his claims but also to attend the first private screening of his completed movie.[21]

Disclosure Efforts 1950- 1960

I knew the men, and I knew that one of them, a general, had passed his opinions on to Bob Ginna (Life Magazine reporter). **Edward Ruppelt, the first head of the USAF UFO Blue Book study.**

1950

....

In 1950, prominent Hollywood author Frank Scully released the book *Behind the Flying Saucers* about four accounts of crashed saucers. The most prominent one that took up most of the book was the 1948 crash in Aztec, New Mexico.

Scully graduated from Columbia University in 1927 and worked as a reporter for the *New York Sun*, *Chicago Tribune*, and *Variety*. He wrote a series of books, including a book on the life of George Bernard Shaw.

Scully's information came primarily from a mysterious Dr. Gee. Scully wrote in a later memoir, "In Armour Bright; Cavalier adventures of my short life out of bed (1963)", that Dr. Gee was "a composite character of eight men who have given me pieces of this story." He always refused to identify who the scientist and engineers were but indicated that they were in a position to know.

His wife reported to researcher Bill Steinman that her husband was given photos of alien beings on a grassy hill. She had seen the pictures and she thought they would be in the thousands of pages of files that she was sending to the University of Wyoming archives. I have checked the files twice, and the photos were not there.

There were a couple of letters there from a woman in New York talking about the fact that military officials had recovered a live alien and couldn't communicate with it. This letter written in 1952 almost completely matches the account of a captured alien (whom they could not communicate with) that an official at Area 51 told George Knapp about in the early 1990s.

Scully's story was written off as a hoax, although Scully always maintained he had legitimate sources and the story was real.

It became one of the first examples of a successful leak, where a story is put out through a researcher or a reporter, the names are withheld, therefore not allowing scrutiny, the event gets written off, and the story gets told without exposing classified secrets.

1950 - November

....

In November 1950, Major Donald Keyhoe sent a six-page draft paper on flying saucers to the Canadian Defense Research Board (DRB), and Wilbert Smith, who headed up the Canadian flying saucer program, through the Canadian Embassy in Washington, D.C.

Donald Edward Keyhoe was perhaps one of the most prominent people in the world of UFOs in the 1950s, 60s, and 70s. He had many contacts inside the Pentagon and many high-ranking military officers on the board of directors of his organization the National Investigative Committee on Aerial Phenomena (NICAP) which had thousands of members. He wrote five best-selling books on UFOs - *The Flying Saucers are Real* (1950), *Flying Saucers from Outer Space* (1953), *The Flying Saucer Conspiracy* (1955), *Flying Saucers: Top Secret* (1960), and *Aliens from Outer Space* (1973).

The DRB was a Canadian defense group responsible for all weapons development in Canada, and a group, which provided "full cooperation" to the Canadian government official flying saucer investigation,[22] which became known as "Project Magnet."

Keyhoe's intention was to publish the article in "True" magazine. It was an article that dealt with the Canadian government's effort to investigate flying saucers and was based on an earlier interview that Keyhoe had done with Wilbert Smith, who would go on to head the Canadian Government saucer study. Dr. Omond Solandt, then the Chairman of the DRB, realized that the article was going to present problems, so he forwarded the article on to Smith.

In a reply letter to Keyhoe, written on November 24, 1950, Smith thanked Keyhoe for "letting us see this advance document and to comment upon it." He stated, however, that he felt "the presentation might cause considerable embarrassment to the Canadian Government since they would be required to make some official statement shortly after the release of the article, which they are not, at present, in a position to do."[23]

On the same day, Smith wrote back to Dr. Solandt notifying him that he had sent a five-page revision of the flying saucer paper to Keyhoe along with a letter explaining the Canadian position. In his memo to Solandt, Smith also suggested that "the article, as revised, be scrutinized by others in the group" for any further revisions they might suggest.[24]

The reference to a "group" associated with the Defense Research Board, dealing with UFOs, directly opposes letters and interviews with Dr. Solandt in the eighties and early nineties. During a 1991 interview, for example, Solandt claimed the Defense Research Board support of Smith was "entirely passive," consisting only of supplying a garage size building in 1953, which was used for the "flying saucer observatory." [25]

In the memo to Solandt, Wilbert Smith also stated that the article was sent to the U.S. Research and Development Board, which was the U.S. equivalent of the Defense Research Board. "The publication of this material," wrote Smith, "if permitted by the United States Research and Development Board, would be in the public interest."

Most importantly, a five-page draft was sent to Vannevar Bush, who during WWII headed the U.S. Office of Scientific Research and Development. Smith already identified Bush, in a Top-Secret memo, as the chairman of a small group that was making a concentrated effort on the modus operandi of the saucers. The Bush role in the January 1951 article also noted in January 1951 correspondence between Wilbert Smith and the Canadian Embassy in Washington, D.C. [26]

The key to the importance of this fact is that Bush was no longer a part of the board, and more importantly, there was absolutely no public indication at the time that Bush played a role in UFO research.

Therefore, Keyhoe was dealing with Vannevar Bush on the subject of UFOs, and it appears Bush was helping Keyhoe in some way. This is the only document we have linking the two, but Keyhoe may have been putting all sorts of UFO material to Bush for comment and direction.

No document has yet surfaced as to exactly what Bush's opinion of the article was. We do know that it was cleared for public distribution, though. The Canadian military liaison to the Research and Development Board, Arnauld Wright, got the article from Vannevar Bush and returned it to Keyhoe.[27] It did not make the 1950 issue of "True" as intended, but was published in Major Keyhoe's `1954 book "Flying Saucers from Outer Space" p. 133-136, minus any mention of Bush or what he said about the article.

The Smith revision of the Keyhoe article forwarded to Vannevar Bush "for clearance" was found in Smith's files at the University of Ottawa.

1951

....

Researcher Linda Moulton Howe reported that government sources told her that *The Day the Earth Stood Still* (1951), depicting an alien landing in Washington D.C., was, in her words, "inspired by the CIA," and "one of the first government tests of public reaction to such an event."

Researcher Robbie Graham wrote, "As farfetched as this may seem, the screenwriter for *The Day the Earth Stood Still*. Edmund H. North was actively serving as a Major in the Army Signal Corps just months before being selected by 20th Century Fox to pen the script. During his time in the Corps, North had been in charge of "training and educational" documentaries. He was the man responsible for overseeing the production of *The Day the Earth Stood Still,* 20th Century-Fox production chief Darryl Zanuck, was himself in charge of an Army Signal Corps documentary unit during World War II. He said that "if you have something worthwhile to say, dress it up in the glittering robes of entertainment, and you will find a ready market... without entertainment, no propaganda film is worth a dime."[28]

1952

....

The official government story is that despite an Air Force investigation into UFOs, the government is not interested in UFOs and is not studying them.

There was one active researcher at the time, however, who reported that the government was quite busy promoting the UFO subject. The researcher was Dr. Leon Davidson, a chemist who was working at Los Alamos, the location in New Mexico where construction of the first atom bombs took place.

> *The CIA secretly sponsored the formation of saucer study groups and contact clubs, including NICAP (under T. Townsend Brown, with whom, incidentally, I have had voluminous correspondence.) The CIA set up many saucer*

publishers, sponsored the publicity received by Adamski's books and others, and sponsored the wave of saucer articles in 1952 in 'Life', 'Look', etc."

"It became clear [to me], early in the 1950's, that the CIA, specifically Allen Dulles, had used legitimate 'flying saucers' events [...] as a tool in the Cold War. Dulles wanted Russia to waste effort on defenses against objects having the extreme capabilities implied by the public saucer stories. [...] Dulles also adopted a concept from his old friend Carl Jung and co-opted the myth that benign aliens have visited Earth for millennia. He used magicians' illusions, tricks, and showmanship to blend in sightings, landings, and contacts, with the legitimate military test sightings. The public perception grew (from comic book to TV show) that space travel was a real possibility, easing Congressional appropriations for the 'moon race' with Russia. Later, Dulles found the saucer believers and their clubs an ideal propaganda vehicle."[29]

Although Davidson didn't believe the saucers were anything more than government operations, he spoke about being brought to the Pentagon in November. There he met with Col. W. A. Adams and Maj. Dewey J. J. Fournet from Blue Book.[30]

"I presented a four-page list of questions," said Davidson. The answers to which proved to me that the A.F. 'investigation' of saucers was completely a cover-up for something else. Col. Adams asked Major Fournet to give me a private showing of the 'Tremonton films' which, at the time, convinced me that the saucers must indeed be real."[31]

Edward Ruppelt, the first head of Project Blue Book, and the originator of the word UFO, admitted that he and others had been tasked with gradual disclosure on the UFO mystery. One example of this was the *Life Magazine* article of April 1952, "Have we Visitors from Space?" It had been under preparation for a year," according to Ruppelt, "and its publication was promoted with the help from the government."

In his book *The Report on Unidentified Flying Objects*, Ruppelt wrote of the help *LIFE* magazine had received:

> *In answer to any questions about the article being Air Force-inspired, my weasel-worded answer was that we had furnished LIFE with some raw data on specific sightings.*
>
> *My answer was purposely weasel-worded because I knew that the Air Force had unofficially inspired the LIFE article. The "maybe they're interplanetary" with the "maybe" bordering on "they are" was the personal opinion of several very high-ranking officers in the Pentagon — so high that their personal opinion was almost policy. I knew the men, and I knew that one of them, a general, had passed his opinions on to Bob Ginna (Life magazine reporter).*[32]

1952 - July

....

Donald Keyhoe had many contacts inside the Pentagon, and rather than a complete cover-up, he stated clearly in an interview with reporter Bob Pratt that he received information in a type of progressive disclosure. He spoke about it when talking about Captain Edward J. Ruppelt, who was the original director of the USAF UFO investigation known as Project Blue Book:

> *Ruppelt had made some statements in public, articles and so forth, and newspaper interviews, and they put the heat on him. Well, after he had gone on inactive, he got a job with an aerospace company, and the Air Force put the heat on him and also the company. If he didn't renege on some of these things he said, they were not going to have anything more to do with the company. So, he added three new chapters to the (revised edition of the) book . . . and he completely reneged on the whole thing and said there was no evidence. It was a ridiculous thing and all that which crucified him. He died of a heart attack shortly after that, and I think that had a lot to do with it. In the three chapters, he added, he takes a crack or two at me, and before that he'd been very*

carefully giving me inside information. He managed to get about 50 cases, really important cases, cleared for me right after that big (July 29, 1952) conference. (General) Samford, who tried to explain away the whole thing, must have been privately in favor of getting it out because shortly after that he allowed headquarters to release all these cases to me with a definite clearance and a statement they were all unexplained, unsolved. [33]

1952 - November

The Early Contactees

The contactees began to appear on the UFO scene a couple days after the detonation of the hydrogen bomb in November 1952. Their stories of contact included "telepathic messages from the space people," an element of the UFO story that is now accepted by researchers.

The late arrival of accounts of telepathic contact with aliens means that from 1947 to November 1952 no one reported having contact with aliens, or being abducted by them.

Many of the early contactees gave indications that they had connections to the United States government. This claim of government contact has led to the theory by many "disinformation theorists" that the contactees were plants by the government to watch what everyone was doing, or to seed silly stories into the field to discredit any serious research.

The reverse theory, however, is also possible. The contactees may have been legitimate contactees that were being controlled by the government, to put out a fact overlaid with fiction about the mysterious flying saucers.

The first public contactee, George Adamski, is an example. He claimed that he had privately met with President Kennedy in late 1961. Adamski claimed he passed on a message from his extraterrestrial contacts about a future world crisis, which Major Hans Peterson from the Danish Air Force, working at the Danish NATO exchange office in Washington DC, identified as the Cuban missile crisis.

Adamski supposedly set up a face to face meeting between the aliens and Kennedy after Kennedy met secretly with Adamski at the Willard Hotel in Washington in May 1963. Adamski reportedly was called to the United Nations to speak with the Secretary General.[34]

Carol Honey, one of Adamski's key co-workers in California, reported many encounters between Adamski and government entities. He told Tim Good "that he was witness to occasions at Palomar when Adamski was visited by highly-placed government and military officials – including a two-star general – and that Adamski was consulted by the USAF regarding an amazing case in which one of their aircraft was several hours overdue."[35]

Adamski also claimed to have an ordinance pass which gave him access to U.S. military facilities. William Sherwood gave support to this story. He had previously worked for the U.S. Ordinance Department and possessed his own ordinance pass.

According to the Riverside Enterprise, in a March 12, 1953, speech Adamski gave to the California Lions Club, he stated: "his material had been cleared with the FBI and Air Force Intelligence."

When the story went public, he was visited by both the FBI and AFI and made to sign an official document stating that he did not have official clearance.

In December of 1953, the controversy was reignited when the Los Angeles Better Business advised Los Angeles FBI that it was investigating Adamski's book *Flying Saucers Have Landed* to determine if it was a fraud.

When they interviewed Adamski, they were shown a document by Adamski with a blue seal in the lower left corner, and at the top of which appeared the names of three government agents – one from the FBI and two from the Air Force.[36]

The FBI investigation determined that the document was a doctored copy of the statement he had signed for the FBI and Air Force a year earlier. A report by the FBI public relations department stated that an FBI agent would visit Adamski, along with AFI if they wished to go, and "read him the riot act," and point out to him that "he has used the document in a fraudulent, improper manner, and that this bureau has not endorsed, approved or cleared his speeches or book, and that he knows it, and the Bureau will simply not tolerate any further foolishness, misrepresentations, or falsity on his part."[37]

The FBI did not, however, press charges for what they claimed was a falsified document.

Finally, Adamski claimed that he secretly briefed the Pentagon about his extraterrestrial contacts.

According to John Keel, in his book *Operation Trojan Horse*, another contactee Howard Menger wrote letters to Gray Barker and 'Saucer News' editor, Jim Moseley. In these letters, he implied that his books were 'fiction-fact.' He added that the Pentagon had given him the films and asked him to participate in an experiment to test the public's reaction to extraterrestrial contact. As John Keel puts it: "He has helped us, therefore, to dismiss his entire story as not only a hoax, but a hoax perpetrated BY THE U.S. GOVERN-MENT!"[38]

Menger was also in contact with Wilbert Smith, the head of the Canadian government flying saucer study from 1950 to 1954.

1956

....

The U.F.O. Documentary

In 1956, United Artists produced the first full-length documentary on the UFO subject called "U.F.O." It was produced by Clarence Greene who at the time was a partner in Greene-Rouse Productions, Los Angeles. He had seen a UFO and was interested in producing something for the public.

According to Robbie Graham, "The director of the USAF's official UFO investigations unit, Project Blue Book, Captain George T. Gregory, was tasked with monitoring not only the film's production process, but its public and critical reception."[39]

The key disclosure part of the story involves the cooperation and involvement from the USAF, and particularly Al Chop who was promoted to Chief of the Press Section at the U.S. Air Force's Air Materiel Command, and then moved to the Pentagon to handle UFO investigations by the USAF's Project Blue Book.

As soon as Greene began the movie, he had a meeting with Chop. Greene told researcher Robert Barrow. "Chop was reluctant to talk at first. But when he realized I was dead serious about the unidentified flying object business, he gave me a breakdown on Project Blue Book, code name for the investigation of UFO." [40]

Chop told his side of his involvement to Barrow, "When first approached about helping with the documentary back in 1954, I was extremely wary about getting involved. However, in subsequent discussions with Greene and Russell Rouse, I became convinced they really wanted to do an unbiased, objective documentary that would shed some light on this subject for the general public."

"A secondary, yet very important objective, was to try to stimulate more interest in UFOs among the scientific personnel in our country."

Not only did Chop agree to cooperate in the making of the documentary, but he revealed to Greene that the USAF was in possession of UFO video, which Greene recovered and used in the film. Chop negotiated for use of the two UFO films Montana (Mariana) and Utah (Newhouse), which had only recently been declassified and made available publicly.

Chop also set up a meeting between Greene and Capt. Edward Ruppelt, USAF Reserve, and former Director of Project Bluebook, and Dewey J. Fournet Jr. (Fournet, as an AF Major, had been the AF UFO Project Monitor).

1957

………………………………..

The Disney Disclosure Initiative

Walt Disney was approached to help produce a UFO documentary in 1957. Ward Kimball, an animator and producer who had been with Walt Disney since 1934, told the 1957 UFO film story. He was one of the original nine Disney animators called the "Nine Old Men" by Walt Disney. As an animator, Kimball was best known for his creation of Jiminy Cricket in the movie Pinocchio, and Dumbo in the movie by the same name.

More importantly, Kimball initiated, produced, and directed three space films that appeared on Tomorrowland, a what-if television show developed to illustrate the possibilities of space. The three films were *Man in Space*, *Man and the Moon*, and *Mars and Beyond*. The first of these was so popular (viewed by over 42 million people) that according to Kimball President Eisenhower phoned Walt Disney from the White House looking for a copy of the production.

Kimball stated, "It impressed President Eisenhower - I can remember this- and the next day he phoned Walt and wanted to borrow a print of it! Walt wanted to know why, and he said: 'Well, I'm going to show it to all those stove-shirt generals who don't believe we're going to be up there!'"

Kimball told the story of Walt Disney's UFO partnership with the government at a 1979 MUFON Convention speech. He stated in the speech that around 1957 or 1958 Walt Disney was contacted by the USAF and asked to cooperate on a documentary about UFOs. The USAF offered to supply actual UFO footage.

According to Kimball, Disney went along with the USAF plan. This compliance was in accord with the many rumors that indicated Disney was a patriotic, conservative, anti-communist who was willing to work with the government.

The FBI file on Walt Disney, for example, stated that on December 16, 1954 Disney was made a SAC Contact, elevated from an informant. The confidential internal FBI memo read:

"Because of Mr. Disney's position as the foremost producer of cartoon files in the motion picture industry, and his prominence and wide acquaintanceship in film production matters, it is believed that he can be of valuable assistance to this office..."

Being a contact would allow him to take reports from other informers. As a part of this association Disney wrote a number of reports to the FBI during the McCarthy communist scare days of the 1950s.

On the day Walt Disney died, J. Edgar Hoover sent a letter of condolences to Walt's wife Lillian. At the bottom of the copy of the letter there was a handwritten notation to remove Walt Disney's name as an active SAC Contact.

The FBI-Disney association gave the FBI "full access to the facilities of Disneyland for use, in connection with official matters and recreational purposes." All Disney movies that involved any references to the FBI had to be sent to the FBI for approval.

Disney had apparently made a deal in 1936 with the FBI to write reports on subversive authorities inside Hollywood in exchange for the FBI determining Walt Disney's true lineage. Disney was apparently very uncertain of his real lineage, and this uncertainty was reflected in many of his film characters. Pinocchio, for example, was alone and desperately wanted to be Gepetto's boy. In the movie, *Dumbo*, Dumbo was the small baby elephant that had been separated from his mother. Finally, the prime character in Snow White was an abandoned stepchild.

Once Walt Disney had met with the USAF, he began to work on the requested UFO documentary for the general public. He asked his animators to think up what an alien would look like. Meanwhile, he waited for the Air Force to deliver the promised film.

After some period of time, the Air Force re-contacted Disney and told him the offer was being withdrawn. There would be no UFO footage as promised. Kimball told researcher Stanton Friedman that once he found out there would be no delivery of UFO film, he personally spoke with an Air Force Colonel who told him there indeed was plenty of UFO footage, but that neither Ward, nor anyone else, was going to get access to it.

Disney, however, carried on without the film. According to one account of the story, Disney cancelled the project but by that time a lot of animated creatures had been completed by his artists and Disney moved forward with the a brief documentary featuring Jonathan Winters impersonating various characters associated with typical UFO lore. Kimball stated, as relayed by Bruce Maccabee:

"I specifically recall Mr. Winters as an old lady/grandmother who saw a UFO and reported it... then he portrayed the Air Force officer who investigated the sightings and offered explanations. He also portrayed a little boy in a room that had a telescope looking up at the stars and, to the little boy's amazement, an alien came through the telescope into his room (I think I've got this right). Of course, the boy's father didn't believe that story."

The movie was never shown in public, but Kimball did show it at the 1979 Symposium. The movie, however, did not contain any of the dramatic UFO footage and live aliens everyone had been promised.

As an interesting footnote to the Disney story, Emenegger reported that he and Sandler had also talked with the Disney people in the time period when they were working on the documentary. The people whom they spoke to at the Disney studios "seemed to be involved and interested, but not have any particularly startling data."

Recent information arising from controversy surrounding the 1995 "Alien Autopsy" indicates that the Disney studio might have gotten some film and just didn't use it, or got it after the movie was finished.

The story that indicates there may have been film comes from a prominent UK photographer Mike Maloney. Maloney is the Group Chief Photographer at Mirror Group Newspapers, a fellow with both the Royal Photographic Society and the British Institute of Professional Photographers. Maloney has won many awards, 96 by one count, including Press Photographer of the Year three times.

In the 1970s, Maloney was dining with the head of Disney, and four of the original nine Disney animators while on a trip to the Disney Corporation in Los Angeles. While this was going on Maloney was introduced to another man, identified in one account as a "well-known Disney employee."

The man offered to show Maloney some unusual film footage at his house. When Maloney saw it, he described it as "old footage of UFOs," and two beings that he was told "were aliens."

UFO investigator, Georgina Bruni, interviewed Mike Maloney about his early 1970s encounter at Disney. She described what Maloney told her about the aliens he had been shown on the film:

"One, which appeared to be dead, was laid out on a table - or slab, the other was clearly alive and moving around on the floor. He was given no information as to the source of the footage, which he was told was "top secret," but he was in no doubt that it was a genuine piece of old film. Mike described it as being similar to the alien autopsy footage that had been shown on television. At no time did he say it was the same, just similar. As to the footage Maloney personally viewed, he said, "If the film that I saw was a fake, it was a brilliant fake."'

This is a promotional poster for the Flying Saucer ride built at Disneyland in 1955. It was a part of the Tomorrowland section of the park.

Disclosure Efforts 1960-1970

1966

....

CBS TV broadcasts a documentary called *UFOs: Friend, Foe, or Fantasy?* It was narrated by newsman Walter Cronkite. In a personal letter addressed to fellow board member of the 1953 CIA Robertson Panel, Secretary Frederick C. Durant, astrophysicist Dr. Thornton Page confided that he "helped organize the CBS TV UFO documentary around the Robertson Panel conclusions."

Although the documentary was very harsh against the reality of ET visitation, Page appeared on the show defending the "we tried to evaluate all reports without saying that they are ridiculous in advance."

Disclosure Efforts 1970- 1980

1-201. Top Secret. Authority for original classification of information as Top Secret may be exercised only by the president, by such officials as the president may designate by publication in the FEDERAL REGISTER, by the agency heads listed below, and by officials to whom such authority is delegated in accordance with Section 1-204. **The law as spelled out In President Carter's Executive Order 12065.**

The events of the early to mid 1970s were some of the most important days in Ufology disclosure. There is almost no doubt that the government was planning some sort of disclosure about UFOs. This is particularly important because there was no pressure to release after the shutdown of Project Blue Book in late 1969.

Once Blue Book was shut down, those who controlled the secret could have sat back and never addressed the subject again. Instead through various people they started to leak the idea that disclosure was imminent. Consider the following statements:

> *...the government will release all its (UFO) information within the next three years." (APRO UFO Organization 1974)*

> *...the government is almost ready to release some of the information it has reportedly withheld from the public for 25 years concerning extraterrestrial life...This super cover-up... concerning UFOs... makes the White House's Watergate mess look like a high school affair." (National Examiner Dec. 9, 1974)*

> *We predict that by 1975 the government will release definite proof that extraterrestrials are watching us. (Authors Ralph and Judy Blum April 1974)*

> *The government will tell us what's been going on, in a series of television documentaries over a period of months... The entire story is slated to be disclosed by the 200th anniversary of Independence on July 4,*

1976. (Robert Barry), head of the 20th Century UFO Bureau)

The most dramatic evidence that some sort of disclosure effort was being planned can be seen from the following incredible story.

1972

....

Film Disclosure Offer

In 1972, Los Angeles Grey Advertising executive Bob Emenegger got a call from Allan Sandler who owned a local production studio. Sandler stated he had received a call from the military that they would like some documentaries done.

Figure 4 Bob Emenegger in front of his Los Angeles home in 1978.

The two men went to a meeting at Norton Air Force Base where all the military film was stored at that time. There they met with Paul Shartle, the security manager. Shartle stated that because of the Vietnam War, the Department of Defense wanted a series of documentaries done that would present the military in a better light.

They were given ideas for the eight planned documentaries, working with dolphins, 3-D holography, and other leading edge ideas. It was after this rundown that Shartle dropped the bomb. He stated that the military would also like a documentary done on UFOs but they would like Emenegger and Sandler to hide the documentary under the other eight films.

Emenegger was shocked at what he was hearing as he was not a believer. He had in fact scolded his wife many times telling her to stop reading all the "I had an alien baby stories" in the tabloids. Now he was standing in front of a military official who was hinting that it was all for real.

"What would you say," said Shartle, "if I told you that an alien craft landed at Holloman Air Force Base in May 1971, and it was filmed from three different angles as the aliens exited the craft and interacted with base officials." That is how one of the best stories in Ufology started.

Emenegger and Sandler were given access to everyone and anything that they needed for the project. Ray Rivas, the director of the final documentary called *UFOs: Past, Present, and Future* was given "unprecedented" access to DoD facilities, with the director saying the "Secretary of the Air Force Robert Seamans gave the order to co-operate."

At the Pentagon, Emenegger and Sandler were offered "800 feet of film...as well as several thousand feet of additional material" of dramatic UFO material. They would be allowed to use the UFO footage in a special film project they had been asked to join.

The 800 feet of film was from Holloman AFB where it was claimed U.S. officials filmed aliens landing and their encounter with them.

The promised film impressed Emenegger who in 1988 described what he saw, "What I saw and heard was enough to convince me that the phenomenon of UFOs is real – very real." Paul Shartle, the Norton Security Manager, who had controlled the film, and made the offer to the two men, described what he saw on the film as:

> *I saw footage of three disc-shaped crafts. One of the craft landed and two of them went away... It appeared to be in trouble because it oscillated all the way down to the ground. However, it did land on three pods. A sliding door opened, a ramp was extended, and out came three aliens... They were human size. They had odd gray complexions and a pronounced nose. They wore tight-fitting jump suits, thin headdresses that appeared to be communications devices, and in their hands, they*

> *held a translator, I was told. The Holloman base commander and other Air Force officers went out to meet them...*

The project was described to the two producers as a documentary on a secret government project. When the two men discovered that the topic of the secret project would be UFOs, they were surprised because "they had assumed that the matter had been resolved with the closure of Project Blue Book in 1969."

Col. George Weinbrenner, as well as former Project Blue Book spokesman Col. Bill Coleman, his bosses in the Defense Public Affairs Department and other defense department officials made the offer to the two men at the Pentagon in late 1972. They were told that the government was now ready to release all the facts about the alien presence on earth.

The two producers actually signed a contract at the Pentagon for producing the documentary, and no questions were asked. Emenegger recalled the bizarre moment:

> *As a matter of fact, you know, one of our agreements was to go over the script at the Pentagon, and if there was any question about anything they had the right to ask about it. Strangely enough, no one even questioned the thing about the landing at Holloman Air Force Base. It was like, "Well OK" . . . I just couldn't believe it. (Emenegger and Sandler began as UFO disbelievers) but said, "Oh well - I'll go along with it." One conversation led to another. Everyone couldn't have been more open about what we were doing. Anyone along the line could have questioned it, which I expected. They could have said, "What the hell are you guys talking about?" This included Col. George Weinbrenner, if you recall.*

Sandler and Emenegger were shown evidence that they could use for their tell-all documentary. This evidence included:

- Photographs and films of UFOs.
- 800 feet of film showing a landed encounter between three aliens and Holloman Air Base officials during a landing that had

reportedly occurred there in May 1971. Several thousand feet of additional material.

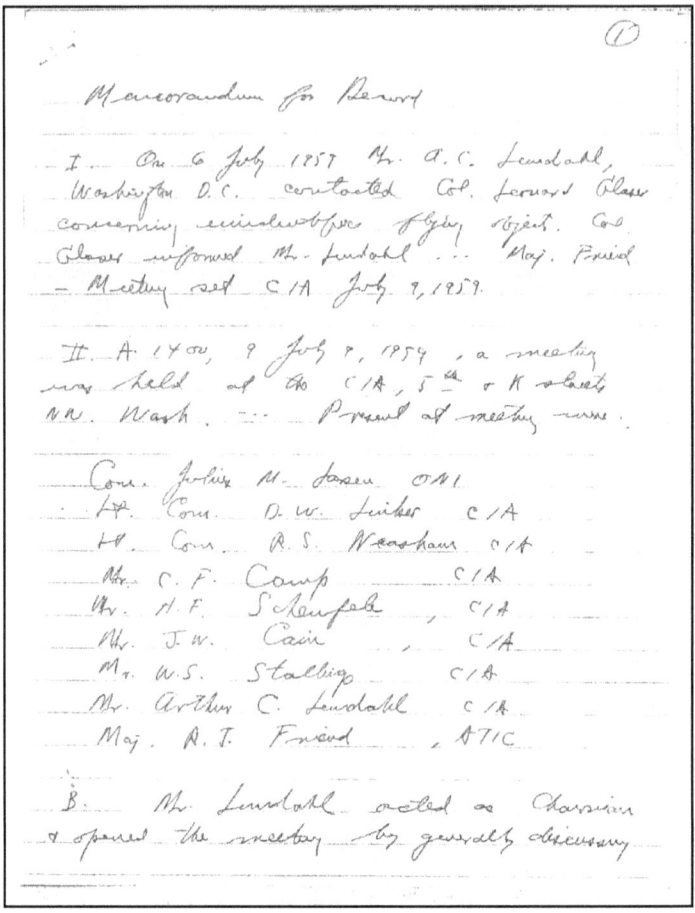

Figure 5 - Page 1 of 11 page CIA Memo

- Photos of UFOs taken by astronauts, which NASA had formally denied the existence of.
- A Top-Secret UFO film of UFOs tracking the launch of a missile launched at Vandenberg Air Force Base. The film canister had the name of USAF Blue Book director Hector Quintanilla on it. **This film was never given back and is still in the possession of the two producers.**
- A memo described an encounter between six CIA officers (including Arthur Lundahl, the director of the most highly classified photo lab for the CIA, head of the UFO desk at the CIA, and a man who claimed he had briefed three presidents on UFOs) and an alien by the name of AFFA. The trance channeled

communication led to a visible fly-by of the building where the CIA officers watched.

Emenegger was given a tour of the CIA's National Photographic Interpretation Center (NPIC) office in Washington where the 1959 communication had taken place with the alien.

The offer by Colonel Bill Coleman to suddenly make public dramatic evidence proving extraterrestrial visitations, and to free up classified information related to the UFO mystery was quite an about face from what he had formally written to NICAP member, Kurt Zeissig. Coleman's 1962 statement to Zeissig related to AFM 190-4, Chapter 4, Section B.2.g, as it applied to Air Force personnel statements on UFOs and other military subjects:

> *By this order, the Secretary of the Air Force Office of Information must delete all evidence of UFO reality and intelligent control, which would, of course, contradict the Air Force stand that UFOs do not exist. The same rule applies to A.F. press releases and UFO information given to Congress and the public.*

In 1988, Coleman clarified and expounded on his 1962 statement in a letter to *Florida Today* columnist Billy Cox, which made his 1972 and 1985 approaches to Emenegger with film footage a strange move indeed:

> *In reviewing material for publication by authors who at the time of creation of the material were under USAF aegis, it was necessary to remove any material that would put the USAF in the position of supporting the thesis that alien intelligence was in fact visiting planet earth. The reason for this is simply the fact that evidence we possessed from the thousands of investigations did not in any way support the thesis. We had a warehouse full of stuff, but non-of it, not one iota, would support the ETIH.*

As plans for the government inspired documentary unfolded, Emenegger and Sandler were invited to Norton Air Force Base in May 1973, where they met with the Head of the Air Force Office of Special

Investigations (AFOSI), and Paul Shartle, former Head of Security and Chief of Requirements for the audiovisual program at Norton.

Emenegger and Sandler were again assured that they would be provided the Holloman landing film to produce their documentary. Shartle would state in a 1988 interview that he had seen the Holloman landing footage. The documentary had been sponsored by the Department of Defense to do a public relations turnaround needed because of the Vietnam War. At least that is the story Emenegger and Sandler were told by Colonel Bill Coleman. A number of different subjects were proposed for the documentaries, but no other subject other than UFOs was brought up.

As the documentary neared completion, the two producers waited for the promised alien landing footage. However, Colonel Coleman, who first made the offer to provide it in 1972, withdrew it. According to what Emenegger told researcher Tim Good, Coleman had declared, "The timing was politically inappropriate, due to the Watergate scandal." The film, according to Emenegger, was driven back to the Pentagon by car.

Once Emenegger was informed he would not be getting the film, as promised, he traveled to Wright-Patterson Air Force Base to see one of the men who had been at the Pentagon, Col. George Weinbrenner. He demanded that the Colonel tell him what was going on.

According to Emenegger the Colonel stood up and walked up to a chalkboard complaining in a loud voice, "That damn MIG 25! We're so public about what we have…all kinds of things we don't know about. We need to know more about the MIG-25."

Moving to his bookshelf, he continued his rant about the MIG-25, while pulling J. Allen Hynek's book *The UFO Experience* off the shelf. He showed Emenegger Hynek's signature and dedication to Weinbrenner on the inside cover while he talked.

To Emenegger, it was clear that Weinbrenner "was confirming the reality of the film while making sure that no one overhearing the conversation would realize what he was doing."

It also illustrated the fact that the Holloman landing must have been a piece of information held by a group that would go to any ends to keep it secret. Weinbrenner was clearly afraid to be caught talking about the film. It was a film "they" wanted everyone to know about, without anyone on the inside officially confirming it.

It was also a film that involved many players below the surface such as the John MacArthur Foundation who put up the $250,000 for the UFO documentary, but who asked not to be listed in the credits.

This appeared to be a clear case of someone supplying the money, and using the foundation as a front in order to protect their identity.

This classification fear is further backed up by a story reportedly told by one of the key figures in the Holloman UFO film story, Colonel Robert Coleman. The reported story, told on the inside, is that Coleman told Emenegger that in order to tell him the true story of the Holloman landing, he would have to take him out into the middle of the ocean on a boat. Then Emenegger said that Coleman jokingly said "and then I would have to kill you."

The Emenegger/Sandler documentary *UFOs: Past, Present, and Future* released by Sandler Films in 1974 was forced to use standard animation, background film taken at Holloman, and "elaborate drawing of the so-called aliens." At least that is what the producers thought when they first ran the film.

Later, the words of the film's narrator Rod Serling took on new meaning when Shartle and Emenegger appeared in a 1988 interview on a nation-wide TV special called "UFO Cover-up? . . . Live" to state that 8 seconds of the film used in the documentary had been actual film of the 1971 UFO landing.

Figure 6 - One actual frame of Holloman film

During the narration of the film Serling had declared, "Let us look at an incident that might happen in the future, or perhaps could have happened already." Those words now took on a whole new meaning.

It slipped through the security net, according to Shartle, and the public never realized that they had actually viewed a flying saucer landing at a highly secure USAF Base.

The film of an alleged interaction at Holloman between "us" and "them" being offered, and then withdrawn, is what Jacques Vallee described as "a dangling carrot case." Evidence would be indirectly provided to convince those who were to carry the message to the public, without those disseminating the message having to violate any security oaths. Vallee should know. He was involved in an almost identical case with J. Allen Hynek in 1985.

Despite the drawbacks of the initial offer made by the government to Emenegger and Sandler, the incident is important because the government didn't have to do it.

Further, it began a pattern of further releases by whoever controlled the UFO secrets that would continue on for the next 30 years and continues to the present day. This pattern appeared to be a process for disseminating the most bizarre, dramatic, concrete, and paradigm-shattering pieces of the UFO mystery into the UFO community, while at the same time destroying the case's pedigree and other marks that would provide proof.

Robert Emenegger, in the book he wrote in conjunction with the UFO documentary, seemed to realize the significance of the Holloman story, when he wrote:

> *But until the answer is found, the challenge remains. The momentum towards finding answers has begun – for a most significant and historical meeting has quietly, and without publicity, taken place.*

It was not the first time that the Pentagon had offered dramatic UFO video evidence, nor would it be the last. Years later, Kit Green, a former high level CIA official dealing with UFOs, would describe the process of gradual disclosure, and why the Holloman film had been given to Emenegger and Sandler:

> *And that is what I think the meaning, the rational, behind things like the Bob Emenegger film is. It's to help people not to get sick later, to calm people down when they find out the truth.*[41]

The final dramatic story was when Linda Howe stated that she and researcher Larry Fawcett met with Emenegger at his home to talk about the story of his documentary experience with the government. She stated that Emenegger had shown her and Fawcett a letter with Richard Nixon's signature that thanks Emenegger for "his discretion on the project they had worked on."

1976

....

Jimmy Carter's Disclosure Efforts

I don't believe in keeping information like that secret, but there may be some aspects of the UFO information, with which I am not familiar, which might be related to some secret experiments that we were doing that involve national security – a new weapons system. I surely wouldn't release that, but if it was something removed from our national security, then I as president would go ahead and release it. I see nothing wrong with that. **Jimmy Carter promises UFO disclosure during the 1976 presidential campaign.**

Twice while campaigning for president Jimmy Carter promised that if he were elected president he would disclose all UFO material that did not fall under the category of national security.

Jimmy Carter entered the White House determined to release the UFO files, inspired by the fact he himself had had a sighting. He informed his close friend, actress Shirley MacLaine, that he knew the secret but that his hands were tied. "It was true…there were occupants," MacLaine told Larry King in 1995. "He wanted to 'shine the sunshine laws on it to see how the people would react,' but he couldn't and wouldn't."

Carter spelled out that if the subject involved "national security" he wouldn't release that material. Anything that the briefers would tie into threat to the security of the nation would be reason for Carter to keep quiet.

Carter's Deputy Press secretary Walter Wurfel clarified what the actual promise on UFOs was:

> *He (Carter) is committed to the fullest possible openness in government and would support full disclosure of material that was not defense sensitive that might relate to UFOs. He did not, however, pledge to "make every piece of information concerning the UFOs available to the public." There might be some aspects of some sightings that would have defense implications that possibly should be safe-guarded against immediate and full disclosure.*[42]

Most UFO histories written about the Carter administration feel that Carter was a failure and that he achieved nothing. Many believe that he was completely cut off from the UFO information and was in effect a puppet for some dark cabal or Wizard of Oz who runs the United States government.

A closer evaluation of the evidence shows that Carter was very much in the loop and that he did a lot to bring disclosure to the UFO mystery. This was hinted at by Carter based on what he told his friend actress Shirley MacLaine. In an April 1995 interview with Larry King, MacLaine was replying to claims made by actor Nicholas Cage that Carter had told MacLaine that he had been given access to the alien bodies and craft. MacLaine replied:

> *He didn't tell me that, but he told me many times when I first wrote Out On A Limb that he would support me [and] that it was true, that there were craft, that he believed there were occupants, why should we be the only people in the universe. He wanted to shine the sunshine laws on intelligence, to expose it, to see how the people would react, but he didn't and wouldn't and couldn't as he explained to me.*

The story that is referenced by those who believe Carter was cut out the loop deals with his president-elect briefing that took place in November 1976. It was conducted, as protocol demanded, by George H.W. Bush who at that time was the CIA director for the outgoing Ford administration.

It was during that briefing, according to Marcia Smith at the Congressional Research Office,[43] that Carter asked for the UFO files. The story continued with Bush turning down the president-elect, saying that there was no need to know and that curiosity on the part of the president did not constitute need to know.

Bush told Carter that if he wanted the UFO files he would have to go through the House Committee for Science and Technology. This is significant because Bush did not turn him down but sent him to a House Committee. This hints that Carter's UFO request had nothing to do with getting the Top - Secret information on UFOs for himself. Sending Carter to the House indicates that Carter was asking for the UFO files to satisfy his election promise to disclose info on all of the UFO info that did not involve national security.

This makes sense because if he wanted the Above Top Secret UFO files, Bush would certainly not have sent him to the House Committee for Science and Technology to find those files. The Top-Secret files for "President's Eyes Only" would have more likely be held by the National Security Agency, CIA, MJ-12, DIA, or some other agency with access to black budget funding. Because Bush sent him to the House the request must have been for files that he could publicly release.

Despite what has been written elsewhere, Carter did many things to disclose the truth behind the UFO mystery. The reason this is not well-known is that Carter did things quietly behind the scenes. In most of his efforts, other officials did the work which kept Carter's fingerprints off what was happening. The UFO disclosure initiatives included:

Freedom of Information Initiatives - When President Carter took office the Freedom of Information Act (FOIA) passed by President Johnson in 1966 was doing nothing to force out secret UFO files held by intelligence, the various executive agencies, and in the military.

When Carter took office, all of this changed. Many of the logjams researchers had incurred with the FOIA regulations were removed. In a news conference, one month after taking office, Carter outlined his personal support for new Freedom of Information Act laws:

> *In general, I favor the freedom of information laws... When there is a sense among American citizens that they are being misled or that illegalities are taking place within our own Government... I think under those circumstances that there is excessive pressure on Government for information. If that same citizen had a sense that he could trust us, there would be much less inclination to demand access to the files... I think I might, as president, assume more responsibility in that field...*

In 1978, President Carter took additional action which strengthened the access to documents using the FOIA. He did this by signing Executive Order 12065, which in effect revamped the government's security classification system.

The new Executive Order changed the way documents got viewed in legal appeals over material releases. President Carter's order introduced the "public interest balancing test" which became an important consideration in the way UFO (and any other subject)

FOIAs were dealt with. The test introduced a new aspect to judicial reviews. Courts in reviewing UFO documents for release "were forced to consider the public's interest when deciding declassification requests under the Freedom of Information Act."

Executive Order 12065 created a flood of declassified UFO documents. In fact, more than 50% of all UFO documents declassified got declassification by the United States government in the four years of the Carter administration. Carter set the stage for the "golden years," during which the UFO documents began to surface. During the four years of the Carter administration, the CIA, FBI, NSA, State, Army, USAF and the Navy Department released thousands of pages of UFO documents.

The Justice Department - Carter sent his press secretary Jody Powell to pressure the FBI to identify how they tracked UFO sightings and what files they had. The Department of Justice was also instructed to tell agencies "to release information that could legally be withheld if the release could not be clearly harmful." The security system was revamped to "eliminate needless initial classification... reduce the time that documents remain classified." Carter estimated that 250 million pages of documents would be released because of the changes.

The CIA - The Carter green-lighting of FOIAs caused panic at the CIA. Citizens Against UFO Secrecy (CAUS) and a UFO researcher specializing in government cover-up, Todd Zechel, had initiated an FOIA lawsuit against the CIA in September 1977 in conjunction with Peter Gersten, a New York attorney, and Ground Saucer Watch, a Phoenix-based UFO group.

This lawsuit along with pressure from the president had initiated a battle for the UFO files at the CIA.

Researcher Bruce Maccabee claimed that CIA officer Kit Green, "Keeper of the Weird," had estimated that "there might be as many as 15,000 UFO-related documents" scattered throughout headquarters based on the one or two thousand he had control over.

One story circulated that Green, who was interested in UFOs, had some personal UFO material in his office which was under threat of becoming part of the FOIA lawsuit. He was called up and asked why the UFO stuff was in his office.

Stories were circulating that lawyers for the government were exerting heavy pressure on the CIA to come up with the requested documents as a result of the lawsuit. At the same time, officers were busy stonewalling and hiding documents.

Domestic Policy Staff - The Carter Domestic Policy staff in 1977 initiated an extraterrestrial communication study at the Stanford Research Institute (SRI) in Menlo Park, California. The study was headed up by Alfred Webre who at the time was the Senior Policy Analyst in 1977 at the Center for the Study of Social Policy at SRI.

> *The over-all purpose of the proposed 1977 Carter White House Extraterrestrial Communication Study was to create, design and carry out an independent, civilian-led research compilation and evaluation of phenomena suggesting an extraterrestrial and/or inter-dimensional intelligent presence in the near-Earth environment.*
>
> *The designed outcome of the study was to have been a public White House report, detailing the compiled evidence and evaluation, together with possible scientific models for the implications of the research. The White House report was to have contained public policy recommendations emerging from the evaluations and conclusions of the Study. These, if warranted, included transformation of secrecy regulations of U.S. military-intelligence agencies.*
>
> *The scientific and public policy goal of the proposed 1977 Carter White House Extraterrestrial Communication Study was to fill a substantial gap in civilian scientific knowledge of the UFO (Unidentified Flying Object phenomenon), Extraterrestrial Biological Entities (EBEs), and related phenomena.*[44]

The program operated during the period from May 1977 until the fall of 1977, and involved input from the White House, NASA, SRI, National Science Foundation, and UFO experts. It was abruptly terminated by an official from the Department of Defense, as told by Webre:

> *They [management of SRI] had received direct communications from the Pentagon that if the study went forward, SRI's contracts with the Pentagon [which were many] would be terminated. He [my*

> *SRI Pentagon liaison] stated that the project, that had just been approved by the White House, was terminated because, and I am quoting him, "There are no UFOs."*[45]

NASA - Carter used his science advisor, Frank Press, to contact NASA and request help with the UFO issue. Realizing the public relations nightmare they would take on, and at a time of their budget being slashed, NASA Director Robert Frosch wrote back to Press on March 21, 1977, saying, "NASA knew of no tangible evidence of UFO reality based on a check with the CIA."

Later, in a letter from Kenneth Chapman, Associate Administrator for External Relations, regarding a report called "UFO Study Considerations," Chapman stated, "We specifically queried the CIA by telephone as to whether they were aware of any tangible or physical UFO evidence that could be analyzed...." The UFO report became suspect for its joint production through both the CIA and NASA.

In September 1977, Carter's administration asked NASA to help with the deluge of incoming UFO mail inspired by Carter's open promise to release the UFO files.

In a July 21, 1977 letter, Dr. Press wrote the NASA administrator, Dr. Robert Frosch, asking for help with the UFO mail problem, but also suggesting it might be time for another study of the UFO issue. Press suggested that a panel of prominent scientists such as Carl Sagan might "conduct an investigation of the validity and significance of UFO reports."

> *We have discovered that the White House is becoming the focal point for an increasing number of inquiries concerning UFOs. As you know, there appears to be a national revival of interest in the matter with a younger generation becoming involved. Those of us in the Executive Office are ill equipped to handle these kinds of inquiries.*
>
> *It seems to me that the focal point of the UFO question ought to be in NASA. I recommend two things: since it has been nearly a decade since the Condon (sic) report (see University of Colorado UFO Project), I believe that a small panel of inquiry could be formed to see if there are any new significant findings. Since this is a public relations*

problem as much as anything else, people who are known to be interested in the problem and also highly known, such as Carl Sagan, ought to be involved. This is a panel of inquiry that could be formed by NASA.

NASA, however, was not receptive to the idea, or even to the notion of having been asked. On December 21, 1977, NASA's Dr. Frosch wrote President Carter's Science Advisor to inform the White House of his decision about not taking up the job of another UFO investigation. The decision was made to help with the mail, but to decline the White House offer of a new UFO investigation.

In response to your letter of September 14, 1977, regarding NASA's possible role in UFO matters, we are fully prepared at this time to continue responding to public inquiries along the same line as we have done in the past. If some new element of hard evidence is brought to our attention in the future, it would be entirely appropriate for some NASA laboratory to analyze and report upon an otherwise unexplained organic or inorganic sample. We stand ready to respond to any bona fide physical evidence from credible sources. We intend to leave the door clearly open to such possibility.

We've given considerable thought to the question of what else the United States might and should do in the area of UFO research. There is an absence of tangible or physical evidence for thorough laboratory analysis. And because of the absence of such evidence we have not been able to devise a sound scientific procedure for investigating these phenomena. To proceed on a research task without a disciplinary framework and an exploratory technique in mind would be wasteful and probably unproductive.

I do not feel that we should mount a research effort without a better starting point than we have been able to identify thus far. I would therefore propose that NASA take no steps to establish a research activity in this area or to convene a symposium on this subject.

I wish in no way to indicate that NASA has come to any conclusion about these phenomena as such. Institutionally we retain an open mind, a keen sense of scientific curiosity and a willingness to analyze technical problems within our competence.

UFO researchers - There were some UFO researchers who claimed receiving invitations for meetings by Carter transitional people. These included Robert Barrow, Jacques Vallee, J. Allen Hynek, and Bill Pitts. Barrow, for example, was contacted about participating in another undefined UFO study.

Figure 7 Professional photographer Linda Arosemena took a photograph of President Carter's helicopter, Army 1, as it departed from Fort Clayton, Panama. June 17, 1978. She took the picture with a Nikon camera using Kodak Tri-X film (black and white) shooting at 1/250 second at F/16. A UFO was sighted the day before in the same general area by some women· while fishing. The object that they drew for police is very similar to what was photographed. Photo Carter Library]

Barrow received no future contact, so no one knows if this particular study went forward. Pitts traveled to Washington, and during a visit to Dr. Press' office, offered to do anything he could to assist the White House in their plan to release their secret information.

A group of UFO researchers in the Los Angeles area prepared a study for President Carter in the early days of the administration. It was known as the "L.A. Study." The researchers have told their side of the story, but no records appear at the Carter library.

1977

....

1977 became famous for the release of the movie *Close Encounters of the Third Kind* directed by Steven Spielberg. Many have viewed this film as a part of the gradual disclosure of the UFO story to the public.

Spielberg became one of the key Hollywood figure for his release of alien-themed movies. His two important productions were *Close Encounters of the Third Kind* (1977) and *E.T. The Extra-Terrestrial* (1982). Other alien-themed Spielberg films include *War of the Worlds, Cowboys and Aliens, Super 8* and *War of The Worlds*.

The CIA provides assets to Hollywood films in exchange for being able to present the agency in the best light possible. As reported by researcher Robbie Graham "The United States Air Force (USAF) provided *Transformers* director Michael Bay with hundreds-of-millions-of-dollars worth of state-of-the-art hardware for use in the 2007 movie, including the F-117 stealth fighter and – in its first ever Silver Screen appearance - the F-22 Raptor fighter. The DoD's support for the Transformers sequel (2009) was no less enthusiastic as Bay was granted every benefit of the Pentagon's coveted 'full co-operation.'"[46]

There have been many rumors that *Close Encounters* was part of an acclimatization program on the part of the government to prepare the minds of citizens for the idea that we are not alone in the universe.

Close Encounters was the first alien movie that took a benign view of human contact with the extraterrestrials, as opposed to the alien invasion movies of the fifties and sixties where evil creatures of all shapes and sizes come to invade and take over the world. Spielberg's *Close Encounters* involved small, shy, childlike spindly beings with large craniums. In making the movie, Spielberg used overexposures of six-year-old girls to make the aliens as real as possible.

Rumor has it that the representation of the grey aliens in *Close Encounters* was so accurate that for Spielberg's movie, *E.T.*, the Pentagon forced him to change the look of the alien.

On March 18, 1978, The *Phoenix Gazette* stated, "Jimmy Carter's favorite movie is *Close Encounters of the Third Kind*. As a matter of fact, the President has seen the movie many times," although there is no evidence in the Carter Library that he saw the film. This omission may have been by design. If the president is running the cover-up, he "cannot be a player," and therefore official documents cannot evidence him watching UFO movies.

In a 1977 Canadian TV interview conducted directly after the film's official release, Spielberg said that Carter had viewed the movie, "Last Saturday."

"We haven't heard the direct feedback," said Spielberg, but added, "We hear he [Carter] liked it quite a bit."[47]

The movie received many bad reviews, such as one by William Flanagan for *New York Magazine*, who wrote, "In my humble opinion, the picture will be a colossal flop." There was a flood of sell orders of Columbia shares in light of the negative reviews. The New York Exchange even suspended trading in the stock at one point. It was a film whose huge budget might have shut down Columbia Studios had it not succeeded.

But the film did succeed. It grossed $72 million in its first two weeks. It was even successful overseas. Spielberg and his wife were invited to London to screen the film for Queen Elizabeth and her husband, Prince Philip. Philip had long expressed open interest in UFOs. He had been a long-time subscriber to *Flying Saucer Review*, the most popular UFO journal in Britain.

Spielberg was a Hollywood sensation whose success gave him access to many U.S. presidents, and Carter was one of them, but that relationship was a secretive one. An example of this can be found in the files at the Carter presidential library.

On August 25, 1978, Carter sent Spielberg a picture with an inscription on it "To Steven Spielberg." It was signed "Jimmy Carter". Enclosed with the photo was an attached White House stationary note from Gretchen Poston, which read, "The President thought that you would enjoy receiving the enclosed photo."

The White House records at the Carter library have a photocopy of the photo, which raises a number of peculiar points. The White House note from Posten had been placed in such a way that it obscured Carter's face in the photocopy. The envelope, addressed to Spielberg, partly covered Spielberg's face. No explanation was ever provided as to why this was done.

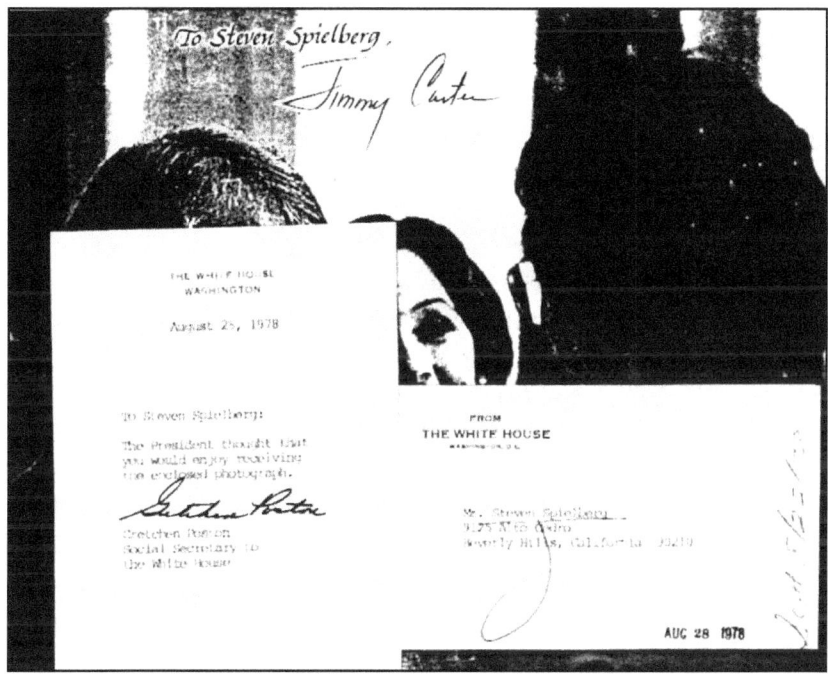

Figure 8 - Photocopy of Carter and Spielberg with faces blocked. Original photo was never located.

A search, with the help of an archivist at the Carter library, for White House photos taken during August 1978 turned up no record of the photo in question.

More unusual was the fact that, according to records held at the President Carter library, Spielberg was never in the White House. No records reflected Carter and Spielberg ever having met, corresponded, or talked on the phone. Yet the photocopied photo clearly shows that the two men met, and the letter and envelope reflect at least one piece of correspondence.

The fact that Carter "could not be a player" in the UFO subject might account for this.

Even *Science Magazine* realized the problems with the president being publicly associated with the UFO film: "In the present climate," wrote *Science*, "then (and who knows when Close Encounters will be shown to the First Family), it may become more difficult to avoid another UFO study." With UFO letters pouring into the White House, and with the president publicly admitting he experienced a sighting, media reports of his seeing Spielberg's film would increase the demands for another UFO study and that was something no federal agency wanted to be stuck with.

In addition to the photo from Carter, there was a second strange incident involving the Carter White House and Steven Spielberg. As will be described below, Carter approached NASA to possibly start a new investigation of the UFO phenomenon, and to help answer the mountains of UFO mail coming into the White House.

NASA declined the offer to reopen the UFO can of worms, and Carter's Science Advisor was accordingly advised. However, behind the scenes, NASA was busy. NASA claimed having no role in the investigation of UFOs, told President Carter they wanted no part of the UFO scene and wrote a letter to Spielberg trying to talk him out of releasing the movie *Close Encounters* (formally called Watch the Sky).

The movie started as a movie idea called "Watch the Skies" which NASA actually tried to stop him from producing. They sent him a 20-page letter objecting to the movie. It inspired him that something was going on and the movie had to be made.

> *I really found my faith when I heard that the government was opposed to the film. If NASA spent the time to send me a twenty-page letter, then I knew there must be something happening.*[48]

The Close Encounters – Holloman Base Alien Landing

Something not well known is that the idea for the movie emanated from the Holloman Air Force Base landing in May 1971, where, like in *Close Encounters*, the government arranged the meeting with the aliens and the whole event was filmed.

I discovered this when I talked to Bob Emenegger, one of the producers who was provided with the Holloman material, including the film, albeit for a brief period of time. As mentioned previously, eight seconds of the actual landing footage appears in the 1974 documentary *UFOs: Past, Present, and Future* and the 1979 remake called *UFOs: It has Begun*.

One of the people who worked with Emenegger and his partner Allan Sandler was Annie Spielberg, Spielberg's sister. When *UFOs: Past Present, and Future* was released, Annie came to Emenegger and said that Steven would like to have a copy of the film. The film was provided and in 1977 *Close Encounters* was released, with a very similar storyline, except the location was changed from New Mexico to Wyoming.

Emenegger told me that after *Close Encounters* was released, he spoke with Spielberg's mother Leah, who said, "I have seen your version of the landing, and I have seen Steven's version, and I like Steven's better."

Another bizarre story that most people don't know relates to the landing story which appears to be an integral part of the acclimatization, and thus it has been recycled over and over. It first appears in the 1974 *UFOs: Past, Present, and Future* documentary, and then becomes the final scene in 1977 Close Encounters. In 1979 it is released again in a documentary called "UFOs, It Has Begun, and then becomes the key to the SERPO story which started to leak on the internet in November 2005.

In 1988 the story of the landing appears in a key documentary "UFO Cover-up? Live," where Paul Shartle appears on camera. He was the Norton Air Force Base security officer who offered the film to be used. This documentary was put out by the same Grey Advertising that has been described as a CIA proprietary agency.

After that documentary aired a constituent for Senator Dodd wrote him a letter demanding that he recover the Holloman landing base film. Dodd filed an FOIA, and Paul Shartle, reviewed the film for release. Dodd was told that the movie was held in a Navy Sync, but it was never released.

When Serpo was released members of the Aviary were reading the material as if there was something to it. At the same time, two people associated with a group known as the Aviary contacted me. They were seriously trying to recover the Holloman landing film. Because I was good friends with Emenegger and had researched the story I was being asked what I knew about it.

One of these people had even made contact with two US Presidents to ask them if their UFO briefing had included the Holloman film.

President Ford stated he had seen the film in his briefing, but he would not identify when the briefing took place, "Don't even go there."

President George H. Bush stated he had not seen it in his presidential briefing, but he had seen it as CIA Director. He spelled out that the film was not of an A-12 plane emergency landing (as Col. Bill Coleman had claimed) or a psychological film prepared to test military officers. He would not say what it was.

In addition to this, a plan had been set up to bring Shartle to Las Vegas to interview him. At that time, many of the Aviary members were acting as consultants to the National Investigations for Discovery Science (NIDS) set up by billionaire Robert Bigalow. The interview would take place as part of a NIDS meeting.

Days before the interview was to take place, Shartle was killed in a roll-over car accident. Some saw the timing of the accident as troubling.

1978

....

Alien Crashes and Bodies

In July 1978, researcher Len Stringfield gave a lecture at the Annual MUFON UFO Symposium in Dayton, Ohio. It was a big moment for the UFO research community because Stringfield was there to talk about UFO crash recoveries and autopsies of recovered ET bodies.

Despite the belief by many in the UFO community, this was the first time these two subjects had been seriously dealt with by UFO researchers. It was a pivotal moment in Ufology.

Although most researchers will never receive a contact from a military person telling them stories of crashes, dead aliens, and autopsies, Stringfield received contacts from up to 300 individuals offering to leak classified information about this area of research. In my 42-year career as a researcher, I have only had two witnesses talk to me about alien bodies. In contrast, 300 witnesses coming forward points to someone giving them the green light to leaked info related to this.

Before Stringfield's lecture, there had been a couple of articles written about the 1948 Aztec crash and the bodies recovered there, but those stories had not received serious attention. Stringfield's sources, talking about the military recovering aliens, were anonymous but conveyed their info via an intermediary. That is how the disclosure game is played.

The paper that Stringfield presented in Dayton was titled "Retrievals of the Third Kind." Despite death threats before and during his talk, Stringfield told the spell-binding story of what he had learned. The story of Stringfield's release at the MUFO Symposium generated massive publicity and attention, and Stringfield described the instant response:

> *UPI picked up the story that, in turn, triggered ABC radio and at least 100 affiliates, coat-to-coast, to call me day and night for interviews and talk shows. These, of course, brought the public into the hubbub and with it a deluge of mail and phone calls.*

One of Stringfield's key early sources was a man known as "Mr. Q." Stringfield believed he was from the CIA. As Stringfield explained:

> *Among my early contacts, one stood out. There was no doubt in my mind, as time went by, that he was what he professed to be – an agent of the CIA. Through "church affiliation" and probably for other reasons unknown to me, he had a close and trusted relationship with Robert Barry of Yoe, Pennsylvania, who served as our intermediary. Known only as "Mr. Q" he was to remain invisible to me; his presence known only by a recognizable voice, terse, commanding, and knowledgeable. I heard it many times as Barry replayed his tapes with information on worldwide events and some useful advisories relative to UFO crashes. In fact, said Barry, he was a member of a retrieval team in a New Mexico crash, 1962, where he personally helped in the recovery of the dead humanoid occupants. Surprisingly, Mr. Q's tips on past UFO crashes, which I had shared with no one, including Barry, often proved accurate.*

Stringfield's work was the first real expose on alien autopsies, and it brought out a number of critics. Stringfield, however, held his ground. Following the convention, he wrote to me stating, "I did contribute some new and valuable data re retrievals, and despite my critics, I'm glad I did!"

Also in 1978, Colonel William Coleman, who was one of the key Pentagon players in Robert Emenegger's documentary, including green lighting and then pulling the Holloman film, produced his own NBC UFO drama series called *Project UFO*. The show was based on cases from Project Blue Book, which Coleman had been a spokesman for. In one the episodes, Coleman promoted a UFO case, but then ended it up pulling it back as he had done with the Holloman film.

1979

....

1979 may have been a key year in the UFO disclosure game. It was late in the administration of Jimmy Carter who had promised to release the UFO files.

It was the year that Navy physicist Bruce Maccabee was contacted by Kit Green at the CIA and went to the agency to give lunchtime lectures on UFOs and the MJ-12 documents. It was this year that Maccabee became aware that there was a connection between UFOs and parapsychology – the phenomenology problem – as it would be described to Dan Smith in 1991 by Ron Pandolfi.

1979 was the year that Dale Graff, chief civilian scientist for the Air Force FTD Division, told Ernie Kellerstrass what was in the "yellow book."[49] This information would become the sensational parts of what was in the MJ-12 documents story and the Serpo story that would appear in 2005.

The yellow book was hard bound and about 100 pages, which talked about who the beings were, where they were from, and many other things. Graff had read it in 1978 and got access through the Foreign Technology Division Chief Scientist Dr. Anthony Cacciopo.

1979 was also the year that USAF Master Sergeant Richard Doty arrived in the UFO community. Doty would eventually become the whipping boy for all disinformation by the United States targeted at the UFO community. Next to the weather balloon story, Doty became the prime military cover story.

Doty was not the only Doty that had been involved in the UFO program. His uncle Edward was an intelligence officer, who became head of UFO investigations at Holloman in the summer of 1951 and was the liaison officer with AFOSI whose primary job responsibility was UFO investigations and who worked very closely with AFOSI.

Doty's father Charles was also a UFO player who according to Edward was "involved in Project Cup, which was more about UFOs than about weather!"[50] Charles also golfed with Col. Lane at Edwards, and Lane was closely involved in Emenegger's first UFO documentary.

Even though Doty was involved in the UFO program from 1979 to 1988 when he left the Air Force, was written up as a one-man disinformation machine. Doty created thousands of pages of leaked UFO documents a decade or more after he left the Air Force, was the creator of the Serpo saga that will be described later in this book, and led researcher Bill Moore to his eventual demise.

Because Doty was assigned to USAF counterintelligence, it is hard to sort truth from disinformation in the info Doty put out during his nine years of contact with the UFO community. A couple of points stand out showing that he was playing some key role in feeding information to the UFO community. He did this in a one-man-story fashion, unconnected to his job with counterintelligence.

UFO researchers are not viewed as a threat in the UFO community and the idea then that Doty was trying to distract researchers, does not make sense. If the government wanted UFO research to cease, they would have told Doty to shut up. On the other hand, if they wanted immediate and full disclosure, they would not have used a low-ranking master sergeant to tell the story but would have sent a top military official to a major newspaper and provided the evidence they would need for full disclosure.

Most importantly, most people relaying "evil Doty" stories leave out the fact that he passed a lie detector test related to what he was telling researchers. The lie detector test result was even discussed at a meeting held in the office of the head of counterintelligence at the CIA in 1988. This came the day after the airing of the documentary "UFO Cover-up Live." Almost every researcher talking about Doty leaves out that important fact.

The other thing that researchers leave out when talking about Doty is the account told by Kit Green who is a fairly respected voice inside the UFO community. Green said that in a meeting he had with former CIA Director Richard Helms, he was told "always believe what Richard Doty tells you about UFOs."

According to Doty:

> *As part of my job I became involved with an official disclosure program starting in 1979 when the United States government assigned me from one Air Force agency to the role of special investigator for UFO reports. It was my feeling at the time alone with my colleagues that the government information on UFOs and aliens should be presented to the public. There is only a small portion that we have gathered from the Extraterrestrials that should be classified or safeguarded. I believe that since we are in contact with extraterrestrials that this information should not be hidden from the public...we then wrote reports and forwarded those reports to superiors in Washington DC meaning the CIA-DCI and Headquarters of the Air Force Office of Special Investigations, Special Projects (AFOSI/PJ), who were our direct superiors.*[51]

Doty reported that there have been "many official government programs for public disclosure" and that their influence on the movie *The Day the Earth Stood Still* is a prime example of how the alien message is moved into the public consciousness.

Doty listed some disclosure projects that have been in operation over the years. They include Project White, Red Snow, Long Silver, Kit Kleen, Silver Stream, Sandal Leg, Walrus, Seven Doors, Seven Princes, Seven Kings, Seven Lights, Seven Pawns, Pawns Right, Pawns Up, Dragger Kings, Dragger Prince, Dragger Lane, Lance Rite, Lance Rite, Lance Green, Lance Red, Gallant Horse, Gallant Kings, Gallant Prince, and Tight End.

The other key player that entered the government UFO disclosure plan in 1979 was USAF Captain Robert Collins who states that he became "involved with an official disclosure program." He stated the whole operation was run like any other intelligence program. He was moved from one Air Force agency to a role investigating UFOs. There were 50 people in sub units, in four regions of the country, assigned to Domestic Collections (Special Project or PJ Office of the Air Force Office of Special Investigations. "We wrote up reports and forwarded those reports to superiors in Washington DC meaning the CIA-DCI and Headquarters of the Air Force Office of Special Investigations, Special Projects, (AFOSI/PJ) who were our direct superiors."[52]

1979 was also the year of the re-release of *UFOs: It has Begun*, which was an updated version of *UFOs: Past, Present and Future*. That documentary had been produced with government help and photographic evidence by Bob Emenegger and Allen Sandler in 1974, and released again in 1976.

The 1979 version added some new material on cattle mutilations, but its third appearance coincided with renewed interest in UFOs due to the release of Steven Spielberg's *Close Encounters of the Third Kind*.

Like the 1974 book, and documentary *UFOs: It has Begun*, the government appeared to play a key role as hinted at the outset:

> *"What you are witnessing is based on fact. Some will find it fascinating, some will find it frightening: but it is all true.*
>
> *With many thanks to the DEPARTMENT OF DEFENSE and NASA."*

Finally, 1979 was the year that Moore co-authored, "The Philadelphia Experiment - Project Invisibility" with Charles Berlitz, who spent 26 years in the Army as an intelligence officer. The next year Moore would co-author "The Roswell Incident" with Berlitz, and everything would change.

A hint of what was about to happen was hinted at in the German version of the Roswell Incident. It had a different title – "Der Roswell-Zwischenfall: Die UFOs und die CIA" – "The Roswell Incident: UFOs and the CIA." On the cover "Die UFOs und die CIA" was in big bold letters, and the "Der Roswell-Zwischenfall" was in small insignificant print.

It was a sign of things to come. Moore who had worked for the CIA while at University would reconnect with the agency and there would be at major attempt to educate the public on the UFO story.

Disclosure Efforts 1980-1990

General Miller told me he had been inside a craft in Northern California...we came to our house. Miller had agreed to meet there. He did show up a little late and his opening comment was "They're voice activated." And "place your hand on the board for more control." The first part of his statement caught Hynek totally by surprise and it registered to him as 'disbelief that all this time he was kept out of the loop.' It seemed to shake him. **UFO documentary producer Bob Emenegger talking about General Glen E. Miller, the head of the Defense Audio Video Agency and Ronald Reagan's first Hollywood agent, talking about how "thought control" was used to fly a flying saucer.**

General Miller invited the three of them (Hynek, Brian Myers, and Tina Choate) out to Norton. While there, he ordered that Paul Shartle (the head of security) show him some of the most sensitive UFO material and the Holloman landing (film). Miller said to him, "I want you to show Hynek all the UFO footage." Shartle replied: "I'll have to have that request in writing." Miller responded: "Do it, or I will have your ass." Shartle did not comply. As to what happened after that, Shartle told me "ask your friends, Brian and Tina." I was not there to know all this craziness that went on, but I do know that three months later Casper Weinberger sent a telegram relieving both Scott and Miller of their posts. Why? I don't know. I don't even know if it was related. **Bob Emenegger talking about General Miller who proposed that a UFO documentary be produced for the American people.**

1980 July

....

Possible Target or Courier - Aerial Phenomena Research Organization (APRO), and possibly Bill Moore

New Concepts Introduced

Aliens working in cooperation with Government

Alien underground bases
Alien implants in humans

APRO was closely connected to Paul Bennewitz, an Albuquerque businessman trained as a physicist who became convinced in the late 1970s that he was monitoring electromagnetic signals (ELF) that extraterrestrials were using to control persons they had abducted.

Bennewitz had set up equipment and tried to decode these signals and believed he was succeeding. In addition to the signals, Bennewitz began to see and film what he thought were UFOs flying in and around the Manzano Nuclear Weapons Storage Facility and the Coyote Canyon test area, just outside of Kirtland AFB.

Bennewitz reported all this to the Tucson-based Aerial Phenomena Research Organization (APRO), and to officers at Kirkland. A couple of the people who became involved with Bennewitz and his claims were Air Force Office of Special Investigations (AFOSI) Agent Sgt. Richard Doty and Maj. Ernest Edwards, head of base security.

APRO was sent a document that became known as the "Wetzel" letter. It was written by Richard Doty and is related to the Bennewitz affair. Bill Moore handled the letter as Director of Special Investigations in 1980 at APRO.

Moore claimed in a speech that he made in July 1989 that the document was "loosely based upon an actual UFO case." He further maintained that it was sent to APRO by Doty as "bait," to recruit someone inside APRO who could keep USAFOSI informed on what Bennewitz was doing and saying.

Since Moore became Director of Special Investigations, he was the one who took the bait. Shortly after the letter arrived, Moore met for the first time with Doty at Kirkland AFB.

One of the key things Moore concluded from the Wetzel document is that "as early as 1980 there were at least two individuals involved in officially creating spurious material and providing it to public sources." Moore discovered this by comparing the writing styles of the Wetzel and Ellsworth documents. The material coming to Moore seemed to be coming from multiple sources.

1980 - September

………………………………………..

Possible Target or Courier - Bill Moore, prominent at the time for having co-authored *The Roswell Incident*.

New Concepts Introduced

MJ-12
DC-5
Project Aquarius

Following the publication of his book, *The Roswell Incident* in the summer of 1980, Moore was contacted while in Omaha, Nebraska by a colonel at nearby Offutt AFB offering to meet with him and talk. While on the same trip, Moore got a call from an individual at Kirkland AFB.

Moore's version of his being contacted (by Falcon) in preparation for being provided with dramatic and conclusive UFO information follows:

> *In early September, 1980, I was approached by a well-placed individual in the intelligence community who claimed to be directly connected to a high-level government project dealing with UFOs. This individual, who subsequently came to be known as "The Falcon" told me that he spoke for a small group of similar individuals who were uncomfortable with the government's continuing cover-up.*

Moore <u>was warned that the information he would receive would be a mixture of fact and fiction</u>. That was the way the government worked. He would have to sort the wheat from the chaff. Moore believed that he would do it, and decided to play. He described the offer he got to be inside:

> *You have a choice – either you are in or you are not in. If you are not in you don't know anything. If you are in, then you see where it goes. Well, of course what do you do? I chose to go with it. I guess I'm really glad I did. If I had it to do over again I would probably do the same thing, and I think most people would if they were approached in the same way I was and given the choice would have opted into it.*

> *Virtually any UFO researcher worth his salt would have.*

Moore received the concepts of MJ-12, the USAF PJ unit, DC-5, and Project Aquarius. Moore, Jamie Shandera, and Stanton Friedman promoted the ideas widely.

1981 - March

....

Possible Targets or Couriers - Bill Moore

Moore was provided a photocopy of the Aquarius Teletype after being shown the original by the Falcon in late February 1981. Moore described the document and its purpose:

> *The Aquarius Document is an actual example of some of the disinformation produced in connection with the Bennewitz case. The document is a retyped version of the real AFOSI message with a few spurious additions. It was apparently created by AFOSI, or at least I assumed it was, and it was handed to me in March 1981, with the intention that I would pass it to Bennewitz.*

1982 - January

....

Possible Targets or Couriers - Bob Pratt and Bill Moore

Pratt was asked by Moore to collaborate on a novel with him in January 1981 or 1982. The basis for the fact as fiction book was "Project Aquarius, MJ-12, and a lot of other things." The working title was "MAJIK-12." The final title was "Project Aquarius." (Alternate titled was "IAC Conspiracy.") Much of the technical proofreading of the 250+ page manuscript was provided through Richard Doty or at least that was Pratt's impression.

Somehow, some researcher made up the story that this was a science fiction book, and that it led to the MJ-12 document and all the claims around it.

This is absolute nonsense. Moore had received many of the concepts that would later appear in the MJ-12 and Aquarius document. He contacted Pratt who had already written a book with researcher John Schuessler on the famous Cash Landrum UFO sighting case called "Fire on the Road." That book did not get published as it was described by the publisher as "not an uplifting treatment of the UFO experience."

In a 1987 letter to me Pratt stated, "The purpose of the book, however, was to try and reveal some things we were certain had happened but couldn't prove."

Pratt knew Moore from his book "The Roswell Incident", and they had considered doing projects together on other things before the "Aquarius" book. They had for example considered doing a project on Abraham Lincoln's Air Force during the Civil War, and the Zone of Silence in Mexico.

Bob Pratt described the book effort:

> *We finally agreed that we couldn't prove any of this stuff, and write a non-fiction book, so we agreed to write a novel, and put all this crap in there you know and pass it off as fact described as fiction. That kind of idea... I wanted to call it MJ-12 or I wanted to call it IAC or something I can't remember. He wanted to call it Project Aquarius. To me that was kind of hokey. Project Aquarius was an old word by then . . . now it turns out that there was a third silent partner in this book, and he gave me the impression that this was Doty. The manuscript was submitted to him for approval.*
>
> *The manuscript came back with a lot of interesting technical details put into it such as weaponry and squads and things of that nature. This supposedly came from Doty. Whether it did or not I don't know [later Bob mentions that at the bottom of the title page it was written "written with the cooperation and assistance of Donald L. Davis"].*

Pratt recalled that the book was ready in late 1983. At that point, Moore's agent took over. In July, Moore phoned Pratt to tell him no one was interested in the book. The book was shelved.

1983

....

Possible Targets or Couriers - Peter Gersten

During a visit to Kirkland Air Force Base to meet with AFOSI Special Agent Richard Doty, CAUS Director, attorney Peter Gersten, is given the whole range of bizarre UFO stories including:

The story of the briefing paper prepared for President Carter on UFOs.
The Cash/Landrum UFO sighting in Texas being "a government exploitation of UFO technology."
Bill Moore being right on in his account of Roswell.

1983 - January

....

On January 28, Bill Moore conducted an interview with the Falcon in the presence of a CBS Executive and an investigative reporter. On the way to the airport the Falcon surreptitiously handed Moore a folded piece of paper saying "put this in your pocket and look at it later after I'm gone." According to Moore he had been given what became known as the "Hilltop" document:

> *The paper turned out to be a single-page document on official stationary bearing a date in the fall of 1982 and "Secret" caveats at both top and bottom. It contained five paragraphs of information about an alleged close encounter incident which had occurred at a remote Air Force radar and space communications site...The document bore the signature of a USAF major at the bottom.*[53]

1983 - March

....

Possible Target or Courier - Bill Moore

Moore received a phone call telling him that he is about to receive information but he would have to pick it up. He was warned "You must follow them (instructions) carefully or the deal is off."

He traveled from airport to airport around the country ending up "in a motel on the edge of a mid-sized city in upstate New York." At exactly 5:00pm, as planned, a man walked into the room with a sealed brown vanilla envelope. Moore was given 19 minutes to do anything he wanted with the material inside the envelope that was comprised of 11 pages that became known as the so-called "Aquarius Papers," which he was told was "a transcription of notes either intended for use in preparing a briefing, or taken down during one and typed later."

Moore photographed the pages as carefully as he could placing a quarter in the bottom right corner of each page. He then read the text of the document into a pocket recorder.

This briefing was later rumored to be the one given President Carter (during a briefing which allegedly took place on June 14, 1977). The Aquarius Papers contained substantially the identical information that Linda Howe says Doty conveyed to her in their April 1983 meeting.

1983 - April

....

Potential Target or Courier - Linda Howe (prominently known at the time for her cattle mutilation investigations).

Linda Moulton Howe, who had just finished producing an award-winning documentary on cattle mutilations called *Strange Harvest*, was told an almost identical story to the one being voiced to Bill Moore. While preparing to make a UFO documentary for HBO, Howe was informed by Richard Doty that higher ups were willing to release and confirm special UFO information for her documentary. She was sworn to secrecy about the offer until the film's eventual release. Howe described the offer:

"The government intended to release to me several thousand feet of color and black and white film taken between 1947 and 1964 showing crashed UFO discs and extraterrestrial bodies in historic footage to be included in the HBO documentary supported with official government confirmation."

Howe's meeting occurred on April 9, 1983 at Kirtland Air Force base. She was taken to a room going through doors with number pads on the door. Doty appeared to know all the codes needed.

In the process of being offered access to the secrets of the government UFO program, Linda asked Doty why they had chosen her instead of just going to *The New York Times* or *The Washington Post*. Doty replied that it was easier to communicate with an individual as opposed to a major corporation with expensive attorneys.

Howe was shown a paper titled, "Briefing Paper for the President of the United States" and Doty stated, "My superiors have asked me to show you this." The paper described the government's efforts from the 1940s on to ascertain the origin and motives of the ETs. This was done through projects described in the paper and given names such as Sign, Grudge, Gleam, Pounce, Blue Book, Sigma, Snowbird, and Aquarius. The paper also mentioned MJ-12.

When Howe asked Doty if he knew about the Holloman film, Doty said he did but that Emenegger had gotten the date wrong. The date he provided for the Holloman landing film was April 26, 1964 [a day after the landing Lonnie Zamora witnessed in Socorro, New Mexico, which Doty said was a screw up to the pre-planned Holloman landing].

Doty then provided Linda with his version of the Holloman landing. When three UFOs appeared at Holloman at six o'clock in the morning on April 26, 1964, one landed while the other two hovered overhead. During the meeting between the UFO occupants and a government party, the preserved bodies of dead aliens were given to the ETs who in turn returned something unspecified. Five ground and aerial cameras recorded this event.

Doty also went on to describe crashes which occurred in 1948, Aztec, New Mexico, 1949, Roswell, New Mexico (which Bill Moore stated Doty had brought up because of a discussion with him days before), 1953, Kingman, Arizona, and 1950, Mexico, and gave a description of the alien bodies identical to Leonard Stringfield's witnesses, and also described a second, taller alien race. He described good and bad aliens but had the greys as good and the blonds as the bad guys.

Doty told Linda about a live alien that had been recovered in 1949 Roswell crash. He stated the alien lived till 1952 when it died of unknown causes. During its captivity, it had telepathically conveyed to military officers that the aliens had long been manipulating human biology and history.

Doty further talked about Nordic-type aliens called "highs" and of conflicting alien factions. As with many of Doty's stories, he appeared to take a common story and twist the facts around. In the case of the blonds and greys, Doty told Howe that the blonds were the troublemakers and the greys were the good guys. Anyone else portrays the reverse (the greys are bad, the blonds good).

Despite Doty's claim that the government had authorized the release of film showing crashed saucers and alien bodies for use in an HBO documentary, it never materialized due to "political delays." When the alleged historical film footage didn't materialize, HBO cancelled the documentary.

Linda relayed her story to the UFO community and concepts about a live alien and various alien species visiting earth circulated widely. Since nothing was officially confirmed, no security oaths were violated.

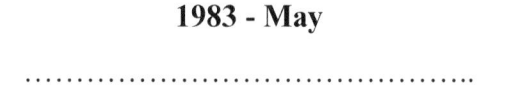

1983 - May

……………………………………..

Potential Targets or Couriers - Bill Moore, Stanton Friedman

Moore and Friedman decided to track documents through FOIAs from various agencies involved in the 1940s green-fireball incidents in New Mexico, thinking that people who investigated these sightings might also have been involved in the Roswell crash.

Friedman had gotten lucky with the Albuquerque Department of Energy recovering 31 memoranda, letters, and reports. The Falcon knew of the find and told Moore on October 25, 1982 that if they looked in the right places they could obtain more documents than those they already had.

In May 1983, during a meeting with the Falcon, Moore was handed a manila envelope with a one-page letter dated January 13, 1949, from Col. E.L. Poland, HQ, 4th Army, to the Director of Army Intelligence in D.C.

The letter was titled "452.1 AKADB, SUBJECT: UNCONVENTIONAL AIRCRAFT (Control No. A-1917)" and Moore was told to request that file from the Department of the Army at the Pentagon and told that "you will find something you have been looking for."

On May 10, 1983, Moore filed an FOIA and received more than 900 pages. They involved early CIRVIS reports (filed under JANAP 146) several dozen early Air Intelligence Reports, a large number of green fireball documents, and many miscellaneous items. Many of the items had been "electronically transmitted" to the CIA and the new National Security Agency (NSA). Also found were references to 44 other files accumulated by the Directorate of Intelligence in the Pentagon, and on loan for 30 days.[54]

Possible Target or Courier - Bill Moore

In May 1983, Moore received a message stating, "A package is ready for delivery." Moore sent Nic Magnuson as a cutout on a specific date to the Sea-Tac International Airport in Seattle, Washington.

Magnuson flew to Seattle and waited at a particular gate for 20 minutes. When no one showed up, he moved to a second gate and at that gate, a "short, elderly, balding man" offered him a newspaper, in which there was a manila envelope "securely sealed with brown wrapping tape."

Inside a second envelope were found eight single-page documents dated from June 24, 1978, and December 28, 1982, all on CIA letterhead and all copied on pale, blue paper. They purported to be copies of internal communications between various members of MJ-12.

1984 - December

…………………………………..

Potential Target or Couriers - Bill Moore, Jamie Shandera, Stanton Friedman, Lee Graham

The now famous MJ-12 documents (reported to be a Briefing for President Eisenhower) were mailed to Bill Moore's research associate and Los Angeles film producer, Jamie Shandera.

The film arrived in an envelope that "was protected by a border of brown tape that ran along its seams." Anyone who has received FOIA documents from the CIA will recognize this taping pattern.

In 1987, British researchers Jenny Randles and Timothy Good also received offers copies of the MJ-12 documents. Randles turned down the offer, but Good accepted and received an identical copy of the MJ-12 documents from what he considered to be a source independent of Moore's.

Good stated that in March 1987 he was contacted by an individual he was convinced "was connected to the American intelligence community." He was told that he should expect something shortly to help his book project. Shortly after he received the MJ-12 document in a packet with the caveats stroked out. Timothy Good decided to publish the documents in his 1987 book *Above Top Secret* forced Moore, Friedman, and Shandera to go public with their documents at the 1987 MUFON Symposium in Washington D.C.

Figure 9 Tim Good

Moore stated that their intelligence people had warned them that "A major story about MJ-12 was about to break in Europe" and that if he and Shandera wanted credit for their research on the MJ-12 document they had better go public before the end of the week.

This led them to publish a heavily expurgated copy of their document in the April 30th, 1987 version of Moore's newsletter called "Focus." This was done to prove they had the document before the European release, and yet be able to check whether what was about to appear in Europe, was the same or different.

1985

………………………………..

Robert Collins became involved in a UFO disclosure effort initiated by President Reagan as described by Collins in his biography. Collins was a former Air Force Intelligence Officer, Captain, O-3

(Chief Analyst/Scientist in theoretical physics. He held a Top Secret/SCI clearance) at the Foreign Technology Division (FTD, now NASIC) and AF Weapons Lab on the Plasma Physics Shiva device. He had an extensive background in Aircraft Avionics Systems, Ground Communications, and Engineering Physics (graduate school), (Electro-Optics, Plasma, and Nuclear Physics) totalling over 22 years (Air Force Commendation Medal).

Collins' first UFO contacts were made at FTD starting in 1985 with Ernie Kellerstrass, Bill Moore, Jaime Shandera and Rick Doty as part of President Reagan's Disclosure Program and continue to this day with research and publications.

1985 - Early

....

Possible Targets or Couriers – J. Allen Hynek, Jacques Vallee, Robert Emenegger

Colonel Bill Coleman, now retired and living in Florida, contacted Emenegger about doing another documentary on UFOs. Coleman indicated the time was again right and that the government might be willing to release key confirming information of the extraterrestrial presence on earth.

He told Emenegger that "Allen Hynek might be willing to participate again." Hynek, therefore, had already been approached. His involvement with the proposed 1985 documentary was independent of Vallee, the final player asked to play. Hynek appeared to have been consulted, even before Emenegger.

A key to getting the information promised by the government is that the film had to be "professional enough and interesting enough to reopen the whole subject before the American people." After hearing Coleman's pitch, Emenegger was convinced the government was about to provide the "final" evidence.

Because he had already done one documentary while working for the Nixon re-election campaign, as soon as the government informed him they wanted another documentary his first question to Paul Shartle, the security manager at DAVA, was "Is Reagan behind this?" He did not receive a reply.

Another reason for believing the documentary was being green-lighted by Reagan was because he was also dealing at Norton with Dr.

Glenn Edward Miller, Reagan's former agent, and his boss, General Robert Scott, the Director of DAVA. Emenegger spoke of their push to get him to do another UFO documentary.

> *During the Reagan administration, I met with Bob Scott and General Glenn Miller... they wanted another program like we had done, and we spent a lot of time discussing it. Bob Scott was a Reagan appointee... He had a Glen E. Miller retired general as his aide, or second in command. We spent a lot of discussion. There was a lot of stuff in the vault that he wanted to get out. I even had General Miller come to our house to meet Hynek and his group to take them out to Norton so they could look around... Miller was, interestingly enough, was head of one of the studios in Hollywood – one of the old ones. He got Reagan his first contract. So, there were these strange connections. I met with Miller and Scott like at Denny's restaurant. It was like "Meet at Denny's and we will discuss this."*

Vallee was negative and skeptical about the offer being made by Emenegger's military contacts. He felt that if the government wanted to release the information they could simply go to someone like the National Academy of Sciences and announce the discovery of the alien presence. Coleman was saying the information had to be "leaked carefully, as part of something else."

For the second time, Emenegger was getting claims that he would acquire sensational evidence of the reality of UFOs. He contacted Hynek and Vallee about there being in the documentary to lend it credibility. He told them he wouldn't go it alone and there were even suggestions that Senator Barry Goldwater, and former President Jimmy Carter "would help."

Both Vallee and Hynek felt the Air Force was again playing games and were trying to use them to mislead the public deliberately. Between themselves they concluded they couldn't support Emenegger's plan, but that if there were "any chance of uncovering genuine evidence" they would pursue it "behind the scenes."

Hynek and his assistants went to Norton Air Force Base to the Defense Audiovisual Agency (DAVA) to meet with Miller and Scott. Both men turned out to be "outright contactees." Vallee and Hynek held against the Generals the fact that they believed the accounts of Swiss contactee, Billy Meier.

On March 27, 1985, Vallee himself traveled out to Norton to meet with Dr. Miller and his assistant, Mr. Atkins. Miller, a man with two doctorates, described three sightings he had experienced including one that involved boarding a landed spaceship, and "further communication with the entity" afterwards.

General Miller told Vallee that he "felt strongly that such data existed," although he did not indicate to Vallee that he knew what "the alleged evidence was, or where it was located."

General Scott was added to the discussion, and he let Vallee know that DAVA was under the control of the Assistant Secretary of Defense for Public Relations, where not surprisingly Col. Coleman worked.

Scott told Vallee that he thought there were many "classes of beings" visiting earth and hinted that they weren't all good. They are here to warn us against destroying ourselves (classic contactee message).

Both Vallee and Hynek felt the Air Force was again playing games and were trying to use them to deliberately mislead the public. Between themselves, they concluded that they could not support Emenegger's plan to pursue a documentary, but "if there was any chance of uncovering genuine evidence" they would pursue it "behind the scenes." Hynek and Vallee did a follow-up on some interviews at Norton Air Force Base, where two "contactee" Generals assured them they could produce the UFO footage. The two researchers, however, weren't buying, and the UFO film offer was withdrawn. This disclosure effort had failed.

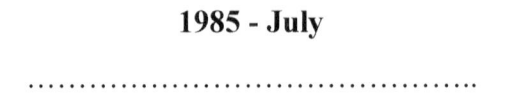

1985 - July

....

Potential Targets or Couriers - Moore, Friedman, and Shandera

This whole incident started when Moore received a postcard addressed to his former mailbox: P.O. Box 189, Dewey, Arizona. It was mailed from New Zealand. Its message read:

> Add zest to your trip to Washington
> Try Reeses pieces

For a stylish look
Try Suit Land

Moore and Shandera discovered an unsigned carbon copy of a brief memo, dated July 14, 1954, to General Nathan Twinning from Robert Cutler, Special Assistant to President Eisenhower regarding "NSC/MJ-12 Special Studies Project." The memo just rescheduled the MJ-12/SSP briefing to take place during "the already scheduled White House meeting of July 16 rather than following it."

The document was found in the declassified USAF Intelligence records from Record Group 341, at the Suitland, Maryland satellite station of the National Archives.

Essential to the account is the fact that for three months Friedman had intended to review the Air Force Record Group 341 files. This happened before the postcard arrived, and because Friedman had often been phoning about the documents, whoever planted the document in the T4-1846 file, Box 189, knew that Friedman (a member of the team investigating the MJ-12 document) would eventually review the records.

Friedman had been phoning the National Archives every week for three months asking if the 64-man Air Force declassification team had finished the review of the files. When he heard the files were finally ready, Friedman realized that he had to go on a UFO lecture tour, and couldn't go.

Moore didn't want to go either. He had already been worn down by the many dead ends of the intelligence game. It was only when Friedman said that the records were not at the National Archives, but at Suitland Maryland, and that to get them the researcher had to go through the military archivist in charge Edward Reese, did the last pieces of the puzzle come together. At that point, Shandera and Moore figured there would be enough of a chance to make the trip across the country.

Like the MJ-12 documents, the discovered document came under heavy attacks from skeptics and critics, with many pointing at Moore as a possible author.

1985

....

Potential Target or Courier - Howard Blum

A secret working group was called together in 1985 to study the hidden government aspects of the UFO phenomena.

According to award winning reporter for *The New York Times* Howard Blum, "a senior official at the National Security Agency" gave him a strange lead. The official was helping him with a book he was doing at the time about the Walker spy case. The lead was "there's been a lot of talk around the NSA about outer space. Weird stuff. UFOs. Heard they got some kind of all-star working group or something. A panel of hotshots is zeroing in on UFOs. Going to get the truth at last."

Blum approached Pulitzer winning reporter for *The New York Times* Seymour Hersh for help on the story, but Hersh was upset that Blum would pursue such a story and took no interest. Oddly, two days later, he phoned Blum to confirm there was some secret working group working on UFOs but stated Blum would have to get the story on his own.

Blum managed to find one of the NSA members who sat on the super-secret inside group known as the UFO Working Group and Blum was able to piece together the story from there.

The UFO Working Group was a spin-off of the remote viewing program and known more accurately as the "coordinate remote viewing" CRV program. One version of the account told by Blum states that the whole thing started in the fall of 1985 during a meeting held in the secure vault of President Reagan's Scientific Advisor, George Keyworth.

Dr. Hal Puthoff, then running the SRI remote viewing program, explained that Ingo Swann[55], a remote viewer, would demonstrate "A new perceptual channel through which individuals are able to perceive and describe remote data not presented to any known sense."

A short series of precise geographical coordinates were read to Swann, and he proceeded to describe a building. Once revealed the target turned out to be the country dacha of Mikhail Gorbachev.

Following this, a demonstration took place to show how the displayed "Scannate" technology was proficient in antisubmarine warfare. They showed Ingo Swann a series of pictures of submarines, some American, some Soviet, some in dry docks, some not built yet. His job was to provide the exact coordinates for each submarine.

As he was set to call up the coordinates of a Soviet Delta-class submarine in one of the photographs, he stopped and reported that he saw something above the submarine. Swann was asked to draw what he saw on a piece of paper, and he proceeded to render a sketch of a classic a flying saucer.

A report was made by the SRI team of the incident and sent to the DIA who was the "primary client." About this same time, money from the Army for the CRV program ended, and the entire program moved to DIA.

The Swann submarine incident led to a DIA/Navy Intelligence sponsored program to use "Scannate" to search for Soviet submarines. According to Blum's information, the DIA was able to detect at least 17 UFO objects connected to Soviet submarines over the next 14 months. The project was called Project Magnet, and the DIA Directorate for Management and Operations supervised it.

Moreover, the incidents of the "hovering UFOs" around submarines provided inspiration to Col. John Alexander, then Director, advanced concepts US Army Lab. Command, Adelphi, MD.

Alexander was a Colonel in the US Army and had been interested in the UFO mystery since 1947 when he was a young boy. He also had done work on "esoteric projects, specifically in the intelligence community with psychokinesis."

Alexander wrote a book on his UFO investigations called *UFOs: Myths, Conspiracies, and Realities*. In the book, Alexander pointed out that although UFOs are real, they are of no interest to the American government, and therefore there is no cover-up of the facts by American officials.

Alexander is also well known in the UFO community for hosting a Top Secret - Special Access series of meetings in the mid-1980s to evaluate a possible new way of the government's approach to the UFO question. Alexander's group was known as the Advance Theoretical Physics Group and bore the same "Top Secret- Restricted Classification" found on the MJ-12 set of documents.

According to Blum, Alexander proposed that the DIA Project Aquarius viewers should view an area above Kickapoo, Texas. It was there that NORAD reported an unknown object had tripped a manmade electromagnetic fence extending up to 15,000 miles above the earth.

The three viewers all were asked to view anything unusual at that latitude and longitude in the last 48 hours. By the end of the day, all three CRV viewers had sent back drawing of a UFO. With this additional evidence in hand, Alexander convinced the DIA to set up a "top-secret working group to investigate the possibility that extraterrestrials were making contact with this planet." (See Appendix 5 for the full story on the DIA connection)

Based on this psychic confirmation of a UFO event obtained by radar, the UFO Working Group formed in February 1985. Col. Alexander sent out the invitations for others he had chosen to generate a top-secret review of the UFO situation.

Researcher Armen Victorian, who squared off with Alexander during the period Howard Blum was researching the UFO Working Group, described Alexander's role and the start-up of the group:

> *Alexander's position as the Program Manager for Contingency Missions of Conventional Defense Technology, Los Alamos National Laboratories, enabled him to exploit the Department of Defense's Project Reliance "which encourages a search for all possible sources of existing and incipient technologies before developing new technology in-house" to tap into a wide range of exotic topics, sometimes using defense contractors, e.g., McDonnell Douglas Aerospace. I have several reports, some of which were compiled before his departure to the Los Alamos National Laboratories when he was with Army Intelligence, which show Alexander's keen interest in any and every exotic subject--UFOs, ESP, psychotronics, anti- gravity devices, near-death experiments, psychology warfare and non-lethal weaponry.*

Having received a lead, Blum decided to investigate the UFO Working Group. The story of what he discovered was written up in a widely distributed 1990 book, *Out There: The Government's Secret Quest for Extraterrestrials*.

One UFO newsgroup reader described the Blum book as "the interesting process of turning bullshit into history." Many other UFO researchers quickly echoed that assessment, and the book ended up receiving little support from with the UFO community.

Blum described the UFO Working Group as a group trying to "settle this UFO question once and for all." The men trying to decide the question were a group of people who had each had some contact with black budget programs and government security.

There are three views as to exactly what the UFO Working Group was. The first view is that they were a group who knew much more than the average researcher, but they were not the important group Blum made them out to be. They were a group of scientists, military personnel, and intelligence analysts who sat around a table and shared anecdotal information and scuttlebutt they had heard directly or second hand through the black budget community or the chain of command. They looked at the relationship of various programs to the UFO program that they believed existed somewhere in the black budget of the United States government.

The second view, exemplified by Howard Blum's account is that the group was a highly classified compartmentalized team working inside the Defense Intelligence Agency's Directorate of Management and Operations which had been granted inordinate power to attack the UFO problem.

The agenda put out by Alexander to the UFO Working Group members (from a recovered file on the meetings) outlined the original objectives and purposes behind the group. It clearly did not mention a search for who was behind the cover-up. A quote from the typed agenda provided to the attendees stated:

1. Objectives
   a. Explore evidence presented/available to determine if further study is warranted.
   b. If evidence from 2(a) is sufficient, is there sufficient evidence to support an R&D (Research and Development) program?
   c. If evidence from 2(b) is sufficient, what would the thrust be?
   d. Develop an action plan (assumes sufficient evidence to proceed).

2. Purposes
   a. Exploration of the facts.
   b. Determine quality of known evidence.
   c. Determine methods to collect more information to fill gaps in information (collection plan).

The DIA Connection

Blum made some references in his book as to the DIA connection to the UFO Working Group. This DIA tie-in is interesting because it parallels stories told at the same time by Bill Moore and others about the vital role played by the DIA in the UFO hierarchy.

The third view is the one put forward by researchers like Jacques Vallee who believed that "Colonel Phillips' secret group is not the real secret group. It is only the latest carrot dangled in front of a public always eager for new revelations. There is clearly an endless supply of such stories, and they are always volunteered to people who are prone to believing them but have no ability to check them."

The UFO Working group, according to all accounts, was able to field CIA assets under cover to investigate UFO sightings. Blum pointed out one case in Wisconsin where two CIA officers were impersonating NASA engineers. This type of internal CIA investigation was possible because of President Reagan's Executive Order 12333, which allowed the CIA to operate within the United States under certain conditions.

The UFO Working Group was a "group of insiders who were looking for the insider group." They were desperately seeking the crashed flying saucers and the MJ-12 group just like the rest of Ufology. They believed, according to some, that there was an unknown mysterious engineering project run by either Admiral Bobby Ray Inman or General John J. Sheehan. A lot of black budget money was known to be flowing in that direction. No one, however, seemed able to get anything concrete on the group.

They had an advantage in seeking the answer in that they knew *some* of the black secrets of the government. Also, they were able to talk to other high-ranking people who would speak to them because of their backgrounds.

The UFO Working Group came together to work on the UFO problem, knowing that together they could share information and achieve more than they would working alone. They worked on four main issues:

- Investigating UFO Reports
- Investigating the MJ-12 Documents
- Investigating the scuttlebutt of UFO crashed saucer stories being told by insiders and witnesses

- Investigating global US intelligence assets being used to detect UFOs
- Many of the 17 men in the UFO Working Group would go on to become members of another top-secret chat group known as the Aviary. In fact, the UFO Working Group might just have been how the Aviary came together.

This informal group became famous for their connections to researcher Bill Moore in the late 1980s and early 1990s. They went by bird names that allowed them to talk to each other without everyone knowing who they were. At least that was the plan.

Many of UFO Working Group, turned Aviary, went on to become members of the National Institute of Discovery Sciences (NIDS), started up by Las Vegas billionaire Robert M. Bigelow. NIDS like the other two groups, have members who shared the common goal of understanding the truth of the UFO mystery. In 2016 many of the same names became attached to the DeLonge story.

The head of the UFO Working Group given the name "Col. Howard Phillips" by Blum was really Col. John Alexander (Penguin).

Other members of the UFO Working Group included former CIA scientist Dr. Christopher "Kit" Green (Blue Jay): USAF Colonel Ron Blackburn, former microwave scientist and specialist at Kirkland Air Force Base; Dr. Hal Puthoff (Owl), former member of the NSA and one of the original researchers who developed the protocols for remote viewing with Ingo Swann. It also included Dr. Jack Verona (Raven), one of the Department of Defense initiators of the DIA's Sleeping Beauty project which aimed to achieve battlefield superiority using mind-altering electromagnetic weaponry; Ronald Pandolfi (Pelican), widely rumored to be at the core of the CIA's involvement with extraterrestrials; Dr. Robert Wood at McDonnell Douglas who would go on to become the chief researcher of the 3700 pages of documents leaked in the 1990s from six different intelligence sources; Hal McConnell from the NSA; and Major General Albert Stubblebine, the Commander of the Army's Intelligence and Security Command.

Ninety percent of the UFO Working Group meetings took place in the BDM secure vault in McLean, Virginia. This is because group member General Albert Stubblebine was the Vice-President of BDM at the time. Only one meeting occurred in the Defense Intelligence Agency secure vault.

They were trying to become an official government sponsored group looking for the answer but failed to get the funding. "They seem like a loose-knit, unofficial discussion group called together on the authority of Phillips, a self-appointed UFO guru within the agency," says Larry W. Bryant, who directs the Washington, DC office of Citizens Against UFO Secrecy (CAUS).

When the UFO Working Group had completed ten sessions, Alexander compiled the information they had gathered in a briefing book, which was presented to the then ready to retire defense authority. Alexander, however, did not want to be involved in controversy and denied the request to make the UFO Working Group into an official formal government funded and operated group. The UFO Working Group then folded, but most of the members continued to interact in what became known as the Aviary.

Blum concluded at the end of his book, based on the material he was fed, that he had been unable to find conclusive proof of UFOs. The actual UFO Working Group arrived at this same conclusion. In fact, Blum became convinced that much of the government's silence was due to lack of knowledge.

1986

....

Potential Targets or Couriers - Len Stringfield

Captain Robert Collins approached researcher Len Stringfield, while Collins was still stationed at Wright-Patterson. Collins phoned him once a week, offering highly technical papers and "a meeting with a Colonel who possessed a lot of information."

Stringfield refused to reveal his sources, and Collins broke off correspondence and moved on to contact Bruce Maccabee.

Collins told me, "I found him too unreliable and dropped him."

As to his connection with the Falcon, Collins stated, "Since being friends with Bill and having a strictly personal interest in UFOs I also knew and understood effective CI methods to cover the identity of a confidential source. Bill was familiar with these methods. Both the use of my name and Doty's to cover the identity of 'Condor' and 'Falcon' worked very well for over 2 ½ years. The tracks were covered just enough now so that it is doubtful that the real 'Condor' or 'Falcon' will ever be found. To this day, I don't know who they are, and Bill won't tell me!"

1987

....

Potential Target or Courier - Lee Graham

Lee Graham was an aerospace worker at Aerojet Electrosystems in Azusa, California, to whom Bill Moore showed documents like the MJ-12 and Aquarius, before their public release. He eventually took the documents to his superiors and came under intense security by the Defense Investigative Service (DIS). Moore who provided the documents, however, was never investigated by DIS even though Lee Graham insisted an investigation should take place.

In 1987, two men paid a visit to Lee Graham's workplace. One of the men identified himself as FBI Special Agent William Hurley. The second man dressed in civilian clothes, who did not identify himself, turned out to be Major General Michael C. Kerby, USAF, who at the time of the visit was Director of the Air Force Legislative Liaison's office.

The bulk of the one-hour interview was encouragement and congratulations for disseminating the MJ-12 document to the public. In addition to this "pep talk," Kerby showed Graham the then Top Secret designation of the F-117 'Stealth' fighter. Kerby had been in command of the operational aspects of the fighter while he was stationed at Nellis AFB, and this was an item of interest to Graham, who had been seeking it through FOIA requests for years.

Strangely, Graham learned the identity of the man in civilian clothes from another mysterious figure in the UFO community, C.B. Scott Jones, then a congressional aide to Senator Claiborne Pell. Jones provided Graham General Kerby's identity, along with a biography and photograph of the general. He told Graham in the accompanying letter that Kerby was a "mutual acquaintance."

When Jones was confronted about how he knew about the mysterious drop-in at Graham's workplace to discuss the MJ-12 document, Jones stated that General Kerby had been at Senator Pell's Senate suite on a courtesy call, and he had mentioned the visit to Jones, knowing Jones' "interest in these matters."

When Graham filed FOIA requests related to his meeting with the FBI agent and General Kerby, he discovered that he was being monitored by AFOSI Colonel Barry Hennessey in Washington, D.C. Interestingly, Hennessey was the boss of AFOSI officer Richard Doty, who had been actively discussing MJ-12 with Bill Moore and Linda Howe prior to the mailing of the MJ-12 documents to Jaime Shandera in December 1984.

In his 1983 meeting with Howe, Doty had said "My superiors have asked me to show you this," as he handed her the document identified as "Briefing for the President." The report had included discussion of MJ-12.

In 1987, the mysterious Kerby/Graham meeting clearly showed Doty's boss was now monitoring Graham who appeared to have been given the job of disseminating the MJ-12 document within the security community.

1987 - September

....

Potential Target or Courier - Whitley Strieber

Strieber received a private letter at his cabin, one of only two in thousands of letters from the public that were received at the New York cabin. The sender left a phone number, which Strieber phoned. The caller related a story of "evil greys" and "appealing blonds." The greys he said were trying to improve their race through the use of human genetic material. "We are in a war here, he told Strieber, "and you are on the front line."

The caller maintained that "public acceptance" of the aliens by the government would be an "open sesame" that would allow the visitors to conclude the takeover. The caller described Strieber as an "enabler" who was working to counter the government "subtle holding action."

When Strieber used a private detective to track the telephone and address of the caller it eventually led back to a Defense Department Exchange located in Colorado. When Strieber phoned the number that was at the end of the mail drops, the person demanded to know how he had obtained the number. A couple of days later the number was disconnected. Boulder, Colorado police threatened to charge the detective who had tracked the number for Strieber with impersonating an officer.

1987 - November

……………………………………..

Potential Targets or Couriers - Linda Howe

Former USAF Officer Robert Collins was "frantically" trying to get Linda Howe to meet with him in Albuquerque. At that meeting, also attended by John Lear, Collins showed them some MJ-12 documents primarily relating to a live alien allegedly held captive by the U.S. Government. According to Howe, Collins stated that he had worked "behind the scenes" with Bill Moore for years.

1987 - December

……………………………………..

Potential Target or Courier - John Lear

New Concepts Introduced

Preying Mantis aliens
Area 51
U.S. Government deal with aliens

Based on information he was receiving from secret sources, John Lear began to tell stories that there was an underground base at Area 51 and that back-engineering work on flying saucers was going on at the base. In addition to these concepts, Lear added a number of new ones he had been told such as:
- The U.S. Government had made a deal for aliens technology in exchange for looking the other way on abductions and cattle mutilations.
- There were underground bases at Area 51 and Dulce, New Mexico, where these alien interactions were taking place.
- The U.S. had recovered a whole series of downed UFOs. One was even buried.

1980s - Late

……………………………………..

Potential Targets or Couriers - Robert Emenegger, Bill Moore, Linda Howe, and Whitley Strieber

Robert Emenegger was told by sources that he was about to get an invitation to meet with a "live" extraterrestrial in New Mexico. Paul Shartle, who worked for DAVA at Norton Air Force Base, made the offer to Emenegger. Emenegger stated the interview never took place.

Linda Howe was offered an interview with the keeper of the live alien. It was a bizarre tale of phone calls from phone booths. In 1989 Howe described the "live alien" offer:

> *I was to have talked to the Colonel, The, I now believe dead, Colonel who was then a Captain in 49', and who retrieved the live alien from the crash at Roswell – the second Roswell crash, and took him to Los Alamos. This Colonel was to have stayed with the live extraterrestrial on a pretty-much 24-hour basis until the alien died on June 18, 1952 of unknown causes according to the briefing paper, and according to what the Flacon/Doty said on the two-hour live special. (UFO Cover-up...Live)... I was supposed to go and film with the Colonel.*

The phone calls went back and forth and Linda bought her plane ticket to go to Texas, where the man was near death. The night before she was to go, she got a call with a simple message. The interview was off. The phone went dead and the interview was over.

Writer Whitley Strieber was also told the "live Alien" story by Master Sergeant Richard Doty. He related the story in his book *Breakthrough*.

I interviewed Mr. Doty after his retirement, although he apparently told this story while on active duty as well. In my interview, Mr. Doty repeated the same tale that he has told many times, of the capture of a live alien, whom, he said, was a mechanic or engineer aboard a UFO. This being, he continued, had not been able to talk until Air Force surgeons had rebuilt his vocal chords, which was done in 1949. He stated that he had seen videotapes of the alien and is the originator of the now-famous story that aliens like strawberry ice cream. Strieber stated:

> *I had some personal experience with them. I was approached by a retired officer from the Air Force Office of Special Investigations with all kinds of stories, how the government had taken 16mm film of an alien that they had done an operation on in 1952 to enable it to talk through otherwise atrophic vocal cords. It struck me as... I wouldn't have written it as fiction because it was ridiculous. They tried to make me believe that aliens had something to do with Jesus Christ and all sorts of ridiculous things which if I had gone out into the public with would have make me look like a fool.*

A few years later George Knapp would have a series of conversations with an official at Area 51. He too would tell the story about the alien they could not communicate with and how they were afraid the alien would somehow escape. Like the other researchers, Knapp did not get to see the live alien or obtain any proof of the story he had been told.

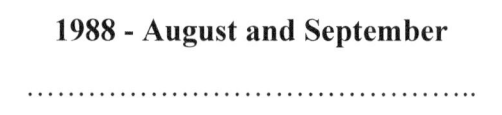

1988 - August and September

....

Potential Targets or Couriers - Len Stringfield

Len Stringfield, after a long period of quiet in contacts from his sources, was contacted by 10 new sources all at the same time. "Each promised," wrote Stringfield, "that useful information about UFO crash crash/retrievals would soon follow. By the end of November, most promises were filled, some were first-hand reports, some second. But, most importantly, some provided new backup information for cases cited in my previously published reports. Most rewarding was the timely emergence of persons serving in covert positions with substantive information in key areas of my work."

1988 - October

....

New Concepts Introduced

Naval Observatory as headquarters for MJ-12
Area 51 as the place where flying saucers were being back-engineered
Parapsychology Research Unit under the DIA
A live alien as a guest of the US government
Bodies and crafts at underground vaults at Wright Patterson AFB

A couple weeks before the 1988 election, as Reagan was finishing up his second term, probably the biggest and most important UFO disclosure took place. It was a UFO documentary that was broadcast live around the world.

A whole series of UFO secrets were revealed, including a flow chart showing the hierarchy of the organizations handling the UFO problem for the U.S. government.

This list included Area 51 which would not become known to the American public till five months later when KLAS-TV in Las Vegas broke the Area 51 story to the world.

It also detailed UFO research being conducted at Wright Patterson AFB where alien bodies and wreckage has been taken. The flow chart also showed the Parapsychology Research Unit under the Defense Intelligence Agency that would not become publicly known until the program was revealed by the government in 1995. In 1988, it was still classified as SECRET/ NOFORN/WNINTEL.

Of interest is the fact that NOFORN means classified with no distribution to foreign nationals. The podcasting of the parapsychology program was therefore a release of sensitive sources and or methods of intelligence as the show was broadcast simultaneously in the Soviet Union, and Canada.

The last key thing that was revealed is that the US government was hosting a live alien as a guest. This would later become one of the main plots in the Serpo documents. The live alien story is also a story that George Knapp would investigate at Area 51, and it was tied into strange coded postcards received by Bill Moore and Jamie Shandera that would lead them to Washington looking for the live alien in a safe house just off the Washington Mall.

Bill Moore, along with a few other people who had been involved with the underworld of UFOs provided material for a two-hour national documentary called *UFO Cover up?...Live*. Richard Doty and Robert Collins conducted the back lighted interviews of Falcon and Condor.

The website Alien Zoo described this part of the documentary:

> *Moore had "sensitive" videotape of FALCON's and CONDOR's testimonies, which painted a picture of reality very much like [the wild stories about Area 51] Bob Lazar claimed. FALCON and CONDOR vouched for the fact that the government had secret dealings with ETs for decades, and that a living alien (EBE-1) communicated much information about interstellar travel and humankind's history. Our "secret history," according to EBE-1, included the fact that we are a species created by aliens via genetic manipulation of primitive hominids. It also included the notion that thousands of years ago, aliens "staged" religion as we know it, including the Biblical miracles, to manage and direct the development of our species. EBE-1, similar to what we think of as a grey alien, was said to have come*

> *from a star system known as Zeta-Reticuli, a double star [system] on a "trade route" with Earth.*[56]

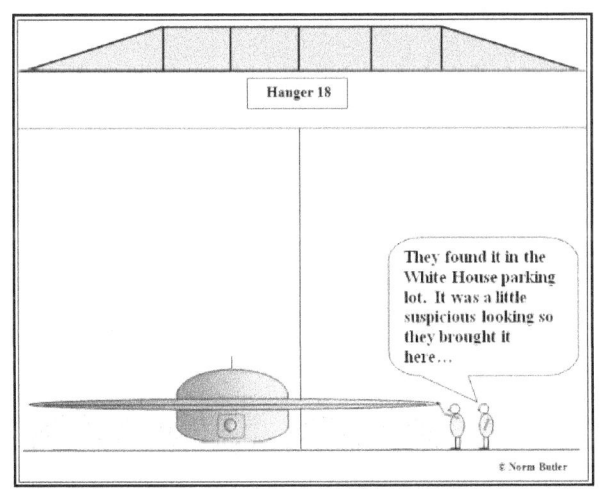

Later, Moore was setting the Doty "20-minute-long, unedited, uncut" VHS video interview of Doty done for "UFO Cover-Up? ... Live," shot in August 1988 "with the permission of the government," in *Focus* magazine.

The Falcon, a man in his 60s, was in the small studio audience for the show. Robert Coleman, who was also present for the live show, recognized the man and was surprised that he was involved.

There were some 75,000 calls into the toll free number the night of the broadcast, but the number was less than expected. Moore, Friedman, and Shandera received a lot of criticism inside the UFO community for the Falcon and Condor interviews, and not surprisingly the info about the captured aliens liking Tibetan music and strawberry ice cream.

The documentary was written off by researchers as a poorly staged event with people reading off cue-cards. Even those on the show hated the fact they had to read their own stories.

When I asked Bob Emenegger why it had been done this way, he stated that the producer, Michael B Seligman, from Gray Advertising in New York was used to doing scripted shows like the Academy Awards. That is one explanation.

The other possibility is that Gray Advertising, known for doing a lot of work for the CIA, wanted people reading from cue-cards to completely control the message that was getting out.

1989 - March

....

Potential Targets or Couriers - John Lear and Las Vegas KLAS-TV reporter George Knapp

New Concepts Introduced

S-4
Element 115
Back engineering work at Area 51

A man claiming to be a physicist named Bob Lazar appeared on Las Vegas TV station KLAS. He claimed to have worked at Area 51, in a section known as S-4, where he worked on back-engineering efforts on 9 recovered flying saucers.

Some in the field were led to believe the appearance of Lazar was an effort by intelligence people to hide the testing of a radically new plane called the Aurora. In 1990, an uncovered financial analysis done for Lockheed corporation showed that the plane was eating up almost a half billion dollars in funding.

This concept is a no-brainer and symbolic of the problem with the whole disinformation theory related to UFOs. If the Air Force wanted to test the Aurora in complete secrecy, would it make sense to start a rumor of crashed flying saucers at Area 51 which would attract thousands of people to the very area where testing was being conducted?

Lazar's story introduced EG&G as a company involved in the UFO program. He also involved US Navy Intelligence as the overseers of the UFO program.

The story created worldwide dialogue resulting in thousands of people heading into the mountains surrounding Area 51 to watch what was going on. The USAF took over public land where viewers gathered in order to stop the tours. Rumors followed of UFO work being moved to a new AFB in Utah or Colorado because of the sudden exposure.

1989 - September

....

Potential Target or Courier - Timothy Good

The director of a "Special Development Group" associated with Ringling Brothers Barnum and Bailey International contacted U.K. researcher Timothy Good. The director stated that one of his colleagues had been at Good's speech a few months earlier at the MUFON Symposium in Las Vegas, Nevada.

Good was told the director's corporation was working on an international touring display on the subject that would provide accurate information on UFOs, and be entertaining. When Good expressed reservations about a circus company getting involved in UFOs, the director wrote back and described a government connection to the UFO International display:

> *Organizations such as NASA, United States Government, Rockwell International, have agreed to work...cooperation to develop the main part of this show, the future of space and the technical advances predicted over the next 100 years. Their reluctance at first was not the fact that we owned circuses, but on how the UFO subject is going to be tastefully handled. We have now satisfied their concerns...*

Tim Good was offered the position of "official Consultant on UFO research" to the Special Development Group. After some delays, Good passed off the project to Bob Oeschler whom he felt he was fully qualified to help, as he had spent years as a UFO researcher, NASA mission specialist and project engineer.

Oeschler also had an intelligence background having given a lecture on crop circles with Bruce Maccabee at the CIA to about fifty agency personnel.

Oeschler had his first meetings with the group on November 1 and 2, 1989, after signing a non-disclosure agreement. The project became known as "Cosmic Journey," and he was told that the project had received the approval of President George Bush, Vice-President Dan Quayle and the National Space Council (an organization based in the White House and protected under Executive Order).

In November 1989, Oeschler had a series of meetings in Washington. One included a meeting at the Pentagon with former Apollo X Astronaut Lt. General Thomas P. Stafford[57] representing the intelligence community attached to the "Cosmic Journey" project. He proposed Oeschler check with NASA and National Photographic Interpretation Center (NPIC) for photos he could use for the exhibit (NPIC was formally run by Arthur Lundahl who is listed as one of the 13 magicians in Appendix 4).

The general according to Oeschler also proposed an exhibit of a dead alien in "a space age looking coffin with blue lighting inside the clear lexan cover." The general indicated that he wanted to use the real thing rather than a mock-up. Oeschler described what he was told:

> *They were devising a series of kiosks that would show the history of UFO sightings. UFOs associated with the space program, and of course aliens commonly associated with the abduction*

> *phenomena. I was shown a photographic rendition that included of what appeared to be some sort of an alien creature typical to the grey alien that had been referred to in the popular publications in the past. The creature was encased in a glass coffin like structure that was being prepared with a lot of apparatuses and tanks and forth. It was probably some sort of cryogenic tank to preserve the body from decay.*[58]

As part of the preparation Oeschler was flown out to an off-shore NORAD tracking facility in black unmarked helicopters landing on what looked like an oil rig which appeared to contain a huge NORAD tracking facility.

On the huge map of the United States they were tracking five AFCs (alternative space craft). No one seemed to be concerned at all over what they were watching.

When Tim Good made the project public in his book "Alien Liaison" there were a series of denials from all the people mentioned by Oeschler and Good. The project disappeared.

Disclosure Efforts 1990-2000

As the Scribe, it is your responsibility to report the incidents as they occurred, not as you hope they had occurred. The future is yours to change, not the past. **Pandolfi posting as the Foot Mann to Dan Smith**

1991 - August

....

The following story is an intriguing case of an actual attempt to disclose the UFO story to the American people. Robert Collins tells it in a chapter of his book *Exempt from Disclosure*. He called it "The End Game that flopped."

The effort to disclose occured as the Soviet Union was dissolving, and President Bush was on a month's working holiday at his Kennebunkport cabin in Maine.

The disclosure initiative involved many of the aviary bird figures that were supporting leaked information to Bill Moore. The manager of the project was the Raven, according to Collins (who was known as the Condor), and UFO bird watchers have attempted to identify who the Raven was.

A short version of the disclosure effort described by Collins included:
- The events took place as the Soviet Union collapsed. The hard line communist coup had failed on August 21, and on August 24 Gorbachev dissolved the Central Committee of the Communist Party.
- The full disclosure briefing of Bush was scheduled for August 23 at Kennebunkport, but moved to the "final weekend of the August break."
- 15 high level Washington officials would conduct an 180-minute briefing (instead of the regular 30), and Bush would green-light the disclosure program.
- Of the 15 officials involved eight appeared to be on board, and it was felt they would convince the other seven. When the actual vote came in, it was 11-4 against disclosure.

- For some reason, success hinged on Robert Gates getting confirmed as CIA director. He had been nominated on May 24th but did not get approval from Congress until November 5th. The hearing had been bogged down with representatives questioning Gates' role in the Iran Contra affair that happened during the Reagan administration.
- NASA was on board, but the Pentagon wasn't. It estimated 2.5 – 3 billion in lawsuits. Some like William Webster, the outgoing CIA Director, was furious he had been lied to about what was going on. Collins summed up the failure of the disclosure plan:

> *They pondered too hard and too long. They made lots of enemies...They could not move forward because they had no protection. Bush, we are told, was never thoroughly briefed. He was only told that a plan was in effect to see if it was feasible to make a release. We were back to plausible deniability.*[59]

1991 - November

....

The failure of the disclosure by Bush was followed closely by another key piece of the government UFO disclosure plan.

Dan Smith had his first encounter with Dr. Ron Pandolfi, who has worked with the office of the CIA's head scientist, at times the DIA, the Office of the Director of National Intelligence, and the White House.

Smith, a physicist, whose father was a Harvard economist and Eisenhower's tax advisor and a descendant of the founders of Throop Polytechnic (today's Cal Tech), had become interested in the crop circles. In late 1991, Smith had phoned NASA with questions and for some reason was given Pandolfi's number at the CIA.

During that conversation with Pandolfi, Smith took notice of a statement made by Pandolfi that he was going to Los Alamos, New Mexico, to talk to a live alien. Smith immediately broadcast Ron's statement to the world via Compuserve.

Smith, who is not scared off by much, quickly picked up the phone and called Los Alamos to confirm the story his new intelligence friend had told him. The next thing he knew he was talking with Col. John Alexander, whose name is a household name in Ufology.

When Pandolfi got back, he told Smith that the call to Los Alamos had caused Pandolfi some trouble. The trip was cancelled, and Pandolfi's phone at the CIA was ringing with people wanting to know what was going on. He encouraged Smith not to tie his name in with the CIA in future posts. However, he did not stop talking to Smith.[60]

The phone call Smith made led to thousands of conversations with Pandolfi about the government UFO situation. Smith reported to me that he has spoken to Pandolfi almost every day for 26 years.

Smith would later blog about the close relationship calling it the "Ron and Dan show."

Included were topics like MJ-12, the 200 people Pandolfi had tracked down who had been given full or partial briefings on UFOs, portals, and discussions of briefing or not briefing the president on the subject.

Many in the UFO community have ignored Smith's stories as he mixes in his belief that there is an eschatological connection to the phenomena and that the CIA knows it.

Later, Smith and Pandolfi would meet with a high-ranking member of the Senate Intelligence Committee, Chris Straub. Straub's name appeared in declassified government records involving a review of the secret paranormal government program then known as STAR GATE[61], which Pandolfi would help shut down once he was able to get control of it from the DIA.

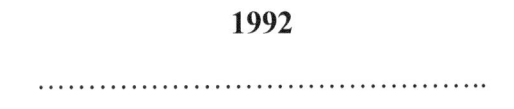

1992

....

Possible Target or Courier - Tim Cooper

Tim Cooper received the Air Accident Report, a three-page report describing the apparent design of the recovered craft, and alluding to the involvement of Oppenheimer, Von Karman, and Paperclip scientists. The secondary source for this document was an American Legionnaire.

Cooper also received the Marilyn Monroe Document in 1992. The secondary source was a CIA archivist. This paper was a one-page memo from the CIA dated August 3, 1962, showing James Angleton's signature opposite "54-12 MJ-12." It referred to Moon Dust, Area 51, and a secret air base for "studying things from outer space."

1982 – June

....

A lot of UFO researchers state that when it comes to disclosure, they will believe the reality about aliens when the president stands up and says ET is here.

Well, that happened on June 27, 1982, in the White House theatre by President Ronald Reagan. That was the night that Steven Spielberg brought his new film *ET: The Extraterrestrial* to the White House for a screening for the president, first lady, and 39 other high level people that included two astronauts, Sandra Day O'Connor from the Supreme Court, Vice President Bush, and the head of NASA.

According to a story Spielberg told producer Jamie Shandera while filming in Japan, Reagan leaned over to Spielberg and whispered, "I bet there aren't six people in this whole room who know how true this all is."

What happened next is Spielberg spoke about the Reagan disclosure in a taped interview:

> *He just stood up, and he looked around the room, almost like he was doing a headcount, and he said, "I wanted to thank you for bringing E.T. to the White House. We really enjoyed your movie," and then he looked around the room and said, "And there are a number of people in this room who know that everything on that screen is absolutely true."*
>
> *And he said it without smiling! But he said that and everybody laughed, by the way. The whole room laughed because he presented it like a joke, but he wasn't smiling as he said it.*

1992 - 1993

....

Potential Targets or Couriers - At first there were no targets other than Tim Cooper who received many of the documents. Cooper approached Stanton Friedman, Tim Good, Dick Haines, and Don Berliner who all refused to investigate the records.

In late 1992, Stanton Friedman received a call from Cooper, who claimed to have found three "new" MJ-12 documents in his mailbox. Friedman sent Cooper to Robert M. Wood, a respected, long-time engineer/scientist with McDonnell Douglas until his retirement in 1993. Robert worked with his son Ryan, a computer specialist, who got involved in 1996.

1993

Cooper claimed the "new" MJ-12 papers arrived in his mailbox by a secretive source named Thomas Cantwheel who was a retired Army Counterintelligence Officer (1993–1996).

The documents released to Cooper included 33 new documents.

1995 - Spring

Dan Smith met three times with Chris Straub, former Chairman of the Senate Select Committee on Intelligence, to discuss the U.S. government's so-called "phenomenology problem" (UFOs). As Clinton had lost the Senate in 1994, at the time of the meeting Straub was a ranking Democrat on the committee and no longer the chair.

It was during these three meetings that Smith received a confirmation that part of Pandolfi's job was to interact and feed him material. Smith wrote that Straub had confirmed he knew about the connection:

> "The first time was to get some feedback on CF (Pandolfi). I was unable to get any until I had three meetings with Chris Straub, c.'95. He was then the ranking staff member for the Senate Intel. Comm. CF joined us for the final meeting that was in the cafeteria. Bottom line: Chris was knowledgeable concerning eschatology, and he told me, 'to rest assured that I was dealing with some very competent people'...

Smith added that this was confirmed by an investigation of Pandolfi dealing with Smith and his UFO associate, Rosemary Guiley, and that the report confirmed these dealings were part of Pandolfi's duties:

> *Recall that I was indirectly responsible for the Inspector General's investigation of CF in '92-93 ... CF reported that it was a six month, $100K investigation in which he was cleared of any wrong doing.*

The story that has often been repeated is that a few key members of the House and Senate receive briefings on Unacknowledged Special Access Programs and because Pandolfi set up the meetings, it appears that Straub was one of the briefed lawmakers.

The Straub story seems to confirm the fact that the government (both president and Congress) have proper rules and regulations to deal with the UFO phenomena.

Smith talked about the last meeting with Straub:

> *In my third and final meeting with Chris, to which Ron invited himself, insisting that it be in the cafeteria, so as to be informal, Ron spent most of the time telling Chris about his tiger initiative, in which I was minimally involved. This had only to do with Siberian tigers, and nothing to do with the [Defense Intelligence Agency technology early warning] Tiger committee.*

```
Approved For Release 2004/09/09 : CIA-RDP96-00789R003100030055-9
                              Secret

                                                        23 May 95
         Memo to:  Record

         From:

               CIA briefed the status of the Star Gate transfer to SSCI
         22 May 1995. The SSCI staff present included Charles
         Battaglia, Christopher Straub, Edward Levine, Melvin Duby,
         Christopher Mellon, Al Cummings, and Donald Mitchell. CIA
         participants included            (D/ORD),            (OCA),
                    (Comptroller), and             (ORD).

                         began with summary of the Congressional Action
         and ORD's response to it, stressing that ORD was conducting a
         blue ribbon panel study and had not transferred people from
         DIA because CIA did not possess the means to task them or
         disseminate their product.           the addressed the
         three main elements of the CDA: 20 year retrospective,
         declassification, and transfer by 1 July of the program from
         DIA to CIA.

               The briefing quickly became a question and answer
         session. Given that no questions were asked specifically
         about "remote viewing," I assume that all present understood
         the general nature of the program activity in this area and
         were concerned primarily with the program cost, utility, and
         transfer issues.

               At the end of the briefing, summary charts were
         distributed to three members, Christopher Mellon, Christopher
         Straub, and Al Cummings (I think). These summary charts
         indicated when Richard D'Amato had been briefed and included
         four highlights of that meeting.

         Some of the questions included:

         Resources and Transfer:

         How much will the study cost, and who is paying for it this
         year?
```

Figure 10 Document showing Straub being briefed on remote viewing.

As we got up to leave our table, I told Chris that I was disappointed that there had been no opportunity to discuss eschatology, which had been the subject on our two previous, private meetings. Chris turned to me and said, "Well, Dan, I guess you'll just have to surprise us."

Ron tells me later that Chris had to get a special briefing prior to that meeting. It was a briefing that allegedly had already been given to some of Chris's colleagues on the Republican side of the committee, a briefing that he had not learned about until he attempted to check who Ron was.

I only had one further conversation with Chris, on the telephone. This was on the same day that I attempted to turn Ron into the FBI for seeming to have had prior knowledge of 9/11. (Yes- Smith did report Pandolfi to the FBI for telling him about 911 before it happened.)

1993 - March

....

Ben Rich, the head of Lockheed Skunk Works, gave a March 23, 1993 speech to the engineering alumni at UCLA after his retirement. He made the following disclosures:

- We now have the technology to take ET home.
- We now know how to travel to the stars. We found an error in the equations and it won't take a lifetime to do it.
- We already have the means to travel among the stars, but these technologies are locked up in black projects, and it would take an act of God to ever get them out to benefit humanity. Anything you can imagine, we already know how to do.
- When asked how they got here he replied, "What do you know about ESP?" Jan Harzan who asked the question asked back, "All things in time and space are connected." Rich replied, "That's how it works."

1993 - December

....

While giving a lecture at the University of Colorado at Fort Collins, Dr. Greer received contact following the lecture by John Petersen, the Director of the Arlington Institute in Washington, DC. He told Greer that he had been following Greer around the country for his last four talks. He claimed he had gotten his instructions at the request of the new CIA Director, James Woolsey.

"I think it is time we help you," Petersen told Greer. In response to the question who he was, Petersen said, "I know a few folks in Washington who I think you need to meet with."

The Petersen/Greer discussion led to a two-and-a-half-hour discussion on UFOs with Woolsey, who it turned out had experienced his own sighting, and was interested in knowing what was going on.

When the meeting became public in the late 90s, Woolsey, his wife, and John Petersen (Arlington Institute), who had set up the meeting, all denied that a briefing took place. They did not deny that the small dinner took place or that it lasted three hours. The denial seemed to center on the definition of the word briefing.

The Woolsey meeting led to meeting with other members of the Clinton administration, and to a new study on UFOs ordered by Woolsey, which the CIA published in 1997.

1994 - February

On February 4, 1994, after a threat by Laurance Rockefeller to the Clinton White House, the president's science advisor, Dr. Jack Gibbons, offered a declassification of one UFO case and then declassification of the rest of the files. Rockefeller had threatened to put a full-page ad in every newspaper in America asking President Clinton to declassify the UFO story if the White House continued to stonewall his UFO disclosure efforts.

Rockefeller took up the offer and demanded a reinvestigation of the 1947 Roswell case. This led to Clinton greenlighting a reinvestigation of the case. The Air Force did not want to get back into the public UFO investigation arena but had no choice.

1994 - March

Potential Targets or Couriers - Don Berliner, Stanton Friedman, Robert Wood

Aviation writer and UFO researcher Don Berliner received an unprocessed role of film in the mail. When developed, he discovered the SOM 01-1 Operations Manual, which claimed to be an operation manual for recovery of crashed flying saucers and bodies.

Special Operations Manual - Extraterrestrial Entities and Technology, Recovery and Disposal (TSMEO, R on cover page) 1954 - 23 pages.

Berliner teamed up with Stanton Friedman and Friedman contacted Robert Wood for help in verifying whether or not the document was legitimate.

"This particular document," according to Wood, "turned out to be a winner. I went to a guy in the government printing office who was involved at that time - 1954. He said 'Based on the content, this is a hoax' because the title was 'Extraterrestrial Entities and Technology,

Recovery and Disposal.' It was telling how we got started on this program, how you keep the public in the dark, how you lie to them, so they don't report UFOs. However, the guy looked at it and said, 'based on the content I would say it is phoney but based on the fact there is a raised z, and the type font is exactly the type font that was used in 1954 that I was responsible for I would say that for sure it was printed by a government printing office in 1954.'"

Wood then got a call from Joe Firmage, known as the Fox Mulder of Silicon Valley. In 1999, Firmage resigned as CEO of USWeb which had merged with CKS (and had clients such as Apple Computer, Levi Strauss and Harley-Davidson with an estimated value of $2.1 billion) because of his campaign to prove the existence of UFOs, which he felt would damage the company's reputation.[62]

Firmage stated that he was not pressured to resign but that he was willing to risk his career to publicize further his theories, such as that high tech advancements could were traceable back to the Roswell crash in 1947. Firmage believed government officials were reverse-engineering materials from Roswell. It was Firmage that told Wood, "I heard that you got questioned on documents about UFOs." He told Wood that he wanted to authenticate the 30 or so documents Wood had received at the time. After he had seen the documents, he gave Wood $500,000 to help authenticate them and $250,000 for a documentary on the documents.

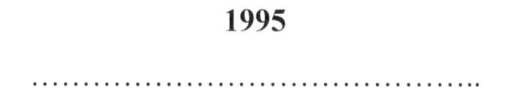

1995

....

Potential Targets or Couriers – Ray Santilli and Fox Television Network

The documentary Alien Autopsy was released. The material was leaked to a British film producer, but the source and eventual market was American, and the film was eventually shown in 20 countries.

Although the film was written off as a hoax, it ties into another story that is not as easy to write off. The second story indicates there may have been more to the alien autopsy than a simple hoax.

A prominent British photographer by the name of Don reported in 1995 that in 1972 he had been in the United States and was having dinner with the head of the Disney Studios and four of the nine original Disney animators. Ward Kimball was one of the four at the table, and the man who was involved in the UFO documentary Disney had created for the government in the 1950s.

While this dinner was going on, Maloney reported that he met another man, identified in one account as a "well-known Disney employee." The man offered to show Maloney some unusual film footage at his house. When Maloney saw it, he described it as "old footage of UFOs," and "two beings that he was told were aliens."

UFO investigator Georgina Bruni interviewed Mike Maloney about his early 1970s encounter at Disney. She described what Maloney told her about the aliens he witnessed on the film:

> *One, which appeared to be dead, was laid out on a table - or slab, the other was clearly alive and moving around on the floor. He was given no information as to the source of the footage, which he was told was "top secret," but he was in no doubt that it was a genuine piece of old film. Mike described it as being similar to the alien autopsy footage that had been shown on television. (The Santilli "Alien Autopsy" film) At no time did he say it was the same, just similar. Of the footage he personally viewed, he said: "If the film that I saw was a fake, it was a brilliant fake."*

Was the "well-known" employee Kimball, or was there a second "well-known" Disney employee who was also a UFO buff? Was the Kimball Disney story told by Kimball in 1979 just a cover for a film that the Disney people had gotten from the government? Maloney has not yet released the name of the man who showed him the movie. If it was Kimball who showed the alien film in his house, then the government now knows where that missing UFO film went.

1995 - March

....

The Disney Company released "Alien Encounters from Tomorrowland." It was only shown on a couple of stations and in some places, it was shown at midnight. It, however, creates a stir in the UFO community because of its dramatic material and statements. Many researchers believed that it was a move to acclimatize the public about UFOs.

1995 - April

....

On April 17, 1995 President Clinton, aided by John Podesta, filed Executive Order (EO) 12958 on Classified Security Information. The EO may have been an attempt to in part expose long-held UFO documents.

The EO spelled out that all records over 25 years were to be declassified unless they fit into six specific exemption categories. It also explained that if there was doubt about the classification of a document, the classification should be at the lower level, and it limited the duration of classification of most newly classified information to 10 years, subject to limited exceptions.

No UFO documents surfaced through the EO. The exemption which may have caused the documents to remain classified could have been Se.3.4.b.4 as they would "reveal information that would impair the application of state of the art technology within a U.S. weapon system."

1995 - July

....

Potential Target or Courier - Tim Cooper

New Concepts Introduced

Counter Intelligence Corps/Interplanetary Phenomenon Unit Intelligence Assessment, 22 July 1947 - (TS Ultra, later M) 7 pages.

Thomas Cantwheel delivered this document in person. The paper was an 18-page report from possibly four different dates and typewriters. Titled in Part, "Investigation of Unidentified Platform Space Vehicles." Included was "a concise summary of our views about a variety of technical, social, and political issues, followed by three 'annexes' that provide data on the history and perspective of the program."

1995 - Summer

....

One of the things that people often ignore in the MJ-12 debate is how long it went on. It started in 1980 with the release of Bill Moore's book *Roswell Incident* and was still going well into the 21 century.

The cynical take on MJ-12 puts the whole affair at the foot of Richard Doty. Doty, however, left the air force in 1987 to be a state police officer in New Mexico. The MJ-12 story and the document leaks were just ramping up as Doty was leaving.

The second person blamed for the MJ-12 story was Bill Moore. He gave a big speech at the 1989 MUFON conference about how he had worked with the intelligence people. Following many adverse reactions, Moore pulled out of the UFO research field.

Moore's partner and the person who received the MJ-12 document in his mailbox in 1984 was producer Jamie Shandera. What every story on MJ-12 leaves out is that Shandera continued to work with the aviary, trying to confirm the inside UFO story until 1999, when he withdrew after remarrying.

When doing an interview with researcher, writer, and podcaster Greg Bishop after he left the field, Moore indicated that Shandera was a long-time CIA asset. This outing of Shandera as CIA is significant because Moore had told researcher Bill Steinman that he had done some work for the CIA while in University and had reconnected once he got into the UFO field. Bishop wrote about the Shandera intelligence link in his book *Project Beta*:

> *Shandera was a producer Moore met while planning a documentary that was never produced. At a meeting with their spook friends some years later, one of the agents told Moore that Shandera had worked for them for many years, and had been called to give testimony on a voice recording in connection with an incident during the Vietnam war.*[63]

Knowing Shandera's long-time intelligence connection helps explain why he rather than Moore received the MJ-12 document in the mail.

In the late 80s, Moore and Shandera, according to Bob Collins, received 17 pages of "Bird Code." It was designed, according to Collins, to give "us directions on how to find the 'Bird Sanctuary' or an apartment in Washington DC near the mall where the (EBE) ambassador was kept."[64] The group included Ernie Kellerstrass, Rick Doty, Moore, Shandera, Collins, and possibly the DIA Falcon and Walter Ferguson from the CIA.[65]

After following the Bird Code and postcards from New Zealand Shandera made a trip to Washington but was too late to find the Alien Ambassador. He did claim he had seen a TS/SCI vault that contained "volumes" on extraterrestrials.

By 1999 he had left claiming that he had seen absolute proof of the reality of a visiting non-human intelligence. When asked, Moore told Bishop he suspected he might have seen the alien crystal which when held in one's hands could show events of history such as the crucifixion of Jesus Christ.

Figure 11 The alien crystal first shown in the 1988 UFO documentary UFO Cover-up Live

1996 - June

Potential Target or Courier - Tim Cooper, Bob and Ryan Wood

1. Cooper received Einstein/Oppenheimer June 47, Twining September 47.
2. Einstein - Oppenheimer Relationships with Inhabitants of Celestial Bodies (TS), 6 pages.

3. 6-page first generation carbon. Pre-dates the July '47 crash.

Report received from Salina, daughter of Cantwheel. According to Bob and Ryan Wood:

> *Cantwheel's daughter claimed to have been employed in the CIA for over 20 years and was a close associate with DDCI James Jesus Angelton (1954–1974). J.J. Angelton ran the agency's most secret directorate and reported directly to DCI Allen W. Dulles until 1961. Salina claims that the Counter Intelligence (CI) ran all the high-level intelligence collection activities outside of normal channels within the agency's UFO program initiated by General Walter B. Smith in late 1952. Smith brought in Angelton and Dulles as consultants for the program under what is suspected as MK-ULTRA, MJ-TWELVE, and Operation MAGNITUDE, in conjunction with a State Department intelligence unit for PSYOP activities and active measures against Soviets.*

1997 - July

……………………………………..

July 1997 was the 50th anniversary of Roswell. Scores of people assembled in Roswell to celebrate. The month also highlighted the release of the book *The Day After Roswell* by Philip Corso. It was described by *The Guardian* newspaper as being in its list of "Top Ten literary hoaxes."

The story told by Corso was that while working for U.S. Army research and development at the Pentagon, he discovered various pieces of hardware from the Roswell craft in a filing cabinet. It was then his job to indirectly seed American industry with the material.

Since Corso's book came out, there has been a lot of debate as to whether Corso was a fraud trying to cash in on the Roswell story. The second more probable explanation is that he was set up to release the idea that night vision, fiber optics, and the transister were developed from materials recovered from the Roswell crash.

He was allowed to write the book but was influenced to change the details to protect the classified version of the story. This same story would be repeated in 2012, on the 65th anniversary of Roswell, when Chase Brandon talked about a Roswell box, and also in 2017 when Pandolfi leaked the story about a box of hardware that President Trump had to show to head of industry.

Also, on July 24, 1997, the USAF released its second report of the UFO crash at Roswell. The 231-page report was titled, *The Roswell Report: Case Closed* and was produced by the Air Force, not because they wanted to get back into UFOs after "getting out" in 1969, but because President Clinton had made a speech in Belfast, Northern Ireland where he stated that if the USAF did recover bodies at Roswell, they didn't tell him about it and that he wanted to know.

The first report on the Roswell UFO crash produced by the Air Force in 1995 did not include small non-human bodies being recovered, and the second report alleged that the bodies were actually anthropomorphic dummies and part of a secret project known as Project Mogul.

1998

In 2002 Catherine Austin Fitts, a former HUD official in the Bush administration came forward with a story about a disclosure effort to get the people ready for the idea of aliens living among us.

After the story had broken, as I was preparing to put the story on my website, I was contacted by John Petersen at the Arlington Institute denying the story. Petersen was also involved in the Greer-Woolsey story. He told me that Fitts (just like Greer) was lying, and he wanted to be able to tell his side of the story, and I agreed.

I sent his denials to Fitts. She replied to every one of Petersen's charges saying "I stand by my story." Following is the story Fitts told in an article she posted on her website called "The $64 Question: What's Up with the Black Budget?"[66]

> *In 1998, I was approached by John Petersen, head of the Arlington Institute, a small high quality military think tank in Washington, DC. I had gotten to know John through Global Business Network and had been impressed by his intelligence, effectiveness, and compassion. John asked me to help him with a*

> high level strategic plan Arlington was planning to undertake for the Undersecretary of the Navy.
>
> I met with a group of high level people in the military in the process --- including the Undersecretary. According to John, the purpose of the plan --- discussed in front of several military or retired military officers and former government officials --- was to help the Navy adjust their operations for a world in which it was commonly known that aliens exist and live among us.
>
> When John explained this purpose to me, I explained that I did not know that aliens existed and lived among us. John asked me if I would like to meet some aliens. For the only time in my life, I declined an opportunity to learn about something important...
>
> When I attended one of my first meetings, I joined in a discussion with about ten people which included James Woolsey, former head of the CIA in the Clinton Administration, Napier Collyns, founder of Global Business Network and former senior Shell executive, Joe Firmage, John, and other members of the Arlington board. The main topic of discussion was whether or not the major project for the coming year should be a white paper on how to help the American people adjust to aliens existing and living among us. I said nothing -- just listened. Not that long after, I dropped from the board due to the continued demands related to litigation with the Department of Justice and their informant.

Like the Greer-Woolsey encounter, some will believe that both Greer and Fitts were lying and that Woolsey was part of some bad UFO smear.

It is possible but not highly likely that Fitts was lying, as she had (and still has) no UFO involvement. She is an economist, and this is the only time she has ever raised the topic.

The chance that Greer and Fitts were lying becomes even more unlikely when we consider that Woolsey pops up again in 2016 and 2017 in connection with UFO briefings done for President-elect Trump.

1999 - September

....

On September 16, 1999 Bob and Ryan Wood received 42 more leaked documents.

1999 - October

....

On October 9, 1999 researcher Tim Cooper received the following items on October 9, 1999, from the same person who gave him the materials on September 16, 1999 (Source S-2).

Disclosure Efforts 2000-2015

2001

....

Dr. Steven Greer started Project Starlight and founded the Center for the Study of Extraterrestrial Intelligence (CSETI - later The Disclosure Project), which sought the disclosure of allegedly suppressed UFO information. He was joined by Adm. Will Miller who advised him on classified program management inside the military.

In May 2001, Greer hosted the disclosure news conference where high-level witnesses testified about the UFO cover-up. Greer had offered amnesty to government whistle-blowers willing to violate their security oaths by sharing insider knowledge about UFOs. It was the biggest news conference since a press conference held by Ronald Reagan year before.

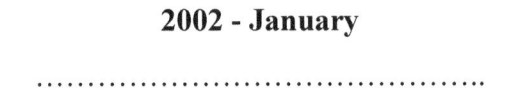

2002 - January

....

Potential Targets or Couriers - Bob and Ryan Wood

Another drop occurred involving 30 pages of material.

2005 - November

....

According to researcher Gary Bekkum, in September 2006, John C. Gannon, BAE Systems vice president for global analysis - a man who previously had chaired the CIA National Intelligence Council, and worked for the Department of Homeland Security - was alleged to be the mysterious source behind Project Serpo, a UFO tale of an extraterrestrial alien-human exchange program, as portrayed at the end of *Close Encounters of the Third Kind*. To most researchers in the UFO community, it came across like poorly written fiction.

The Serpo story would become one of the biggest UFO leaked stories of all time. It began with the words, "First let me introduce myself. I am a retired employee of the U.S. government. I won't go into any great details about my past, but I was involved in a special program."

I heard of top scientists reading the material carefully, implying that there was valuable classified information contained within the "garbage."

Kit Green who was formally responsible for UFOs at the CIA told writer Mark Pilkington, "There are certain facts in there, certain references in there that prevent me from being able to reject the material out of hand, even if the story that it's telling is not patently true." The Serpo material Green suggested, "might have served a purpose to someone, somewhere, perhaps conveying information in a heavily codified form." He reminded Pilkington that SERPO had caught the attention of some of the senior players in the defense intelligence field – perhaps some of the most senior players.[67]

2006

……………………………………..

Richard Doty was involved in the UFO program from 1979 to 1988. When he left the Air Force, he was written up as a one-man disinformation machine. Supposedly, Doty created thousands of pages of leaked UFO documents a decade or more after he left the Air Force, was the creator of the Project Serpo saga and led researcher Bill Moore to his eventual demise.

Because of Doty's assignment to USAF counterintelligence, it is hard to sort truth from disinformation in the info Doty put out during his nine years of contact with the UFO community.

A couple of points stand out showing that he was playing some key role in feeding information to the UFO community. He did this in a one-man-story fashion, unconnected to his job with counterintelligence.

Most people relaying "evil Doty" stories leave out the fact that he passed a lie detector test related to what he was telling researchers.

In 2006, Pandolfi leaked a series of e-mails detailing the 1988 meeting in the office of the director of counter-intelligence at the CIA.

In that meeting, Pandolfi, Green, Air Force officials Col. John Barry Hennessey and Col. Richard L. Weaver attended. Smith described what happened:

> *The way I originally heard the story from Ron [Pandolfi] was that there was just one such meeting, attended by Ron, wherein [Dr. Green] displayed a polygraph chart allegedly demonstrating Rick's [Richard Doty] veracity ... the discussion centered on whether or not Richard Doty had passed a lie detector test as to the knowledge he had shared in connection with the UFO mystery.*[68]

2009 - March

....

> *"I received an email yesterday morning, sent from Gordon Novel, confirming a dinner meeting for that evening in Roslyn. Also on the list were Paul Murad, Steve Greer and CK (Ron Pandolfi), and some other names I didn't know. I called Gordon to make sure I was actually invited, and whether the others were coming. I left a message with CK.*
>
> *(The meeting took place on 3/16/09). CK and I sat at one end of the table, Gordon at the other. Steve was in the middle and did most of the talking. There were six others present. Steve has been a member of the RAM team since that last meeting, a few months ago, that CK told me about in January. This was CK's fourth dinner meeting with Gordon & Co. in the last two years.*[69]

This meeting was the first meeting regarding a proposed official U.S. Government UFO/ET Disclosure Program. It included a UFO Potus Briefing for President Obama, and a documentary proposal written for producer Steven Spielberg. This was described as a part of a civilian-government liaison UFO operation by the CIA.

It listed Pandolfi as the U.S. Government Liaison Control Officer, Gordon Novel as Production Control Executive, and Dr. Steven Greer as Executive Producer. Other names attached to the program were Jim Marrs, Richard M. Dolan, Steven Greer, Harold Puthoff, Bruce

Maccabee, Stanton Friedman, Producer Bob Emenegger told me in an interview that he had been contacted by Pandolfi to help with the program.

The film part of the program was pitched as follows:

POTUS Briefing -- Eyes Only™ is a total disclosure and demonstration of an evidentiary chain that will be put before the President of the United States (POTUS) regarding UFOs, exo-biological life forms, commerce with these life forms, UFO Technology, and the inherent impact of such upon our world. The production also will propose solutions to the seemingly intractable challenges of this new reality.

The program started with a document called "Supreme Cosmic Secret" that was prepared by Gordon Novel and written solely for the CIA's internal review. According to Novel the document led to the "CIA now sanctioning the group responsible for creating the SCS document – RAM Gravonics, LLC. – in its developmental effort to replicate this technology... From mid-2004 to 2009, the CIA covertly authorized, supported, and sanctioned a comprehensive effort by RAM Gravonics to organize a science team and develop a plan to once again reverse engineer this extraordinary transport technology."[70]

Later Pandolfi would distance himself from the claim that he backed Novel, stating, "Looks like something Gordon Novel created as part of a scam. Hard to believe anyone falling for this scam."

According to researcher Ed Komarek who also dealt with Pandolfi, the reversal is not unexpected based on what Dan Smith told him. "Dan says that Ron really has no choice but to be this way because of the high-level position he holds in government. Ron may have to publicly deny some of what Dan has said about him here and elsewhere."

Novel interest in the project was mainly about submitting an energy related proposal to the government for grant money. Pandolfi stated that opportune.[71]

Greer however wanted to add two films, POTUS Briefing 1 & 2. The first, shorter one would be for the president to view. The second would be for subsequent commercial release. The pitch was;

POTUS Briefing -- Eyes Only™ is a total disclosure and demonstration of an evidentiary chain that will be put before the President of the United States (POTUS) regarding UFOs, exo-biological life forms, commerce with these life forms, UFO Technology, and the inherent impact of such upon our world. The

> *production also will propose solutions to the seemingly intractable challenges of this new reality.*[72]

On June 2, 2010 Novel appeared on the New Realities Show with Alan Steinfeld:

> *We (Novel and his Replicated Alien Machine group of which he claimed Pandolfi was a member) are trying to make a movie "Potus Briefing – Eyes Only – the supreme cosmic secret – which is what we are trying to do in Hollywood. It's a total expose of it. We want to be the disclosure – the full-blown disclosure of the whole thing. So, we've got a) the technology and b) we've got all the information because we know where all the bodies are buried. A lot of bodies are buried out there...I think we are going to make a movie – the most sensational movie in the history of the world. It is going to expose the whole thing. Then I think there is going to be a hue and cry and demand from people who are going to say, 'You mean I can be rich if you release this technology. We are all rich'... we are going to create the demand for it and Congress is going to have to satisfy the demand for it. They going to say 'All these guys are criminals. They're covering it up.' ... Potus Briefing will expose all the politics and how everything fits together.*[73]

Asked by Steinfeld how he could prove that the CIA was taking him seriously, Novel replied, "How many people do you know can go around Hollywood handing out scripts [at which he picks up the script and points to it) with this on it: 'Prepared for the Central Intelligence Agency and Steven Spielberg - Potus Briefing – Eyes Only – Classification Umbra Red – Supreme Cosmic Secret – US government Liaison Control Officer Dr. Ronald Pandolfi... Proposed Official Government Disclosure Program.' Isn't that about as formal and official as it gets?"

"Why aren't they stopping you?" asked Steinfeld.

"Because I have their authority," replied Novel. "I have their authority to put those seals there. They all know that this is going on."

"They're for this disclosure?" asked Steinfeld.

> PROPOSED OFFICIAL U.S. GOVERNMENT UFO/ET
> DISCLOSURE PROGRAM
>
> Prepared for the
>
> CENTRAL INTELLIGENCE AGENCY
> and
> STEVEN SPIELBERG
>
> # POTUS BRIEFING
>
> EYES ONLY
>
> CLASSIFICATION – UMBRA RED
>
> U.S. Government Liaison Control Officer: Dr. Ronald Pandolfi
> Production Control Executive: Gordon Novel

"Sure," Said Novel.

Pandolfi would later deny that he and/or the CIA gave any authorization to Novel. I know this to be untrue based on two pieces of evidence.

1) Producer Bob Emenegger told me he had received a call from Pandolfi asking for help with the production.
2) In Smith's February 2007 chat board, Best Possible World Hypothesis, he details a series of e-mails back and forth between Novel and Pandolfi that indicate that Pandolfi not only helped Novel but actually met with Spielberg on two occasions. Smith begins the posting by quoting an e-mail from Novel, "Langley's major players are indicating they or their business surrogates will support financially - the pending RAM Conference announcement. Do you object to being Bcc'd in the RAM broadcast lists? RP has had Dan contact Alison yesterday in L.A. to advise her RP has had surprisingly two previous meetings with Spielberg and has the official - albeit covert - support of the 'company' and his new boss as Deputy Director of ODNI (Office of the Director of National

Intelligence). Adm. Mike McConnell the new Director of ODNI is also the current or former MJ- #1 Director General."

When Novel died in 2012, the RAM project to build a flying saucer and the Potus Briefing Movie faded away. The RAM story resurfaced on *Open Minds Forum* in February 2017, but there are not enough details known as to what new disclosure effort is underway.

2009 - July

In 2009, bestselling author James Bamford released his book *The Shadow Factory* with the latest inside information related to United States intelligence.

When UFO researchers reviewed the book, one of them found carefully hidden on the front cover the security stamp "Top Secret-MJ-12."

The discovery on the cover of Bamford's book was important because Bamford is perhaps the top American author and journalist on the topic of United States Intelligence Agencies, notably the National Security Agency. The NSA had long been rumored to be a major player in the UFO cover-up. The other reason it was important because the government had made a clear statement that there was no MJ-12. Now "Top Secret-MJ-12" mysteriously appears hidden on the cover of the top writer about the intelligence agencies.

When asked how "Top Secret/ MJ-12" ended up on the front cover of his book, which had nothing to do with UFOs, Bamford replied that he had no idea.

2012 - March

In 2012, during a speech in Roswell, New Mexico, Obama said that the Roswell alien question was the question most asked by young nine and ten-year-old boys. The Top-Secret subject of UFOs is one that he didn't have to bring up, but he did:

> *We have landed in Roswell. I announced to people when I landed that I had come in peace. (Laughter) Let me tell you – there are more nine and ten-year-*

old boys around the country when I meet them – they ask me, "Have you been to Roswell and is it true what they say?" And I tell them, "If I told you I would have to kill you." So, their eyes get all big...so...we're going to keep our secrets here.[74]

2012 - June

....

This material has been reviewed by the CIA to prevent disclosure of classified information. **The disclaimer at the beginning of the book is *The Cryptos Conundrum.***

Inside the courtyard of the Central Intelligence Agency, there is a fifteen-foot-tall steel sculpture. It is emblazoned with a message that no one can decipher. The three-inch-high letters on the sculpture form a coded message that is claimed to be central to the survival of mankind – a message hidden in plain sight, displayed in a public space, with the full text available to anyone who has an internet connection.

Another message hidden in plain sight was delivered by the CIA on Coast to Coast AM which is the biggest late night talk show in America with an audience estimated in the millions. UFOs are a common topic of conversation on the show.

On June 23 and then July 12, 2012, Chase Brandon, a 43-year-old veteran of the CIA, was a guest on the show. Brandon was promoting a science fiction book *The Cryptos Conundrum*. According to Brandon, the book was vetted extensively at least twice by the CIA, and he stated they requested many changes. These changes would ensure that he revealed no official secrets to the incredibly dense and easily manipulated UFO community which the agency targeted for the book.

The book was promoted just before and after the 65th anniversary of the infamous 1947 Roswell crash. That made the timing of the book critical as it dealt with a fictional version of the CIA's handling of the Roswell crash. Brandon stated the draft of the book was heavily reviewed at least twice before its release. Therefore, everything that appears in the book has the blessing of the agency and they approved the messages the book contains.

Like other fictional books reviewed by the CIA, the classified aspects of the story were protected, but the premise of what occurred was revealed. Brandon's book is a classic example of gradual disclosure on the subject of UFOs.

Brandon was a key member of the CIA, having spent 25 years as a covert officer around the world. Then from 1995-2005, he held the key job as the chief CIA liaison to Hollywood.

Brandon stated that that job made him the second most powerful official (after the director) inside the CIA and he was able to make public statements on behalf of the agency. His job involved helping movie producers in Hollywood portray the CIA in a positive light, leaving the right impression on the public. Brandon indirectly confirmed that he is still under contract with the CIA, when he said on Coast to Coast AM that "No one ever really retires from the CIA. Everyone likes to help out."

The account Brandon told the audience that evening was that while he was at CIA headquarters he was waiting for a film crew to do some filming in the collections area:

> *I absolutely know ... that there was a craft from beyond this world that crashed at Roswell, that the military picked up remains of not just the wreckage but cadavers and all of that was made public for a short while ... One hundred percent guarantee, in my heart and soul I say - Roswell happened.*

Although Brandon stated that no one was allowed in the area without an escort, he claimed that he was wandering around looking at the archived boxes when he saw one that had "Roswell" written on the label.

He stated that he pulled the box down and looked inside. What he saw was a collection of materials which he would not specify. He said that at no time would he ever spell out what was in the box, but that what he saw confirmed to him without a doubt that the 1947 Roswell UFO crash had been an extraterrestrial event and that it involved cadavers.

Brandon did not specify whether or not the material in his Roswell science fiction book had come from material he had seen in the box, but he did hint that the book was much more than fiction. He stated that if readers read the book they would get an interesting read but if they read between the lines they would learn something.

The story that Brandon told is the fictionalized version of the real story. That story probably involved Brandon being read in on the CIA's role in the Roswell crash. Because that material would be very classified, Brandon and the CIA reviewers drafted an unclassified fiction version of how Brandon got the material. This is standard procedure when CIA officers write books through fictional spy novels. The idea gets out but no one is able to detect what is true and what is false.

Therefore, it's likely that there was no Roswell box. That was simply a prop in the stage play used to tell the classified story. It delivers the story and at the same time, a cover story providing plausible deniability

The release of this Roswell tale by the CIA raises important questions about Obama and the White House. Why would a high-level agency man like Brandon throw the CIA under the extraterrestrial Roswell bus, after the CIA has spent 65 years covering up any involvement they might have had in the 1947 crash?

The simple explanation that explains all these seemingly contradictory stories is the fact that the CIA approved Brandon's disclosing that it was an extraterrestrial event. Brandon revealed events and he broke no secrecy laws in the way that that he did it.

Brandon in his half dozen interviews about the Roswell box was very specific in pointing out that the CIA works for the 'people at 60,000 feet' (President, executive branch, congressional intelligence committees). The CIA is contracted to provide intelligence, and therefore only do what they are told to do. They answer to the president and the president is responsible for their actions as they work for him. Therefore, Obama would have been aware and would have green-lighted the disclosure of a Roswell box to the American people, as he would have been held responsible if the story had backfired with serious questions asked by opponents in an election year. Obama was probably behind the story, which seemed to be set up as a "Happy 65th Anniversary of Roswell" event.

The UFO community, as it usually does, just wrote off the Brandon story as a hoax and went off to chase the next UFO story, picture, or video. The story got out, no classified information was exposed. There was only one rough moment in the second Coast to Coast AM interview when there was a long pause after Brandon was asked if he had ever been asked by the CIA to influence Hollywood productions about UFOs.

The only reporter to push the CIA for further details was reporter Billy Cox. He wrote about his attempt to get to the bottom of the story:

> *Someone here is clearly lying. Last week, De Void asked the CIA if a) its HIC was in possession of Roswell data, and b) would Brandon have had access to that material? Agency PIO Jennifer Youngblood responded Tuesday afternoon: "Our historians have found nothing in the Agency's holdings to corroborate Mr. Brandon's specific claims. The CIA has fielded numerous inquiries related to UFOs over the years, and the definitive account of the Agency's role in UFO studies was published in 1997 and can be found — without reduction — on our website."*

Lee Spiegel had the opportunity to ask Brandon if the CIA had asked him for the location of the documents he claimed to have seen. He said they did not. The story ended, Brandon walked back into the shadows, mission accomplished.

Brandon proposed a second book called *Hour Glass* which he stated would be out in 6-18 months, once *Cryptos* has run its hard back and paper back period of time.

Brandon stated that "actually that one – Hour Glass – got hammered more in the publications review process, because it's not science fiction – it's just fiction but it is pretty realistic fiction, and it's classic espionage spy thriller where Cryptos is science fiction, but has an awful lot of real history and real names in it – and real information having to do with other things including UFOs."

For whatever reason the book was never released.

2013 - April

....

In April of 2013, John Burroughs was one of the researchers, activists, and military witnesses who came forward from ten countries and gave testimony in Washington, DC to six former members of the United States Congress about events and evidence indicating an extraterrestrial presence engaging the human race.

Burroughs testified about his encounter with a landed UFO at the Bentwaters AFB in 1980. Part of his testimony was that he was unable to access his military medical files because they were classified, which shocked Congressman Cook on the panel. Cook had been a congressman with responsibility over Veterans Affairs, and said he didn't know there were classified medical files.

In July 2013, Kit Green, a former member of the CIA, and still under contract with the CIA, contacted Burroughs' lawyer and interceded by writing a two-page memo to the military in order to help Burroughs get a heart operation for damage caused by the RF radiation given off by the landed UFOs.

Green's action was one not of cover-up, or full disclosure, but of just plain disclosure. He helped Burroughs get the help he needed and the medical records remained classified. Green wrote in part:

> *It is true, his records...about a thousand pages, and to this day, still many hundreds, were in fact legally classified. In my 46 year career as a Medical Officer and physician with CIA [including as Staff Officer, Chief of Medical Intelligence/ Life Sciences Division, and Assistant National Intelligence Officer for Science and Technology]...I had, until a year or so ago...only seen a handful of truly 'classified' medical records: those of Adolph* Hitler, John Kennedy's Autopsy, and recently ... John Burroughs.[75]

2013 - December

On December 8, 2013, President Obama became the first president to talk about the fact openly that there was a place called Area 51. He did this at the Kennedy Center, the night Shirley MacLaine and four other artists were honored. MacLaine has claimed to have seen UFOs.

Obama used a joke directed at MacLaine to talk about Area 51. MacLaine joined Billy Joel, Carlos Santana, Herbie Hancock and opera star Martina Arroyo at the event, where they were awarded the nation's highest honour for influencing American culture through the arts. Here's what Obama said:

> *Now, when you first become president, one of the questions that people ask you is what's really going on in Area 51?*

> *When I wanted to know, I'd call Shirley MacLaine. I just became the first president to ever publicly mention Area 51. How's that, Shirley?*

The key to understanding the significance of this is that Obama did not have to bring up Area 51. In doing so, he was inviting questions about a location that has been Top Secret for 60 years, and which still has many classified programs taking place at the base, including possible back-engineering of UFOs. The questions, however, never came.

2015 - October

....

In October, 2015 a stunning development took place. The CIA suddenly showed up at a special event panel that was held at the Atomic Energy Testing Museum just off the main strip in Las Vegas, Nevada. The panel of former and current CIA employees answered questions about Area 51 and included discussion about UFOs. The three CIA panelists included Chief CIA Historian, Dr. David Robarge, former CIA senior scientific intelligence officer, S. Eugene Poteat, and re-engineering expert, Thornton Barnes.

This was a striking new openness for the agency. The official CIA position was, and still is, that they have not been involved in the UFO phenomena since 1952, but control Area 51, which was officially denied to exist till 2013.

Suddenly, in July 2013, in reply to a Freedom of Information Request about the base, the American government suddenly admitted that Area 51 was in fact a reality.

At the October 2015 event in Las Vegas, the CIA officials tried to downplay the former secrecy about Area 51 saying, "What happens at that secret base called Area 51 is known by everybody, there's nothing secret." They then contradicted hinting that there were secrets when Robarge stated, "I can neither confirm nor deny that secrets can be kept."

The back-engineering of UFOs at Area 51 was denied when they faced a question about scientist Bob Lazar, who claimed he had worked on back-engineering at S-4, located at the base. Robarge said they were not working on UFOs, but the CIA panel refloated their contention that a lot of UFO sightings had been caused by people misinterpreting test flights of the U-2 and SR-71 planes that were tested at Area 51.

The appearance of the CIA was a form of disclosure, because they didn't have to appear at the closing of an exhibit telling the rumored story of crashed UFOs held at Area 51. They could have just remained silent as they have officially done for decades.

2015 - November

Hillary Clinton, during her campaign for president, appeared on the late nigh Jimmy Kimmel show. Documents leaked through WikiLeaks showed that she was expecting and hoping to be asked a UFO question. The same document pointed out that she was disappointed at not getting the question as she had for five minutes rehearsed a response.

The fact that she wanted a UFO question is significant because UFOs have always been seen as a toxic issue to politicians. She eventually received the question from Kimmel in March 2016, and stated that despite the fact that her husband has said he hadn't found anything on UFOs, she would look again, and would disclose as much information as she could.

2015 - December

Daymond Steer, a reporter at the *Conway Daily Sun* newspaper, in Conway, New Hampshire asked Hillary about UFOs.

Speaking of the UFO cover-up Clinton said, "Yes, I'm going to get to the bottom of it…I think we may have been (visited already). We don't know for sure."

The statement was pure disclosure as she was married to a former president of the United States who would have known the truth. Hillary became the highest-level politician ever to mention not only that there may be life "out there," but that they might already have visited the Earth.

2016 - February

....

On February 11, President Obama appeared on The Ellen DeGeneres Show with 6-year old presidential trivia wizard Macey Hensley.

Hensley was invited to ask Obama a question and she chose to ask if aliens are real. Obama replied, "We haven't actually made direct contact with aliens yet. But when we do, I'll let you know."

After the interview had aired, I asked Ben Hansen, former host of Syfy's "Fact of Faked: The Paranormal Files" to perform another painstaking analysis of President Obama's response.

He used his experience and FBI training to analyze Obama's body language and voice to determine if he exhibited stress by the questions he was asked or deception in his response. Based on his analysis he told *Open Minds TV:*

1) We can prove that this interview was pre-planned with questions and answers known beforehand (we speculate that the Kimmel interviews had some of this, but it's not as obvious as this interview).

2) Everything indicates that Obama deliberately and precisely delivered his words to answer Macey's question, yet he didn't directly answer it. His selective wording leaves a lot open for interpretation. This could allow him to still "technically" tell the truth, while covering up what he knows.

3) Obama's answer asserts that he IS in a position to know. Whether true or not, he speaks as if he's coming from a position of authority, being informed by those who have information.

4) His statement is contradictory to his previous statement on Jimmy Kimmel that he can't reveal any information. His inconsistency could indicate that the disclosure situation is evolving or that he's been told to issue blanket statements of denial instead of continue the cloak and dagger routine that he may know something.[76]

Most importantly, Hansen pointed out that both Obama and Hensley appeared to be reading off cue-cards as "several times we can see both Obama's and Macey's eye-line move slightly off to the side of the camera lens."

If this is true, then Obama knew the UFO question was coming and was prepared for it. He or his staff could have vetoed the question from being asked and didn't.

The answering of the question and the lack of any denial about the UFO subject was revealing – and is thus disclosure.

2016 - March

....

On March 24, Hillary Clinton took a planned question about UFO subject on the Jimmy Kimmel show. In his question, Kimmel also brought up the comments made on his show by Bill Clinton where he stated he had looked but could not find anything. He asked Hillary what she would do in light of that reply.

With a big smile on her face and great confidence Hillary responded, "I am going to do it again. I would like us to go into those files and hopefully make as much of that public as possible. If there's nothing there, let's tell people there's nothing there."

2017 - January

....

Two days before the inauguration of President-elect Trump, on January 18, 2017, the CIA announced it had uploaded to the internet 13 million pages of previously declassified documents only accessible on computer terminals at the National Archives.

As the CIA only carries out the instructions of the president, there is little doubt that President Obama was behind the release.

These files included many UFO and psychic research files and the info was released two days before the inauguration. This supported the statements made by Pandolfi that we are dealing with a phenomenology problem and not just UFOs.

Stephen Bassett from the Paradigm Research Group stated, "PRG believes that two days before the new president took office the CIA made a powerful statement that only increased public awareness and added new pressure on the truth embargo."

Actually, it was the president who was making the statement as the CIA does not do anything without authorization from the executive office of the president.

2017 - February

....

Dan Smith posted material that he received from the Footmann, Ron Pandolfi, who in in charge of UFOs for the Director of National Intelligence. The claim being made by Pandolfi would seem to be easily dismissed as nonsense. As pointed out in this book, that dismissal is part of the plan to get the message out without spilling the milk. On February 3, Smith posted to *Open Minds Forum*:

> *In the meantime, there were two items from the Footmann...... a goodie bag, and something that would be nine months hence.*
>
> *My first reaction to the goodie bag was negative, but, on further reflection, not so much. It sounded rather like a replay of Philip Corso's story of a 'file cabinet' to which he was granted custody by Gen. Trudeau. Allegedly, the items in the cabinet, which were retrieved from Roswell, were reverse engineered by various government contractors, and substantially contributed to the subsequent technology boom. The present day 'box' will supposedly put our technology back in first place.... make America great again.*
>
> *Corso's book assumes an ETH..... we're not talking wishing well stuff (non-physical), here. I was provided no further information. Rather than Corso's crash retrieval-type scenario, I would speculate that we're looking at something like a time capsule from the future... just what the president ordered. Hey, Donald (Trump), go ahead and take the bait.... make our day.*

The goodie bag was actually just a rehash of not only the Corso story of finding pieces of crash debris in a filing cabinet and handing it off to industry, it was a rehash of the 2012 Chase Brandon story. In that story, instead of finding the stuff in a filing cabinet he found it in a cardboard box at Langley.

The Wiki-Leaks UFO Story

Background

....

On October 7, 2016, Wiki-Leaks started to publish thousands of emails reportedly retrieved from Podesta's private Gmail and Georgetown email accounts. Podesta and the Clinton campaign refused to confirm or deny the authenticity of the emails choosing instead to declare the whole thing to be an attempt by Vladimir Putin and the Russian government to help Donald Trump get elected.

The Clinton campaign received support from the United States Intelligence Community. They released a report directly accusing Russian intelligence of involvement.

Julian Assange, the head of Wiki-Leaks who published the emails on their website told Russian RT reporter, John Pilger, "That's false. The Clinton camp has been able to project a neo-McCarthy hysteria that Russia is responsible for everything."

On the eve of the election, Assange defended just publishing material from the Clinton campaign, "we cannot publish what we do not have. To date, we have not received information on Donald Trump's campaign, or Jill Stein's campaign, or Gary Johnson's campaign or any of the other candidates that fulfills our stated editorial criteria."

What is clear from the research is that at least when it comes to the UFO related emails they all seem to be legitimate. I contacted a number of the people whose UFO emails appeared on the Wiki-Leaks site. Everyone claimed the emails had been sent and were unaltered.

Of the close to 60,000 emails there were about 200 that were related to UFOs. Searches produced the following results:

91 UFOs
20 Extraterrestrial
35 DeLonge
26 Edgar Michell
13 Rebecca Hardcastle Wright
20 X-Files
3 Astronaut John Glenn

The reason that there were so many UFO related emails is that Podesta has had a long-time interest in UFOs and the X-Files. This interest went back to his time inside the Clinton administration where he was known as the X-Files man.

The UFO and X-Files interest was also well known among the media. One example of this is a January 2016 Wiki-Leaks email sent to Podesta from Glenn Thrush at Politico who had received an email related to the X-Files. He forwarded it to Podesta with the comment, "I feel like this reader email needs to be routed to the US Department of Podesta."

John Podesta

The Madison Man

....

A popular government without popular information, or means of acquiring it, is but a Prologue to a Farce or a Tragedy, or perhaps both. Knowledge will forever govern ignorance, and a people who mean to be their own governors must arm themselves with the power which knowledge gives. **Words written by President James Madison in 1822 and inscribed outside the Library of Congress Madison Building in Washington D.C.**

As Wiki-Leaks exposed the Podesta plan to get some sort of UFO disclosure, many in the UFO community turned on him. Questions were raised questioning his motives.

Part of the reason for this is that the UFO community loves conspiracy. Many researchers feed of and repost the most bizarre theories appear on websites that have been discredited many times over.

Podesta has always held "openness in government" as one of his key beliefs. It was one of the items noted about Podesta by *The Washington Post* in a biographical article they wrote on him. They listed encryption technology, the declassification of government documents, agricultural policy, and the impact of the Internet as Podesta's main focuses while at the White House. Other evidences of the Podesta commitment to "openness in government" include:

- He served as a member of the Commission on Protecting and Reducing Government Secrecy chaired by Senator Daniel Patrick Moynihan.
- He was a member of the board of The James Madison Project, a non-profit organization established in 1998, committed to "promoting government accountability and reduction of secrecy."
- He announced on Clinton's behalf the rejection of appeals made by President Clinton the day before the end of his final term. The appeals rejected were those of the President's Foreign Intelligence Advisory Board and the Secret Service. Both groups were attempting to block the release of "assassination records" related to the death of former President John Kennedy.
- Appearing in front of a group of intelligence officers at the National Reconnaissance Headquarters, Podesta made a major speech on classification and declassification, as it related to the Clinton EO. He reminded the agents of the words Supreme Court Justice Louis Brandeis that, "Sunshine is the best of disinfectants." He also pointed out to them that, "our founders knew that democracy cannot function in the absence of public information." Finally, he noted the importance of "balancing the vital interests of national security with the genuine claims of public openness...For over two centuries, we have prospered and won because -- at our best -- we have found ways to do both."
- Appearing in front of the Senate Committee on Commerce, Science and Technology Subcommittee on Science Technology and Space, in May 2002, Podesta testified that he had been "deeply involved in the development of budget and policy priorities in this area" within in the Clinton White House. He spoke out against the Bush administration policy of renewed scientific secrecy, and for encouraging scientific research to be done by the Defense Department and black programs. He encouraged "public knowledge, public scrutiny with free exchange of scientific information" which would "not only provide the basis to make the breakthroughs necessary to stay ahead of our adversaries, but may provide a better long-term security paradigm as well."

Of the many speeches Podesta has made on secrecy, the following excerpt spells out why he might want UFO disclosure.

> *Many consider the tension between secrecy and openness as a balancing act between civil liberties and national security.*
>
> *According to this theory, the decision is how much or how many of our democratic principles are we willing to sacrifice for our security.*
>
> *But, of course, when the choice is between survival as a people or as a nation against an abstract principle, the outcome is predetermined.*
>
> *History has shown the fallacy of this analysis – excessive secrecy does not lead to improved national security. Just the opposite has proved true. Of course, there are secrets worth protecting, but a culture of secrecy has led to regrettable policy choices, wasted resources and a decline in public trust.*
>
> *It is my view that the current administration has ignored the lessons of the past and has compounded our security problems by withholding vital government information from the American public.*[77]

The Puppet Master

....

We cannot lead if the American people are kept in the dark. We cannot lead if the world does not know the principles and laws that guide us, or if others can credibly say that our commitment to a government of the people, by the people and for the people is simply window-dressing, or that we sacrifice our constitutional principles when it is expedient. **John Podesta**

The story of Hillary Clinton, and UFOs was a big story inside the 2016 campaign, and it all goes back to John Podesta. He was the driving force behind Hillary Clinton getting and then answering three UFO questions from reporters.

Podesta is the former Chief of Staff to President Bill Clinton, a job which was described by former Vice President Dick Cheney and others, as a job that holds more power and authority than the vice president. Podesta also served as legal advisor to President Obama.

Hillary left many of the strategic decisions to Podesta, as everything in a primary campaign is polled to find out how it will play out. In many ways, Hillary was the puppet and Podesta was the puppet master.

Podesta was perhaps the main idea man of the Democratic Party in 2016. He founded the key Democratic think tank known as The Center for American Progress that has 180 employees and a yearly budget of 25 million dollars.

The Center's employees are made up of experts on national, foreign affairs, and national security issues. Podesta estimated that by 2009, 40 of them had gotten jobs in the Obama administration.[78]

Many consider Podesta the smartest man in the room. *The New York Times* described his power in Washington stating, "Perhaps no other unelected Democrat has shaped his party as much over the last two decades."[79]

Podesta was a longtime advisor to the Clintons. He was with President Clinton on the first day of his administration and with him the day he walked out the door. He has been an advisor to Hillary for decades.

As Chief of Staff to President Clinton, Podesta was responsible for directing, managing, and overseeing all policy development, daily operations, Congressional relations, and staff activities of the White House from October 1998 until January 2001. He coordinated the work of cabinet agencies with a particular emphasis on the development of federal budget and tax policy. He served in the President's Cabinet, and as a Principal on the National Security Council.

As Chief of Staff, he was on the list for the Top Secret Presidential Daily Briefing (the PDB goes to the vice-president, national security advisor, chairman of the Joint Chiefs of Staff, White House chief of staff, and secretaries of State and Defense). He would, therefore, be familiar with Top Secret level material dealt with by the president.

He gave himself the title "Secretary of (expletive)" for his role as the person who cleaned up all the Clinton scandals in the second term of the administration. Senator Tom Daschle stated, "I've never seen John lose it…. He's also able to take disparate people and groups and find common threads and common ideas."

In 2008, Podesta took on the role of helping to pick the members of the Obama administration. He spent a segment of time as a principal advisor to Obama on things like energy policy, and possibly UFOs.

Dr. Steven Greer, who headed up the Disclosure Project, stated that Podesta helped him provide a UFO briefing to the newly elected Obama. Greer said:

> *An attorney working with Mr. Podesta requested the briefing, and we assembled an extensive file for Mr. Podesta to provide to the newly- elected President Obama. There was also support for this process from a senior CIA official who is friendly to Disclosure, and the briefing was also provided to then-CIA Director Leon Panetta. Mr. Podesta came out publicly in support of Disclosure the year after the historic 2001 National Press Club Disclosure Project event organized by Dr. Greer.*
>
> *We are encouraged that Mr. Podesta remains a stalwart supporter of Disclosure, and we continue to advocate for the release of illegally classified information and technology related to UFOs.* [80]

Besides his political skills and power, he was very well known as the X-Files man inside the Clinton administration. While still at the White House, Podesta told *U.S. News* about the Sunday night show which he never missed. "When the show about the aliens comes on," said Podesta, "I get glued to the tube and try and figure out which government agencies to call to determine if the show's story is real or not."[81] U.S. News further reported that Podesta had even sent a letter to one of the show characters, FBI agent Dana Scully."

The Washington Post also referenced Podesta's "fanatical devotion to the X-Files." They quoted Clinton Press Secretary Mike McCurry, who stated, "John can get totally maniacal and phobic on certain subjects. He's been known to pick up the phone and call the Air Force and ask them what's going on in Area 51."[82]

Podesta spoke about his X-Files obsession at a June 1998 Commencement Address given at his Alma Mater, Knox University. He began by describing the upcoming X-Files movie as the biggest event of the year, and then described his White House office.

"Some people at the White House have coffee tables full of White House trinkets. Others have what are known as "me walls" filled with candid shots of them and the president. In my office at the White House, I have a little table that I've converted into an X-Files shrine, with copies of books, fan magazines, CD-ROMs, photos of David Duchovny and Gillian Anderson."[83]

Despite his apparent yen for things extraterrestrial, in public Podesta has taken a much more conservative political stance when talking about extraterrestrials. The Las Vegas Review-Journal, for example, quoted Podesta as being "skeptical that there is extraterrestrial life."

Podesta's public position on UFOs is also conservative, saying, "I think it's time to open the books on questions that have remained in the dark on the question of government investigations of UFOs."

When asked about Area 51, Podesta stated, "My tendency is to try and err on the side of openness rather than on the side of secrecy, and I think a thorough review about whether more information could be brought to light (about Area 51) would be a worthwhile enterprise." Asked if "Area 51 harbors government information about UFOs," Podesta said, "I can answer that, no." [84]

On October 22, 2002, the Sci-Fi network hosted a Washington UFO news conference to encourage the government to disclose the truth about UFOs. Podesta appeared as a member of the public relations firm, which he founded with his brother Tony.

In that news conference, Podesta stated, "It's time to find out what the truth really is that's out there," he said. "We ought to do it, really, because it's right. We ought to do it, quite frankly, because the American people can handle the truth. And we ought to do it because it's the law."[85]

In reporting on the news conference, CNN quoted Podesta as saying "It is time for the government to declassify records that are more than 25 years old and to provide scientists with data that will assist in determining the true nature of the phenomena." [86]

He also spoke about the benefits of scientific openness in an appearance before Congress. "A new culture of secrecy is bound to influence the direction of discovery," said Podesta.

> *The efficient advancement of scientific knowledge, and the public, or at least their representatives in Congress, provide an opportunity to assess the costs that come from a science program unchecked by public scrutiny. Before we rush headlong into this new era of scientific secrecy, we should pause to remember the nuclear exposure experiments carried out in this country on human subjects, including the mentally retarded and*

even children, and remember also, that the Ames strain of anthrax that was used in the attacks last fall was probably developed in a classified military program, ostensibly for defensive purposes. Public knowledge, public scrutiny with the free exchange of scientific information may not only provide the basis to make the breakthroughs necessary to stay ahead of our adversaries but may provide a better long-term security paradigm as well.[87]

Podesta's Own Knowledge

....

Podesta has been at the center of power in Washington for decades but likes to be in the shadows. He says almost nothing, even on the UFO subject. In his most influential position, Chief of Staff to President Clinton, he would have been involved in the scheduling for any briefings Clinton got on the subject of UFOs, and in any actions, Clinton made to get answers.

He has come out of the shadows from time to time, such as helping Leslie Kean file an FOIA on the 1965 reported UFO crash at Kecksburg, Pennsylvania.

The question then arises, what does Podesta know and what has he disclosed?

A small hint came when CNN picked up the story of Hillary promising to reveal what she could about UFOs if she was elected president. The reporter Jake Tapper asked Podesta about the promise to release documents and then pressed Podesta hard about what he thought the truth was. The numerous hesitations and stonewalling of answers hint Podesta may know a great deal, but is not able to talk about it because it is classified.

Tapper: Have you seen any of these documents? You were White House Chief of Staff years ago?
Podesta: Well you know, ah, President Clinton, ah, asked for some, ah, information on some of these things, ah, and in particular, ah, in particular some information about what was going on at Area 51, ah, but I think that ah I think that the US government could do a much better job, ah in answering the legitimate questions people have, ah, about what is going on with ah unidentified aerial phenomena and

they should the American people can handle the truth, so they should just ah do it.

Tapper: What is the truth? Is there evidence of alien life?

Podesta: You know that - that's for the public to judge once they've seen – seen all the evidence...

Tapper: What do you think personally?

Podesta: What do I think? I think there are a lot of planets out there.

Podesta's power combined with his openness and interest in UFOs made him the center of attention in the UFO community when his personal emails started to be leaked on the internet in October 2016.

John Podesta - The UFO Queries

As Podesta's emails started to appear, he told reporters that it "doesn't feel great," to have his personal information and exchanges aired out for the world to see, but acknowledged, "I'm kind of zen about it at this stage."

The leaks may not have been helpful for Podesta or the Clinton campaign, but they were a windfall for the UFO community, as they gave a hint about the fact that secret UFO conversations are going on in Washington that are not made public.

Some of the more important UFO emails that appeared in the Wiki-Leaks releases included the following topics.

Stephen Bassett

....

In the UFO community, Stephen Bassett is the key disclosure person. For twenty years, he has acted as the only lobbyist for what he refers to as "ending the UFO/ET truth embargo."

Bassett was one of the first to realize the important role Podesta played in the Clinton administration. Bassett promoted knowledge regarding the Rockefeller Initiative during the Clinton administration, which tried to get UFO/ET disclosure, Podesta's great interest in UFOs and in the X-Files, and his efforts to get UFO/ET disclosure through the hoped election of Hillary Clinton.

There are 25 Wiki-Leaks e-mails from Bassett, or emails sent to Podesta, referencing Bassett and his work.

One of the key emails was the one sent by Bassett the day after Podesta made his famous final tweet, the day he was leaving the Obama administration, about his failure to obtain UFO disclosure "once again."

Referencing *The Washington Post* article written about Podesta's tweet regarding UFO disclosure, Bassett was short and to the point.

> Mr. Podesta:
>
> Isn't it time for you and I to have a private, off-the-record meeting?

Podesta didn't reply to this or any of the other emails Bassett sent his way. "I've corresponded with Podesta for 10 years," Bassett told NBC News, when asked about his emails to Podesta being found in the Wiki-Leaks releases, "and I've never gotten a response. There's like a chess game going on between the Paradigm Research Group and the Clinton Team."

Bassett believed that his efforts had exerted tremendous pressure on the White House, Hillary Clinton, Podesta, and the many other players involved in the 1993-1996 effort by Laurance Rockefeller effort to get UFO disclosure from the Clinton White House ("The Rockefeller Initiative").

Bassett therefore believed that many of the actions of Hillary Clinton, Bill Clinton, and Podesta were reactions to pressure he was exerting through tweet storms on targeted Washington officials and congressmen. Bassett was also working with a lot of reporters and they were phoning Podesta and the Clintons looking for comments about what Bassett was saying.

After the loss, he told radio host George Noory at Coast to Coast:

> *"The greatest lie in history continues, the greatest intellectual failure (American academia) in history continues, and the shame of American journalism continues. There are 70 days left to effectuate disclosure under President Obama assuming the intellectual elite the wealthy elite and journalistic elite are willing to lift a finger. And if they choose not to, then they will reap the whirlwind."*

Robert Fish

....

Robert Fish started sending emails to John Podesta about three weeks after Podesta tweeted about his disappointment at not getting UFO disclosure through President Obama.

Podesta started by sending emails to Leslie Kean who had written the book *UFOs: Generals, Pilots, and Government Officials Go on the Record*. Podesta authored the foreword for Kean's book and helped her file a Freedom of Information Act request for documents related to a UFO crash that occurred in Kecksburg, Pennsylvania in December 1965.

When Kean did not reply, he started e-mailing Podesta. In his first email, he implied that researchers working on the UFO mystery were looking in the wrong place:

> *John - I know you are busy as heck so I appreciate your taking a moment to read this email and put it in a file for future use. I emailed Leslie Kean ten days ago, but have not received any response. Based on significant personal experience, I can attest that UFO hunters are looking in the wrong places. Random personal observations, fuzzy photographers, and crop circles will never "prove" the existence of anything, especially since UFO appearances to humans are transitory and somewhat related to the observer's state of mind. What needs to be collected and publicly disseminated is hard scientific data collected from instruments that are known to be accurate and reliable. Within the US, this information has existed for many years and is still available today, if one knows "where to look" and "what to look for." Radar data and thermal imaging data is a good start, especially if one knows the flight envelope and maneuvering characteristics of a UFO. If/when you might be interested in gaining more specific information (program names) please feel free to contact me by email to arrange a phone call or meeting (I live in northern Cal but occasionally travel to DC for business activities)! While I am publicly known by my work with the USS*

> *Hornet Museum, this communication with you is entirely PRIVATE and CONFIDENTIAL and has nothing to do with the museum. Regards, Bob Fish, Danville, CA*[88]

The next day Fish wrote another email to Podesta. In this email, he was a lot more revealing. He referred Podesta to secret UFO information that he had heard while in a secure facility in California:

> *John - Just tuck this in your UFO files for future reference. One of the government programs that collects hard data on unidentified flying objects is the USAF DSP satellite program. I can add a little insight to rumors published on the web. While I was never fully briefed into the DSP operation directly, I was introduced to them as the US prepared for Operation Desert Shield and Desert Storm. On occasion, I had lunch with a few of them in the cafeteria of a highly classified organization in El Segundo, CA. No one could get into the cafeteria without TS/SCI clearances, so this was not "lightweight group of gossipers." One of these times, a member of that group was really excited - said they'd just picked up Fastwalker (I assumed that same day). He described how it entered our atmosphere from "deep space" (origin actually unknown, of course, but from the backside of the satellite) and zipped by the DSP satellite pretty closely on its way to earth. Not only was it going very fast but it made a 30-degree course correction (turn) which means it did not have a ballistic (free fall) re-entry trajectory that a meteorite might have. So, it was under some sort of control - although whether it was "manned" or just "robotic" there's no way to tell. Although it's now 24 years later, one factoid makes me think the USAF is still collecting information on these Fastwalkers. Reading the current official USAF "DSP Fact Sheet" there is this' line near the end: In addition, researchers at The Aerospace Corporation have used DSP to develop portions of a hazard support system that will aid public safety in the future.*

> http://www.losangeles.af.mil/library/factsheets/factsheet.asp?id=5323
>
> Also, much of the information on this site is accurate although I do not know the author or his sources:
>
> http://ufodigest.com/shadowmag/extra/topsecret.html
>
> Somewhere within that USAF program office is many years' worth of Fastwalker data. If someone were to collect and analyze it, patterns will emerge that provide information about the various types of craft and their destinations, which would add substantiation to eyewitness claims on the ground about UFO activity. Furthermore, it would be interesting to understand the dates of these appearances - is there a certain time of the year they swarm in (which might indicate a resource mining operation) or might there be a correlation with major events on earth, (such as the detonation of the first atomic bomb at White Sands in 1945 although no DSP's existed to provide any info on that particular event)? Regards, Bob Fish

Podesta did not reply but forwarded the email to Kean with a note "FYI." Kean replied immediately, stating:

> Another confirmation of yet more documents kept from the public. This knowledge belongs to the people under the law! Can we get the ball rolling during this transition window - perhaps a quiet meeting with the right people - before your next assignment? I already have the perfect briefing package, and a highly-qualified staffer ready to go. The timing seems ideal. -Leslie[89]

A couple hours after his second email, Fish sent the final e-mail that appeared on the Wiki-Leaks site. It had dramatic claims about UFO tracking being done by the military and a possible UFO base in the Atlantic off of Florida:

John - Just tuck this in your UFO files for future reference too. Recently, I noticed this Sentry Eagle information, even though the original book was written in 1998:

http://exopolitics.org/nsa-document-supports-whistleblower-claim-of-alien-ufo-communication-program/

I don't know Dan Sherman and I don't know if this non-ECI program is real. Caveat – I did work with Ft. Meade on several classified communications projects, including President Reagan's dedication of the new HQ building in September 1986 when I was a contractor to WHCA. But this report did trigger the memory of another event that may be of use should you ever want to follow up on the UFO stuff. In that same TS/SCI building cafeteria in El Segundo, I had lunch with a senior USAF NCO who had worked for Project Blue Book in the 1970s (after it had been "officially disbanded). He was an ELINT technician (electronic intelligence) who flew in RC-135s from MacDill AFB in Florida. The "normal" target was Cuba where they did lots of snooping and sometimes challenging the Cubans to turn on radar and other systems. He said there were times when they were diverted from these missions to track UFOs off the east coast of Florida. His claim was they UFOs had a landing and takeoff spot in the ocean east of Miami, north of Bermuda. He also claimed there was a specific electronic signature (frequency) emanating from them when they were going into or coming out of the water, so they were easy to track. On several occasions, they filmed the UFO as it transitioned from water to air or vice versa. One last item is he was occasionally assigned to fly in a USAF weather aircraft (WC-135) when they had a hurricane hunting mission over the usual UFO area, where his specific assignment was kept secret from the other crew members. He would always report back to a dedicated USAF intelligence officer on base when they returned from a mission.

He did not know where the intel that he collected was sent for processing or storage (WPAFB in Dayton would be the obvious choice). High quality film of UFOs is "out there" somewhere! So, if true, Blue Book was not disbanded – only the outer layer of the onion (the "public information layer) was stripped away in 1970. And, this may be part of the Sentry Eagle program with the USAF and NSA sharing UFO elint information. Might be some leads in that area too. Regards, Bob Fish[90]

Jim Davidson

....

Jim Davidson was described by Reuters "one of the most powerful lobbyists in Washington." Davidson "represented Fortune 500 companies and leading industry groups on issues involving taxation, agency regulations, government information policy, media regulation, privacy, regulation of advertising, health care, appropriations, and budget policy."

Davidson was also interested in UFOs, and a month after Podesta put out the tweet asking reporters to ask Hillary about aliens, Davidson wrote about a UFO show he had just seen on TV:

You are now "legitimately" famous - one of my favorite programs on 116. It quoted you as trying to get to the bottom of UFO reports but that the CIA had "frozen" out the Clinton administration.[91]

Thirty minutes later, Podesta replied with a cryptic reference to the future. He replied simply, "More to come."[92]

Daniel Oberhaus

....

Oberhaus was a journalist who has written for *Vice Magazine*, *Popular Mechanics*, *Slate*, *Motherboard*, and *The Atlantic*. On January 26, 2016, he wrote an article for *Vice* titled "An Alien Hunter's Guide to the 2016 US Election."

On January 17, 2016, which was a week before meeting with high-level military officials to discuss a plan proposed by Tom DeLonge for

UFO disclosure, Podesta received a letter from Oberhaus requesting an interview:

> *I am writing an article for VICE on the subject of the politics of searching for alien life. I've spoken with SETI researchers and ET disclosure advocates about the political aspects of their work, and was hoping to get your opinion on the matter given your intimate knowledge of capitol hill and history of promotion of UFO disclosure. If you are at all open to answer a few questions about ET disclosure advocacy and the importance of SETI science via email or the telephone in the coming days, please let me know at your earliest convenience.*

Podesta rarely granted interview but for some reason he agreed to this one replying on the same day:

> *Easiest to shoot me some Q's via email.*

Oberhaus sent the questions, and on January 19th Podesta gave direct answers to UFO questions. Here are the questions and answers.

Why do you think that the disclosure of UFO related documents is important?

Throughout my career, from my work on the staff of the Senate Judiciary Committee to the White House, I have been a strong advocate for government openness and transparency. When I was White House Chief of Staff I led the effort to declassify over 800 million pages of historically valuable previously classified documents. Disclosure of files related to unidentified aerial phenomena is completely consistent with the goal of a transparent and open government. It might also be good material for future X-Files plots.

It seems like a lot of UFO documents would contain sensitive military information - how would you go about getting these released?

The government has processes in place for redacting material that should remain classified, even if it's decades old. I'm confident that it can be handled appropriately.

Do you think if Hillary is elected she would make good on her promise to get to the bottom of this UFO business? Why?
She promised me she would!

Other than Hillary, are there any other alien-friendly candidates in the running? If not, why do you think this is?

Notwithstanding the fact that serious scientists, military leaders, business people, and average citizens are interested in the subject of intelligent life in the universe, political leaders tend to worry about whether they will be lampooned if they broach the subject. I, on the other hand, am interested in just making the UNIVERSE GREAT AGAIN.

What makes you think there is information on UFO and extraterrestrials that the government is not sharing with the people? What would the motive be for this? If it turned out that there was information being withheld, how do you think people would react to it? Are we ready to hear this? Why/why not?

Look, I believe that the government, in the name of transparency and openness should declassify and release information in regards to unidentified aerial phenomena. Obviously, there have been decades of speculation about what, if anything, is contained in these files, and I'm confident that the American people can handle the truth.

Judge David Tatel

....

In Late December 2015, reporter Daymond Steer in Conway, New Hampshire, took up John Podesta's challenge to ask Hillary Clinton about the aliens. It created a story that went around the world.

The first reaction Podesta got for his tweet prompting a reporter to ask Hillary about the aliens came on January 7, 2016. It came from Ann M. O'Leary, a senior policy adviser in Hillary Clinton's 2016 Presidential Campaign.

As well as mentioning the fact that Hillary had talked about promising UFO openness to Steer, O'Leary raised the name of a very prominent man in Washington who was also interested in UFOs. The man was Judge David S. Tatel, who was a judge on the United States Court of Appeals for the District of Columbia Circuit since 1994. O'Leary wrote to Podesta and Tatum:

> *This article on Hillary's comments about extraterrestrial life made me think of you two and remind me to connect you.*
> *John - As I was telling David the last time I saw him, the two of you are the biggest believers in ET life who I know and I think you'd enjoy talking with one another. I know that neither of you have much time, but I think you'd have a fascinating time discussing it if you ever get together!*

On January 11, 2016 Judge Tatel wrote an email to Podesta, copying O'Leary, where he expressed happiness that Podesta was also interested in extraterrestrial life.

> *I'm delighted to hear from Ann that you too are interested in extraterrestrial life. If you'd ever like a break from politics, let me know and we can find a way to get together to talk about this fascinating subject. In the meantime, you might want to watch NOVA's latest film, "Life's Rocky Start," this Wednesday on PBS. I saw a screening of the film last week at the Carnegie Institution. The film is based on some important new research about the origins of life on Earth and leaves no doubt that life must exist throughout the universe.*
>
> *http://www.pbs.org/wgbh/nova/earth/life-rocky-start.html*
>
> *I'm also very excited about Yuri Milner and Steve Hawking's announcement of a $100 million program to support SETI.*
>
> *https://www.washingtonpost.com/news/speaking-of-science/wp/2015/07/20/stephen-hawking-announces-100-million-hunt-for-alien-life/*

> *I know the people involved in this project: They're all serious radio astronomers and deeply devoted to the search for extraterrestrial intelligence.*
>
> *Looking forward to talking to you. David*[93]

Podesta never replied to the Tatel email in the time frame of the Wiki-Leaks emails.

Apollo 14 Edgar Mitchell

....

In the Podesta emails, there was a lot of Edgar Mitchell correspondence attempting a meeting with John Podesta to discuss Zero Point Energy and UFO disclosure.

Although the letters appeared to be from Edgar Mitchell they were written on his behalf by Terri Mansfield, Dr. Suzanne Mendelssohn, and Dr. Rebecca Hardcastle Wright.

The first of the emails sent to Podesta was on January 14, 2014, just a month after Obama appointed Podesta as a special counselor to the President. Wright, who was writing on Mitchell's behalf, stated:

> *Now within the Obama administration, you are in the unique position to address disclosure of the extraterrestrial presence in a manner that promotes science, technology, peace, Earth sustainability, and space.*

The email continued with the central theme that would become the focus of the Mitchell-Podesta emails over the next two years:

> *John, I would like to schedule a phone conversation at your earliest convenience to discuss what I feel are intensifying imperatives for extraterrestrial disclosure. For many years, you and I have shared a mutual vision of disclosure. I highly commend your public record urging disclosure which includes the forward you wrote for Leslie Kean's book and your call for the Pentagon's release of 25-year-old classified government papers on UFO investigations.*

> When our government releases this classified information, we become the twenty-fifth country to make public disclosure. You and I also share a mutual vision for earth sustainability apparent in the escalating demand for a change in global energy policy. Our phone discussion will also include the zero-point energy research and applications developed by my Quantrek international science team. Advanced energy science is linked to consciousness research and public disclosure of the extraterrestrial presence.
>
> Global consciousness remains one of my top priorities. I envision our species entering deep space as advanced, cooperative, consciously aware and nonviolent. We are not alone in the universe. How we relate to other intelligent life matters. Understanding how nonviolent ETI from the contiguous universe travel to Earth by means of zero-point energy is key to our acceleration as space-faring humans.
>
> Thank you for letting me know your availability for our phone call. Rebecca Hardcastle Wright, our Washington DC representative for Quantrek, will be in contact with Eryn Sepp regarding scheduling.

Podesta did not reply to the email according to the Wiki-Leaks emails. The reply, however, may have come from one of his two assistants, as there was no hacking of their emails.

In June 2014, another email was sent on Mitchell's behalf asking for a meeting with Podesta and President Obama. Mitchell told Podesta that he would be meeting with a childhood friend of Obama's, and would be bringing up disclosure and zero-point energy:

> This 4 July weekend I will meet with President Obama's friend, Ambassador Hamamoto, at the US Mission in Geneva during their Independence Day Celebration. While in Geneva I will also speak at the UN and the European Space Agency regarding why we must move forward with disclosure and specific programs such as manned moon missions, since some scientists and others are calling for moon

colonization due to what they perceive is happening on Earth. John, with this email I am requesting a conversation with you and President Obama regarding the next steps in extraterrestrial disclosure for the benefit of our country and our planet.

Fifty years ago, Battelle, Brookings and RAND studies on UFOs convinced the government to remove knowledge of the extraterrestrial presence from the citizens of our country. These organizations advised with their best information. However, today much, if not most, of the extraterrestrial reality they examined is known by our citizens. These organizations' resultant strategies and policies of 50 years ago, no longer hold credibility or benefit. Five decades of UFO information have dramatically shifted the public awareness of an extraterrestrial presence. And yet, our government is still operating from outdated beliefs and policies. These are detrimental to trust in government transparency, science, religion, and responsible citizenry embracing the next step in our country's space travel and research.

Three disclosure issues are prominent: 1) planet sustainability via next generation energies such as zero-point energy, 2) galactic travel and research undertaken as an advanced species aware of the extraterrestrial presence, not as uninformed explorers who revert to colonialism and destruction and 3) the example of a confident, engaged government who respectfully regards the wisdom and intellect of its citizens as we move into space.

In an October 1, 2014, email written by Terri Mansfield, Mitchell wished to talk about the connection between UFOs, the Vatican, and the Roman Catholic Church, with Podesta having been raised Catholic. "As John is aware," the letter said, "more than 20 countries including the Vatican have released top secret papers discussing extraterrestrial incidents on Earth over many years. The US has NOT participated in disclosure, yet."

Mitchell was going to bring Mr. Dan Hill (Catholic philanthropist), Dr. Michael Mansfield (Catholic retired Air Force Colonel), and Mrs. Terri Mansfield (Catholic consultant). Mansfield wrote:

> *It is urgent that we agree on a date and time to meet to discuss Disclosure and Zero Point Energy, at your earliest available after your departure. My Catholic colleague Terri Mansfield will be there too, to bring us up to date on the Vatican's awareness of ETI (Extraterrestrial Intelligence).*
>
> *Remember, our nonviolent ETI from the contiguous universe are helping us bring zero-point energy to Earth. They will not tolerate any forms of military violence on Earth or in space.*

At the end of the letter, there was an important note where Mansfield thanked Eryn Sepp for letting her know "3 possible dates and times for our meeting with John so that we can prepare travel logistics." This offer of dates to meet indicated that Podesta was interested in having the meeting.

This email was followed up by another email requesting a meeting to discuss UFOs and the Vatican that was sent January 18, 2015, less than a month before Podesta left to chair the Hillary Clinton campaign:

> *It is urgent that we agree on a date and time to meet to discuss Disclosure and Zero Point Energy, at your earliest available after your departure. My Catholic colleague Terri Mansfield will be there too, to bring us up to date on the Vatican's awareness of ETI...*
>
> *I met with President Obama's Honolulu childhood friend, US Ambassador Pamela Hamamoto on July 4 at the US Mission in Geneva, when I was able to tell her briefly about zero-point energy.*

At the end of April 2015, Terri Mansfield sent one of the most significant emails to Podesta. In the email, there was a request for a meeting with Podesta ASAP. Mansfield mentioned that Mitchell had just shut down his Quantrek company for health reasons.

In June 2015, Podesta's assistant Eryn Sepp provided three dates and times Podesta was willing to Skype with Terri Mansfield and I about Disclosure and ETI. For some reason this meeting did not take place, and seven months later, on February 4, 2016, Edgar Mitchell passed away.

The meeting with Podesta and the president never took place. Dr. Karlyn Mitchell, Edgar's daughter, sent an email to Podesta inviting him to the funeral.

Podesta addressed what to tweet about Mitchell, as some of what Mitchell believed was far beyond the straight ET story. Part of the discussion that Mitchell wanted to have was disclosure about the "difference between our contiguous universe, nonviolent obedient ETI and the celestials of this universe."

This statement by Mitchell implied that there were extraterrestrial intelligences that were working for God and extraterrestrials in our universe that perhaps are not as nice.

In reply to an email query from his assistant, Milia Fisher, as to what to put in the tweet re Michell, Podesta emailed back:

> *We should tweet something like Sad to learn of the passing of Edgar Mitchell, an American hero. Check his Wikipedia page to make sure that won't seem too goofy. He's a big UFO guy. Former astronaut.*

The DeLonge Podesta Connection

....

The biggest story in the Wiki-Leaks emails was the correspondence involving Tom DeLonge, who was the lead singer and the co-founder of the rock band, Blink 182, and also the band, Angels and Airwaves. DeLonge has sold 30 million albums.

In an interview on Coast to Coast, DeLonge described how he approached Podesta:

> *I reached out and told him what I was trying to achieve with the project and he was very quiet on the phone. He was listening. I kind of went through what may objectives were. I have my pitch down and I am speaking very respectfully. I am trying to lay out all*

> *the reasons this needs to happen, but I didn't think I really got through to him. For all I knew he thought I was just some crazy rock star that wants to talk about something weird. I knew he was into this stuff but I just didn't know how much.*
>
> *He said, "Call me in a couple months. I am pretty busy, and we'll see where we're at." I said, "okay, cool."*
>
> *I didn't call him back because I didn't really think he was absorbing what I pitched him, and then all of a sudden out of nowhere, I just get these flurry of e-mails, from his office that he wants to be in this and I have to come out to come out to DC and it's a major priority, and the rest is history.[94]*

The fact that Podesta agreed to be a part of a UFO disclosure project is significant considering the high level White House positions he has held and the fact that he was in the process of trying to get Hillary Clinton elected as president.

The fact that it took a long time for Podesta to get back may have been because he was busy. A second, more tantalizing possibility is, that Podesta knowing that the UFO subject was classified needed time to go to those in charge and ask if government people were talking to DeLonge as he was claiming, and if so what their aim was, and what role Podesta should play.

This is how the system would actually work, as opposed to the belief that if a rock star suddenly starts asking about classified material, they are going to give it to him because they want him to reveal to everyone in America what they have been denying for decades.

It's also interesting to point out that this flurry of key emails, where Podesta talks about being involved in a UFO disclosure effort, did not appear in the Wiki-Leaks Podesta emails that were posted to the internet in October 2016. That is probably because as DeLonge pointed out they were coming from Podesta's office and not Podesta himself. The emails were probably written on Podesta's behalf by one of Podesta's two assistants, Milia Fisher and Eryn Sepp.

DeLonge traveled to Washington and interviewed Podesta for his Sekret Machines documentary in July 2015. Before he arrived, on July 19, 2015, one of DeLonge's producers sent Podesta the some of the questions they were going to ask during the July 22 videotaped interview. A later email said there would be a more "a candid and organic conversation on all these types of issues."

> *Q: In the long run, do you think that the Church Committee - with what it exposed and the regulations that followed - helped curtail the rise of secrecy and the trend towards becoming a national security state? Or did it merely cause the executive branch and the intelligence organizations under its control to become more aggressive in their pursuit of creating and maintaining protection from any oversight?*

> *Q: Kenneth Mayer (a professor at the University of Wisconsin who wrote a book on the President and Executive Orders called "With the Stroke of a Pen") said, "What is especially striking about debates over classification and secrecy is that presidents have asserted almost complete command over the institutions and processes that both produce and protect secret information... In practice, classification remains an outpost of almost absolute executive prerogative." Do you agree with this statement? If so, what can be done to lessen the President's dependency on secrets and classification within executive programs? If not, who is responsible for the proliferation of secrets within the US government?*

> *Q: The Privacy and Civil Liberties Oversight Board has been created to provide oversight of covert actions on behalf of Congress and the American people. However, in the Intelligence Authorization Act for Fiscal Year 2016 that was passed by the House - Section 306 states that "[n]othing in this section shall be construed to authorize the Board, or any agent thereof, to gain access to information that an executive branch agency deems related to covert action, as such term is defined in section 503(e) of the National Security Act of 1947 (50 U.S.C. 3039(e))." While the companion Senate bill, S. 1705, does not include a similar provision, why do you*

believe there is a desire by members of Congress to limit the ability of a committee like the PCLOB to provide oversight of covert executive branch programs?

Q: State secrets have proliferated far beyond the government's current ability to review and clear them for release. What can be done to reduce the creation of - and dependency on - classified documents in future administrations? What can be done to increase our ability to process the massive amounts of "sensitive" date - much of which was born secret and was never reviewed prior to classification?

Q: In your opinion, why are the files having to do with UFO investigations being kept classified and who gains by continuing to keep these files classified? Q: If you were to create a set of guidelines or a group to handle the declassification of UFO-related information and material - how would you go about it?

The same day that Podesta received the questions, he forwarded them to individuals who would be considered experts on the subjects DeLonge raised. The replies must have taken place in person or on the phone as there was no email responses from the people who were sent the questions. Podesta sent DeLonge's questions to the following people from the Clinton campaign and from the Center for American Progress, the prime democratic think tank found by Podesta in 2003:

Jennifer Palmieri is Director of Communications for the 2016 Hillary Clinton presidential campaign where she handles she manages candidate message, media-relations and trouble-shooting. She left the Obama administration with Podesta in February 2015.
Daniella Leger - Senior Vice President for Communications and Strategy at Center for American Progress.
Sara Latham - Chief of Staff to the Chairman of the Hillary Clinton campaign - Special Assistant to White House Chief of Staff John Podesta and Deputy Assistant to the President and Deputy Director of Presidential Scheduling from 1996 to 2000.

Ken Gude - a senior fellow at the Center for American Progress specializing in civil liberties and terrorism.

Ian Millhiser - a policy analyst for the Center for American Progress, the think tank created by Podesta. Millhiser's work focuses on government efficiency and transparency.

In the trailer for the documentary, which DeLonge posted on the internet and then took down, Podesta made a couple of revealing statements about UFOs that indicated he had some knowledge of how UFOs are dealt with in government. The statements are particularly important because Podesta knew that this would become public and would be seen by a lot of people who would see him as a government spokesman, especially if Hillary were to win the election, which we now know she did not.

Here are quotes of what Podesta said, in part:

> *The Pentagon has special access programs deep inside the bowls of the Pentagon bureaucracy. Little sunlight (laughs) emanates from there.*
>
> *You have to start by knowing what is the right question.*
>
> *The Pentagon has a 600-billion-dollar budget. It is hard to keep track of everything.*

When the interview was over, Podesta asked DeLonge to update him from time to time on his "sensitive meetings on the project." Two weeks later DeLonge wrote an email to Podesta telling him he was ready to provide an update, but there is no Wiki-Leaks email evidencing that that update took place.

On October 26, 2015, DeLonge contacted Podesta again in an e-mail titled "Important Things." In that email, DeLonge updated Podesta as to a deal he was trying to get with Steven Spielberg, and he offered to bring some of the key government officials advising him, to see Podesta:

> *Things are moving with the project. The Novels, Films and Nonfiction works are blooming and finishing. Just had a preliminary meeting with Spielberg's Chief Operating Officer at DreamWorks. More meetings are now on the books -*

> *I would like to bring two very "important" people out to meet you in DC. I think you will find them very interesting, as they were principal leadership relating to our sensitive topic. Both were in charge of most fragile divisions, as it relates to Classified Science and DOD topics. Other words, these are A-Level officials. Worth our time, and as well the investment to bring all the way out to you. I just need 2 hours from you. Just looking to have a casual, and private conversation in person.[95]*

Then in a second email dated November 16, 2015, forwarded to Podesta from his special assistant, Milia Fisher, DeLonge again requests to meet with Podesta and again offers to bring along someone important, perhaps Steven Spielberg:

> *I created this teaser as a way to open conversations and excite Spielberg's people. It worked. I just left my meeting at DreamWorks, and they are very, very interested.*
>
> *On another note, I have somebody important that is willing to fly out and meet with Mr. Podesta. A member of my Committee. I am awaiting a time in January that might work for Mr. Podesta. My goal is for Spielberg to be there, too. And if not him, somebody of his stature. Please show Mr. Podesta this private teaser. Let him know that I am spending all afternoon interviewing a scientist that worked on a spacecraft at Area 51 tomorrow.[96]*

The Media Wing

………………………………………..

Tom DeLonge owns his own media empire and much of what he will reveal will be rolled out by his company To The Stars Inc., which his website describes as "an independent production company built on transmedia story-telling experiences that reach across music, entertainment, licensing and publishing."

Much of what we know about how DeLonge's company will partner with other media entities comes from the Wiki-Leaks emails sent by DeLonge to Podesta.

Aside of DeLonge, I have heard that one of the top people at Paramount, two Hollywood writers from Warner Brothers, and Spielberg may be involved.

DeLonge also mentioned Spielberg and in a letter to Podesta's assistant Milia Fisher, where he talks about discussions with Spielberg's company in connection to his documentary Sekret Machines:

> *I created this teaser as a way to open conversations and excite Spielberg's people. It worked. I just left my meeting at DreamWorks, and they are very, very interested. On another note, I have somebody important that is willing to fly out and meet with Mr. Podesta. A member of my Committee. I am awaiting a time in January that might work for Mr. Podesta. My goal is for Spielberg to be there, too. And if not him, somebody of his stature. Please show Mr. Podesta this private teaser. Let him know that I am spending all afternoon interviewing a scientist that worked on a spacecraft at Area 51 tomorrow.*

In one email dated February 23, 2016, DeLonge talked about some of the meetings he was conducting with major producers who would carry the message through movie, TV, and print.

> *Great things happening.*
>
> *I had an incredible meeting at Spielberg's Amblin/DreamWorks Pictures. They are taking their time on reading the book. For them story comes first.*
>
> *I met with ScottFree (Ridley Scott's company) last week - they did the Martian film that has won incredible acclaim over this past year. They were blown away by what I am doing, they need a couple weeks to dig through the Novel. Like everybody else I meet with, their faces drop halfway through the meeting and can't believe that I am spearheading a project that has support from the shadows. They look comatosed... Ha. But they it's so incredibly excited that this topic may start to come out. *I did a*

general introduction with NetFlix. They want a company-wide meeting on it ASAP, but I need to wait until I go in with a Producing Partner that we pick- Like Amblin or ScottFree.

I met with Allie Shearmur's company, she used to Run LionsGate Films and produced all the Jason Bourne films as well as the new Star Wars film that is coming out later this year. The execs were again, blown away. They should have thoughts for us this week actually.

I have an Amazon meeting and VICE NEWS in next 2 weeks. Amazon, Netflix are biggest TV studios now and doing the most prestigious shows, actually. VICE NEWS just raised $300 million to start doing fictional television based on Nonfiction. Sounds like our model.

I am meeting with Ron Howard's and Brian Grazer's company Imagine tomorrow...

Rolling Stone is embedding a journalist with me for 2 days to break the story on my project. It will be an international story for print. This is huge as they are known for big cutting edge stories that have political and geographic effects. I have gone through rules with all Advisors on what can and cannot be said. It will be tricky, because they will want to know what kind of support I am getting, and I cannot and will not say anything to them- But they should get the idea that this is important and real.

NY Times, WSJ, or Washington Post will follow Rolling Stone with the Foreword of my book that I wrote, and the Trailer for the Documentary. This will lay the foundation that there are many pieces to this puzzle and it will all come out over the coming years.

The documentary will most likely be a Miniseries. 8 - 10 one hour episodes on an elevated network like HBO. One major producing house wants to do it, but we cannot choose a producer for this until we choose a producer for the Fictional television series. I think VICE news, HBO, Netflix, Amazon may be good candidates for this. I don't *know if you heard of the latest miniseries that got a lot of attention, one called JINX, another called Making a Murderer, another called Going Clear. All of these won awards, and got multiple showings on their networks. I actually think most of these were on HBO.*

-- Sorry this was long, but lots going on. Thank you again for your valued time. I hope this project can be an exciting and good addition to your already crazy life.

After Podesta

....

After Hillary Clinton lost the election, the plan for Hillary to be the disclosure president evaporated. That is, at least, how it seemed on the outside.

As soon as the election was over, I contacted my source who was dealing with high level government officials and who also had an inside on what DeLonge had been doing. I asked, "Has the time table changed after the election?"

The answer came back quickly, "No sir!! There is a huge group of serious people involved with this thing Grant. Very big - millions - and old money involved! This thing is going to be a huge effort by lots of people...Hang on to your seat belt."

DeLonge also posted basically saying that the election had changed nothing, "Big things are coming. Project is still on, believe it or not, things just got bigger." [97]

The "official disclosure" idea appeared to be dead, but the DeLonge and Greer efforts seemed alive at well. It harkened back to a message Greer reported getting back from Bill Clinton after a "friend of Bill" presented him with briefing materials on the UFO subject. The message said, "I can't do this, but you can."

It also harkened back to what my insider friend had told me over a year earlier, "The government wants the story out, but they don't want their finger prints on it." I wondered how this could happen without the government's fingerprints. Now it made more sense. It appeared that they would continue to support the gradual disclosure effort of raising coconsciousness through controlled leaks, and Hollywood.

The Tom DeLonge Disclosure Story

We cannot be involved with anything that has anything to do with that subject, especially since there has been absolutely no evidence whatsoever that it exists. **Top Lockheed Skunk Works official to Tom DeLonge**

I landed on the tarmac, walked off the plane, and met a smart and fit man in his 60's. Never seen a multi-star General before. Let alone talked to one. He led me to a table in the back of a large room. He leaned across the table and said "It was the Cold War, and we lived under the very real threat of nuclear war every day... And somewhere in those years...We found a life-form." I said, "Sir, I need help telling young adults this story..." He said, "What do you need?"...."Advisors", I responded. "I need high-ranking advisors in the military, intelligence and DOD to help guide me." So - I was given 10 advisors, each with knowledge in different areas that pertain to UFOs and the very real National Security issues associated with them. **Tom DeLonge Facebook Post July 5, 2016**

Things like this do not happen at the White House. They don't happen at the hill. They happen at places like this, at places like this where a few men get together and decide to push the ball down the field. **The statement by one of two men in suits who met DeLonge at a table at a room near the Pentagon in the first meeting where they started feeding him information about the classified Top-Secret UFO program.**

    The key element to the DeLonge UFO story is that he got access to what DeLonge described as, "10 people that I'm working with that are at the highest levels of the Department of Defense and NASA and the military… three of them are of the brightest scientific and engineering minds in the entire military and industrial complex. These are the guys that work nine months out of year over at Area 51."
    This was not a one-man leak from some military type who might have been deluded, or looking for his 15 minutes of fame. DeLonge was dealing with a group of high-level officers, scientists, and intelligence officials. He was dealing with some sort of group or agency within the government.

His encounter with these people is therefore very important as he may have been tapping the brains of the people who hold the answer to the UFO mystery. As DeLonge described it, "I have been given a gift, the ability to tell you all, our biggest secret." Every statement, however, must be checked to see if it is information or disinformation.

DeLonge believed that "he brought an idea to the table that they did not have…a thesis on the phenomena that is correct."[98]

The way he was contacted, how he was connected to other officials, and the bizarre locations where the meetings took place was almost a complete carbon copy of the stories told by researcher Bill Moore in the 1980s.

The short version of DeLonge's story is that he gained access to classified information which he was then allowed to roll out to the public, but as history has shown, that is not how it works.

An example is the story told by George Knapp about six witnesses that came to him after he first aired the story about UFOs being stored and back-engineered at Area 51. The six witnesses all approached Knapp with various pieces of information about the Area 51 and UFOs connection. In each case, just before they went on camera to tell their story they were visited by agents of some sort that reminded them of their security oaths, and what might happen if they were to come forward. In all six cases, the witnesses contacted Knapp and told him that they would no longer be going on camera to tell their story.

DeLonge's contention that if you know how it works they then "let you talk" is not correct. If it is classified information, they do what they can to stop people from coming forward, or compromise their stories with disinformation so no one will believe it. The only time they let you come forward is when you have it wrong, or the compromised story you will tell suits the purposes of the security program that surrounded the SCI program or operation.

DeLonge told *Rolling Stone* why he thinks he has been allowed to talk about classified information to *Rolling Stone Magazine*, "It's very hard to think, 'How did this guy in a band get access like that? It sounds crazy'. But it's because I can speak to a very specific audience. I earned their trust. I knew my material."[99]

He described how he managed to get access to the secret world of government UFO research after bring invited to an event which consisted of "the most classified and the most advanced group of engineers and scientists that work within the military industrial complex that work under one specific group." This is important because it showed he WAS INVITED which would have required top company officials to agree, and showed clearly, they made the first move.

Going into the meeting DeLonge knew exactly who the men were and what they did for a living. Based on their invite, they also knew exactly who DeLonge was and what he believed about UFOs. Talking about the event, DeLonge told reporter George Knapp:

> It's a very quiet group but for the very first time they were doing an event where family members can come, and not go in the buildings, but at least celebrate in the parking lot what their loved ones do during the day. They asked me to come up because I knew this one individual that told me to be very careful. He said, "This is a way for you to come up and see what we doing." He said, "Do you want to introduce the head of the company to the crowd?" I said "I will if I get to sit with him for five minutes."
>
> I got that opportunity. I went up and introduced him to the crowd and then I got five minutes to sit down alone and say whatever I wanted to say. I didn't say anything about this subject. I just said I have an idea for a project, and if done right will reverse the cynicism that people have about government..."
>
> He said, "Great" and "I said can I come up in a couple weeks and tell you more about it," and he said "yah."
>
> I go through four layers of security and machine guns, and then I get escorted into a very specific building...this is out in the middle of the desert somewhere. Then I go through two layers of electronic codes entry systems...I am in a hallway and its lined with speakers playing white noise like TV static and that's there so you don't hear anyone's conversations...then I am in the center of the building where the top three engineers work with the head of the company...I walk in and they are sitting there ready for whatever it is that I am going to pitch them.[100]

At this point a very important thing happened. This seemed like a carbon copy of the second interview that Bob Lazar did with EG&G before being hired to work at S-4 with the recovered saucers.

In the 1988 Lazar interview, Lazar was asked "what's your relationship with John Lear, and what do you know about him?" The question indicated that EG&G officials had done research on Lazar. More importantly, they knew that he was friends with Lear, who was heavily into UFO conspiracies at the time.

Lear was so heavily into UFO conspiracies at the time that when Lear was the chief organizer of the big MUFON UFO conference a few months later, the MUFON organizers over-rode Lear's selection of speakers, as they were regarded as crazy conspiracy people. When this happened, Lear broke with MUFON and held his own UFO conference at the same time at a location down the street.

Lazar's reply in his interview was, "I do know John Lear, I go over to this house, I think he sticks his nose in places where it doesn't belong."[101]

DeLonge had not yet brought up the subject of UFOs, but as he was making his pitch he was cut off. One of the three men suddenly indicated, that like Lazar, they had done research into DeLonge's background, and they knew that he like Lear, was into UFO conspiracies. (In interviews DeLonge would defend writing about many UFO conspiracies, saying that because of the lack of confirmed material – "where else are you going to go.")

> *I had no plan for even bringing up UFOs...so we're talking and one guy did a bunch of research on me and knew I was into the subject, so halfway into the conversation this person says, "So, what about all the conspiracy stuff you're into?"*

The situation for DeLonge was suddenly very difficult because in 2011 he began a conspiracy website where he made money promoting theories that didn't say nice things about the men he was now talking to.

In his website called "Strange Times," he promoted the "use of Freemason imagery in videos and on his guitar, "his belief that "he believes at least some of the 9/11 inside job theories," "shadow government," and he published all manner of conspiracy stories.[102]

He was now facing the men he had accused of these evil acts, so he quickly started respectfully about his interviewers and started to build a story where these men were painted as heroes who had saved the country. As he was trying to figure out what to say about his conspiratorial past, the head of the company walked in the room.

> *Now I am being eyeballed...I tried to talk myself out of it and in comes the head of the company...he got introduced to the conversation right at that point.*
>
> *I said, "You come in right at a very interesting part of the conversation where this person brought up the whole UFO issue with me. I just want you to know that I don't plan on treating that disrespectfully with this project," and then I got interrupted. The head guy says "we cannot be involved with anything that has anything to do with that subject, especially since there has been absolutely no evidence whatsoever that it exists."*
>
> *So, I am just cut off, and my heart is racing... all I could say is that Edgar Mitchell, the 6th man to walk on the moon is out telling all the young people that this is real so we have a credibility issue that we have to attack...so they said continue.*[103]

The bait was set, and the meeting ended.

DeLonge then asked to talk to the head guy alone. When they were alone DeLonge said "I just want you to understand something...I understand the national security implications of what I am about to say...I think if you hear me out you will see that there is merit in what I am about to propose."

The man asked him what topic he was talking about, to which DeLonge replied, "UFOs sir."

DeLonge then laid out his entire concept for the Sekret Machines project to tell the entire UFO story to the young people of America. He offered to send something to the official that would outline his proposal and the official said okay.

He sent his thesis on UFOs in an email, and then realized that he probably shouldn't have used that approach as he did not hear anything for a couple weeks. At that point he received an email saying that he was to meet a particular person outside the Pentagon at a specific time, and a specific date from the CIA.

The man who he would meet was a retired respected high-level CIA officer with almost three decades of service. He was an experiencer, having had a dramatic encounter, along with his wife, with beings in their bedroom in the 1990s. One of the people I dealt with who had been involved with him called him the "big man."

According to DeLonge, the meeting at Lockheed led to "multiple clandestine encounters across the United States from desert airport to vacant buildings in Washington DC."[104]

As to the 10 individuals who were set up to guide DeLonge, he identified his contacts as "sources within the aerospace industry and the Department of Defense and NASA." And added, "That sentence, specifically, was approved for me to say."

Based on his beliefs going in, and on the information that DeLonge gathered from these sources, his plan was to reach the young people of America with the story behind the UFO phenomena in a way that readers would be entertained and educated. His plan involved songs, major motion pictures with documentaries, and 6 novels and non-fiction books.

Not all the material that appears in DeLonge's project will be from the government sources. Much of it is just stuff he has read or pulled off the internet.

The co-author of his first book, a British-born American novelist, who writes mystery/thrillers and fantasy adventures by the name of Andrew James Hartley spoke a bit about the where the material for the first book *Sekret Machines* came from.

> *There's a lot to learn. Tom is sending me books, he's sending me links to documents online, YouTube videos, and all sorts of stuff.*[105]

When asked why he thought the government had decided to play the disclosure game with him, DeLonge stated:

> *I came in with a voice that they don't have – the ability to speak to your children I like do. I also walked in there with a thesis on the phenomenon that is correct, and that is totally different than just visitors from another planet. So when they knew that I actually knew what I was talking about I think that caught them a little bit off guard. I also said I have a plan to do that looks something like this, and I laid out the entire Sekret Machines project, and they thought that was really interesting. When I started*

> *executing and pulling the people together and getting all these advisors, and writing the novel which was good, and the documentary was good, and everything happening the way I said it would I think I built up an enormous amount of trust with these guys.*
>
> *I think that I came and brought an idea to the table that speaks to the young people the way that I do. I also walked into there with a thesis on the phenomena that is correct and is totally different than visitors from another planet so that when they saw that I actually knew what I was talking about that sort of caught them a little bit off guard, and I also said I have a plan to do something that looks like this and I set out the whole Sekret Machines project, and they probably thought that was pretty interesting. When I started doing the work and pulling the people together, and getting all these advisors, and writing the novel, and the novel being good, and the documentary being good, and everything happening the way I said it would I think I built up an enormous amount of trust with these guys.*

The Wiki-Leaks emails released some of the names of these people, which confirmed that DeLonge had the sources he claimed he had. This was extremely important because it showed government involvement in what may be some sort of UFO disclosure or acclimatization effort. There had to be some sort of green light as there was no doubt the government was aware of the DeLonge meetings and conversations. These meetings with sitting government officials would not have occurred without approval.

Not only had they approved the encounters, the group of government officials had reviewed and approved all the things DeLonge had done. One example mentioned by DeLonge was a fake interview set up in the early days of the project by DeLonge's company to see how a rock star could handle talking about national security.

The interview was taped and DeLonge sent it to his key advisor who sent back four pages of advice on what to say, how to say it, and what not to say.

DeLonge outlined how his partnership with government officials operated:

> *I had the rare opportunity to present my ideas to an executive in the Department of Defense who worked in special access programs in an area known as Watertown, also known as Area 51. That meeting led to multiple clandestine encounters across the United States, from desert airports to vacant building deep within Washington DC.*

The person DeLonge initially met with was probably Robert Weiss, a retired U.S. Naval Reserve Captain, who went on to become Executive Vice President and General Manager of Aeronautics Advanced Development Programs at Lockheed Martin Corporation. Weiss would later be identified in the Podesta Wiki-Leaks emails as having attended a Google hangout meeting on January 25, 2016, with DeLonge, Podesta, and two USAF generals on a UFO disclosure plan initiated by DeLonge.

DeLonge had always been interested in UFOs. When Dr. Steven Greer held the disclosure news conference in May 2001, DeLonge contacted Greer and flew him out to California. Greer arrived with 100 hours of video testimony in a backpack which impressed DeLonge.

DeLonge continued to meet with Greer in California, and at Greer's home in Virginia. Greer gave DeLonge 36 hours of testimony which DeLonge hid, fearing what the authorities might do if he was caught with the testimony.

This fear was heightened by the fact that once DeLonge met with Greer, he started to experience phone problems. He told reporter George Knapp that his phone was going crazy and that in four years that he dealt with Greer he experienced buzzing and clicking noises on the phone. This happened despite the fact that DeLonge moved four times during the three-year period.[106]

The Greer DeLonge Quandary

Although DeLonge met with and supported Greer, their association came to an end, and perhaps highlights the main problem with DeLonge's entire view of the UFO question. Greer believed there were no evil aliens, and DeLonge had come to the conclusion that they were all evil. (See "Tom DeLonge and the Evil Aliens" later in this chapter.)

DeLonge claimed that the government officials agreed with his evil alien theory, but that presented a problem as Greer, who was saying there were no evil aliens, was also talking with high level officials, and probably with many more insiders than DeLonge had on his team.

Both men claimed to have the government's ear and they were telling two different stories that could not be farther apart.

At some point DeLonge and Greer took separate roads as to what is behind the UFO phenomena and how the government is dealing with it. Both men have been confronted with the discrepancy and each basically had the same answer to explain the difference.

According to DeLonge, he believes that the reason he and Greer are being told different things by the government is that Greer is being used:

> *Someone is using him to send out information and they want to study how the information gets out. They want to see how it goes across the internet and what kind of articles this information goes into.*[107]

Greer, in turn, stated DeLonge was being used and provided false information that was scripted by a dark hand of the United States military.

> *He is being used. He has been brought in by General McCasland at Wright Patterson, who is feeding him disinformation about a threat, so it will get to the young people. That's like the new movie "Independence Day" where they had the big recruiting ad from the Army to get the people to buy into this – the us versus them alienism.*[108]

The fact that high-level officials are apparently backing two key disclosure figures with opposing views as to the intelligence behind the UFO phenomena is interesting. The officials dealing with both appear to have allowed them both to believe what they want about the intelligence behind the phenomena. The primary focus of the officials, therefore, seems to be using both researchers to get out a particular message.

It appears that both men are telling the truth claiming that high level officials are giving them information related to UFOs.

The most important thing to note is that neither man has a security clearance. Each, however, believes he is being leaked Top-Secret material with no repercussions. Each believes he is being given information that the president is not even aware of.

Another important observation is that both men have huge egos that may blind them to what is happening as opposed to what they think is happening.

People don't usually change their beliefs, and the people behind the control of the UFO phenomena would know this. Getting the story out comes down to overcoming or changing peoples' long held beliefs. This has to have been a huge part of the work done behind the scenes on UFOs - how will it affect peoples' beliefs and how do you change those beliefs.

Tom DeLonge	Steven Greer
The ETs are evil - "UFOs are Bad News."	The ETs are good "Anyone who believes in evil aliens is an idiot."
The UFO officials are heroes	The UFO officials are evil.

DeLonge and Disinformation

Everything I do gets approval. **Tom DeLonge**

Ever since DeLonge came on the scene, he has been accused by many researchers of being used by the government to spread disinformation about UFOs. DeLonge agrees that this has happened in the past where the government had initially planned to slowly release the information to the public but never did. Instead, they disseminated disinformation, and have ridiculed the topic, to keep people off the trail of what is going on.

Both DeLonge and Peter Levenda, who is co-authoring all DeLonge's non-fiction books about UFOs, both deny charges against the military possibly using him.

DeLonge stated the people he is dealing with are not counter-intelligence people:

> *Because of how I met these people and brought them together. That's how the relationship works. I know exactly who they are. I know their full bios. I know their current positions, and they are not counter-intelligence people. It would be a different situation if they were different people.*[109]

Levenda also claimed there was no disinformation plan stating:

> *The information we are getting is exactly as Tom said. It is not that someone has come to us. It is not a Doty Bennewitz situation. We don't have an Air Force intelligence officer coming to us and saying "guess what," and opening up his black raincoat and saying "I've got some dirty pictures here I want to show you." It's not that kind of thing. It's not that kind of deal. First of all, the people that we are dealing with, without getting into any details...Doty would not be in the same room.*

DeLonge's co-author AJ Hartley did admit that using non-fiction was a way for the government to control how they want the UFO story told. He told reporter George Knapp, "Yes, that's a great way... it's a novel – a work of fiction, so yes... We were constantly being presented with material where we believed we were being led in very particular directions, but there was that house of cards type line if you are familiar with the original of the British TV show where someone would say, and then the minister would say 'you might think that but I can't possibly comment.' That's their way of saying 'Yes, that is exactly what is going on, but I am not going to tell you officially.'"[110]

DeLonge and Levenda may say that they are different than the situation where Doty was running a counterintelligence operation on Paul Bennewitz, but their story sounds almost like a movie rerun.

Bennewitz saw and filmed UFOs over the Marzano weapons storage area, and believed that it represented some sort of alien invasion, meant to control and subjugate the human race. DeLonge thinks the same thing saying, "Well guess what? UFOs are bad news. Deal with it. They just are."

Bennewitz approached Major Ernest Edwards who headed the Kirtland AFB Security Police to report what he was seeing. They invited him to a meeting on the base to sell his idea. In attendance were several major Air Force officers and Sandia personnel, including Brigadier General William Brooksher.

DeLonge, on the other hand, went to Area 51 and met with Lockheed Skunk Works director Robert Weiss and his two assistants where he presented his Cargo Cult theory of alien invasion. At that point he, like Bennewitz before him, was offered help.

The story of how DeLonge got to the initial meeting at Area 51 is also important as it shows how he was set up.

His interest in the dark side of the UFO story came with his support and encounters with Steven Greer. DeLonge stated that he flew Greer out to Los Angeles and Greer came off the plane with a backpack with over 150 hours of testimony from high level witnesses that had not been made public.

He left 36 hours of testimony with DeLonge who suddenly became paranoid that he would get bumped off so he hid the tapes:

> *The top 36 hours that summarized the best parts of all of that footage, I had it hidden in my house for a period of time, and during that time I was flying this person out along with somebody that was Wernher von Braun's right-hand assistant...and I was flying them out to Los Angeles and we were taking certain meetings. At that time a lot of weird stuff started happening.*

Part of the weird stuff that was happening, according to DeLonge is that his phone was being tapped for the years in interacted with Greer, even though he had moved a number of times during the period.

Levenda stated that they were not led, implying that they are in control of the story and the people telling it to them:

> *More than that it's a question of, as Tom says, we're the ones asking the questions. They are not trying to lead us on, and its different people in different parts of society, different parts of the military industrial complex. It's different people in different parts of*

knowledge of influence, of whatever you want to call it.

Therefore, the UFO intelligence people knew all about DeLonge and his plans long before he made his first trip to Area 51. This idea that they knew who he was and had studied him came during his first meeting at Area 51 when he was directly asked about all the conspiracy theories that he was into.

The most powerful evidence that he had been chosen to carry a UFO message comes from the story of how he got to Area 51 in the first place. DeLonge told Jimmy Church that he had gotten an invitation to attend a party for Skunk Works families where he would introduce the president.

There is no way that the most classified military research unit in the country would pull in a civilian to introduce the president without it being approved by the president and the management team.

DeLonge stated that he would do the introduction if he could sit with the president for five minutes and they agreed.

During his five minutes, he stated that he did not talk UFOs but stated that he wanted to make a proposal down the road to the president, and the president, without knowing what it was, agreed.

Two weeks later, DeLonge is at the Area 51 base behind the levels of security, without a security clearance, or investigation by the FBI, and America's top secrets are being told to him.

Every step of the process is against every security protocol there is. It seemed clear that they were leading the dance and DeLonge was calling none of the shots.

DeLonge stated that as soon as he outlined his Cargo Cult theory explaining UFOs, he suddenly got offers of help. Once they expressed interest, DeLonge said, "Sir, I need help telling young adults this story..."

The official he was talking to said, "What do you need?"....

"Advisors," I responded. "I need high-ranking advisors in the military, intelligence, and DOD to help guide me." So - I was given ten advisors, each with knowledge in different areas that pertain to UFOs and the very real national security issues associated with them.

He like Bill Moore and Steven Greer had advisors who knew what he was doing and planning and managed/approved the story he would be putting out.

This is not to say that DeLonge is being used to spread disinformation. He is carefully directed to put out a story. The game that is being played is the controlled leaking of the inside UFO story, much the same way as scores of people who have done the same thing over the last 70+ years.

It is not "classified" information as DeLonge is claiming because as I pointed out at the beginning of the book, leaking classified information is punishable by ten years in jail for every violation.

That was even pointed out to DeLonge early in the process when a General he was meeting with, reminded DeLonge, "I took an oath to my country."

In the promo for DeLonge's first book *Sekret Machines: Chasing Shadows* DeLonge says that the book will reveal "fascinating secrets" and "actual events and other truths drawn from sources within the military and intelligence community." The government knows who is talking to DeLonge and his team, and what he is being told. DeLonge and his two writers do not have a security clearance for the material or a need-to-know. If classified secrets were being illegally leaked, all ten of his inside sources would be in jail, and so would DeLonge, Levenda, and Hartley.

DeLonge made the same mistake many researchers make when it comes to offers of UFO information by "insiders."

All officers take an oath to obey the law and uphold the constitution. Officers who leak classified information about UFOs, which is the most highly classified subject in the country, are violating that oath. No one, including DeLonge, ever brings this up. No one asks them how they can be telling the truth if they lied to the American government about taking an oath not to release classified information to people without proper need-to-know.

Everyone just goes along with the person leaking assuming that they are receiving unauthorized classified information and that for some reason the government doesn't know the leak has occurred or they are letting people walk around and violate the law.

Did DeLonge ask his ten advisors why they were sharing unauthorized classified information with him so he could put it in books and make money? I very much doubt he did.

The Cargo Cult Theory

Fear sells. Fear makes money. The countless companies and consultants in the business of protecting the fearful from whatever they may fear know it only too well. The more fear, the better the sales.

Daniel Gardner

Everyone believes something different about God, and we are killing each other over it, and we all have advanced weaponry based on crashes that just happen to fall on our borders...the pain and the anger and the emotional energy of war. Maybe there is something there that they are interested in – the emotional side of things. It's hard to think of but it's still energy. **Tom DeLonge**

The Cargo Cult theory is how Tom DeLonge has defined his theory of what is behind the UFO mystery. It is a theory that describes the UFO phenomena as an existential threat which should initiate fear in every human being.

"UFOs are bad news," DeLonge told radio host Jimmy Church. In an interview with *Motherboard* he stated, "There are things so terrifying and unimaginable that certain interests believe that they should never ever be made public."

What is important to note is that DeLonge held this theory BEFORE he made his first approaches to high military, NASA, and government officials. These are not ideas that he got from the government.

This is important because DeLonge has indicated that he thinks the military people that he talked to agree with him. DeLonge described that he developed the theory when he first started touring the world with Blink-182.

He was raised a strong Catholic, but had a loss of faith once he started encountering other religions around the world. This led him to the idea that all religion comes from encounters with UFOs, and that all the death and destruction in the world is caused by religion. (Note that this runs contrary to the evidence that the biggest genocides of the 20th century – the Soviet Union, the Chinese cultural revolution, the North Korean genocide, and the killing fields of Cambodia all happened under secular non-religious regimes. (See Appendix 1 for a listing.)

The idea that religions are caused by seeing UFOs is also countered by the fact that two of the main religions Hinduism and Buddhism were created by internal discoveries made through meditation, and both religions describe the visual senses as illusion.

In an interview with George Knapp in March 2016, DeLonge stated:

> *The entire UFO phenomenon is about multiple gods that fight among themselves, and by design factionalize mankind into different religions, to step back and let us fight each other, so it has other things that it wants to accomplish, and we don't notice them because we're too involved fighting each other.*
>
> *The various UFO crashes might have been done on purpose for the aliens to translate their technology to humanity in order to give us greater weapons of war to use on each other.*

In an interview with radio host Jimmy Church, DeLonge expounded on what he called the Cargo Cult theory, and how he thinks that he got access to high level sources because he had figured out the UFO mystery:

> *I went to them with a thesis called the Cargo Cult. Cargo Cults in World War II where indigenous tribes that had never seen man watched planes come in and drop off ammunition in the jungle and to this day they still worship those planes. They are worshiping the cargo. I said we are all Cargo Cults. Me and Peter Levenda created this theory for the non-fiction books. So, I went in there are said, "The first thing that it does is it creates religious experiences, and it dances in the sky in star of Bethlehem type stuff, and you have all these different religions, and now everyone hates each other. Now we are all killing each other, and then it happens to crash, and it crashes in a few different places, in a few different countries and a few different ways.*
>
> *What happens? We got better weapons of war now – big weapons of war. Now we have anti-gravity craft. Now we have all these things. So, I am sitting there telling these guys this. I said "Something smells fishy to me, really fishy and right at that point when I said that is when I got a communication that says, "Meet right next to the Pentagon at this date and this time."*

Greer talked about how the evil alien story is being used to influence the progressives. "People have to understand that there are consequences to these kind of tales...when you have rock stars and other and millions of people who otherwise would otherwise be new age progressive or whatever buying into a mannequin black and white, us versus them, good versus evil – they are just being brought into alienism. They are being brought into a paradigm of interplanetary war. The question is who would benefit from this?"

Whether DeLonge believes this or not, the argument that there are "evil aliens out there" can be used by military elements that are motivated by fear in the same way that 911, the "weapons of mass destruction" in Iraq, or the Gulf of Tonkin were used. The evil alien theory can be used to arm the planet for an interplanetary war that will dwarf any past wars known in the present day.

There is, in fact, a story being circulated by the Defense Intelligence Agency that aliens were in fact playing one group against another. The difference in the story being told by DIA was that rather than religious wars, countries, such as China, Russia, and the United States were being influenced to engage in war against one another.

Buying into the Cargo Cult of evil aliens will allow the militarist-congressional industrial complex that Eisenhower warned of in his final speech to sell fear and accumulate more power with promises of protecting the population from invading ETs.

These elements will hijack the disclosure effort and spin it into a scenario where the aliens are here to eat us or put us to work in gold mines. In such an environment, it will be very easy to gain taxpayer authorization for increased defense spending in preparation for World War III, in the same way the public was motivated in the 2016 U.S. presidential election because of their fear of invading "evil Mexicans, Chinese, and Arabs."

As Greer accurately points out, the evil alien theory "coopts the progressive community" of UFO researchers into a dualistic worldview of good blond human aliens versus evil grey and reptilian races, which seems to be an extension of many humans' racial and ethnic tensions with one another. We are therefore projecting on to outer space our existing frailties.

Logic would dictate that if there is indeed an enemy that can disappear at will, abduct high level officials without interference, and walk through walls, that no such a war cannot be fought and won, regardless of how advanced the hidden technologies are. After all, if Lockheed developed advanced technologies by reverse engineering

Roswell artifacts, it would be like a kindergarten kid learning the alphabet and thinking he is now a genius.

Logic, however, does not play a factor as populations are manipulated by the use of emotional advertising, and people make most of their choices based on their emotions before logic comes to bear.

Alien False Flag

Mr. President. Anyone that can cross millions of miles of space to get here will know how to take care of themselves once they arrive. Don't start something you can't finish. **Albert Einstein to President Truman after Truman issued the 1952 UFO shoot down order.**

What a wonderful recipe for war. **A favorite expression used by DeLonge's military advisors.**

Using fear of aliens to build up the military industrial complex is not a new idea. It has been discussed in the UFO research community for years and is known as the "alien false flag."

Most people, who are aware of UFOs, want some sort of disclosure by the United States as to what is going on. The question is what will this disclosure lead to?

The final story could be that beings are here to visit or warn us of our misuse of nuclear weapons and the ecological damage we are inflicting on the Earth. The final story, however, could be an alien invasion where we are enslaved, destroyed, or devoured.

The DeLonge material described the third option, which is that there are evil aliens here, they are up to no good, and "money and resources will be needed by the military industrial complex for the battle ahead against the alien invasion."

Dr. Greer, who has for years campaigned for the government to reveal what they know about UFO mystery, described his fear that the DeLonge material plays right into such a false flag scenario:

> *I would rather stop what I am doing than to propel further disclosure if what it leads to is piggybacking onto this fearsome new world order of interplanetary conflict and hatred. That is not what I have dedicated my life to.*[111]

The ET false flag was first described by Dr. Carol Rosin who was the first woman corporate manager of Fairchild Industries, and was the spokesperson for Dr. Wernher Von Braun in the last years of his life.

Rosin testified that Von Braun had warned her that an alien threat would be used by the military industrial complex to finance a massive increase in military funding:

> When I was a Corporate Manager of Fairchild Industries from 1974 through 1977, I met the late Dr. Wernher Von Braun. We first met in early 1974. At that time, Von Braun was dying of cancer but he assured me that he would live a few more years to tell me about the game that was being played - that game being the effort to weaponize space, to control the Earth from space and space itself.
>
> Von Braun had a history of working with weapons systems. He escaped from Germany to come to this country and became a Vice President of Fairchild Industries when I had met him. Von Braun's purpose during the last years of his life, his dying years, was to educate the public and decision-makers about why space-based weapons are dumb, dangerous, destabilizing, too costly, unnecessary, unworkable, and an undesirable idea, and about the alternatives that are available.
>
> As practically a deathbed speech, he educated me about those concepts and who the players were in this game. He gave me the responsibility, since he was dying, of continuing this effort to prevent the weaponization of outer space. When Wernher Von Braun was dying of cancer, he asked me to be his spokesperson, to appear on occasions when he was too ill to speak. I did this.
>
> What was most interesting to me was a repetitive sentence that he said to me over and over again during the approximately four years that I had the opportunity to work with him. He said the strategy that was being used to educate the public and decision makers was to use scare tactic. That was how we identify an enemy.

> *The strategy that Wernher Von Braun taught me was that first the Russians are going to be considered to be the enemy. In fact, in 1974, they were the enemy, the identified enemy. We were told that they had "killer satellites". We were told that they were coming to get us and control us -- that they were "Commies."*
>
> *Then terrorists would be identified, and that was soon to follow. We heard a lot about terrorism. Then we were going to identify third-world country "crazies." We now call them Nations of Concern. But he said that would be the third enemy against whom we would build space-based weapons.*
>
> *The next enemy was asteroids. Now, at this point he kind of chuckled the first time he said it. Asteroids-against asteroids we are going to build space-based weapons.*
>
> *And the funniest one of all was what he called aliens, extraterrestrials. That would be the final scare.*
>
> *And over and over and over during the four years that I knew him and was giving speeches for him, he would bring up that last card.*
>
> *"And remember Carol, the last card is the alien card. We are going to have to build space-based weapons against aliens and all of it is a lie."*[112]

The warning given by Rosin and also Greer does seem to be playing out in the material DeLonge claims the United States military is giving him or what he interprets the officials are giving him.

In an interview with Jimmy Church, DeLonge even indicates how he thinks the invading aliens will be dealt with by the military. The whole thing, according to DeLonge, goes back to a high altitude 1.4 megaton nuclear test conducted in 1962 called Operation Starfish Prime where a nuclear device was detonated in outer space, 250 miles up. This test, hinted DeLonge, had brought something that was alien down indicating that nuclear weapons could be used to find and destroy UFOs hiding high in our atmosphere. "Nuclear weapons," said DeLonge, "will f'up those little ankle bitters, and they know it, and they as advanced as they are cannot get away from it."

The implication by DeLonge is that his advisors have told him that they are prepared to use nuclear weapons to fight back again the evil alien invaders. If true, a worst-case scenario will play out.

The Starfish Prime test disrupted electrical system and telephones in Hawaii. The test created new radiation belts around the earth, which lasted for five years. According to Wikipedia great damage was done to orbiting satellites at a time when there were almost none in orbit, "The weaponeers became quite worried when three satellites in low Earth orbit were disabled, although Brown et al. seem to be skeptical that electrons caused the damage. The half-life of the energetic electrons was only a few days. At the time, it was not known that solar and cosmic particle fluxes varied by a factor 10, and energies could exceed 1 MeV. These man-made radiation belts eventually crippled one-third of all satellites in low Earth orbit. Seven satellites failed over the months following the test, as radiation damaged their solar arrays or electronics, including the first commercial relay communication satellite, Telstar, as well as the United Kingdom's first satellite, Ariel 1."

Today literally everything is controlled by satellite. All telephone, TV, military and civilian Earth observation, communication, navigation for aircraft and GPS, weather, space telescopes, humans in low earth orbit would all be affected if not destroyed.

If DeLonge is accurate in the belief there are evil aliens that must be destroyed, and that it can be done with nukes, the situation is an almost end of the world scenario.

Evil Aliens

The material DeLonge has put out indicates that he considers UFOs to be evil invaders, and that the government is working hard to provide protection us against "the threat." DeLonge has made the following statements about the UFO situation.

- "Well guess what? UFOs are bad news. Deal with it. They just are."
- "There are things that are so terrifying and unimaginable that certain interests believe that they should never ever be made public."
- "There is a very, very, strong link to what people think demons are from the Bible and other religions, and the UFO phenomenon. What you have is something that does not like man – period. And something that either feels jealous of, or has some kind of plan for what man is to be...."
- There was cooperation between the Russians and the Americans during the cold war against the evil aliens.

English Phase 2 Survey

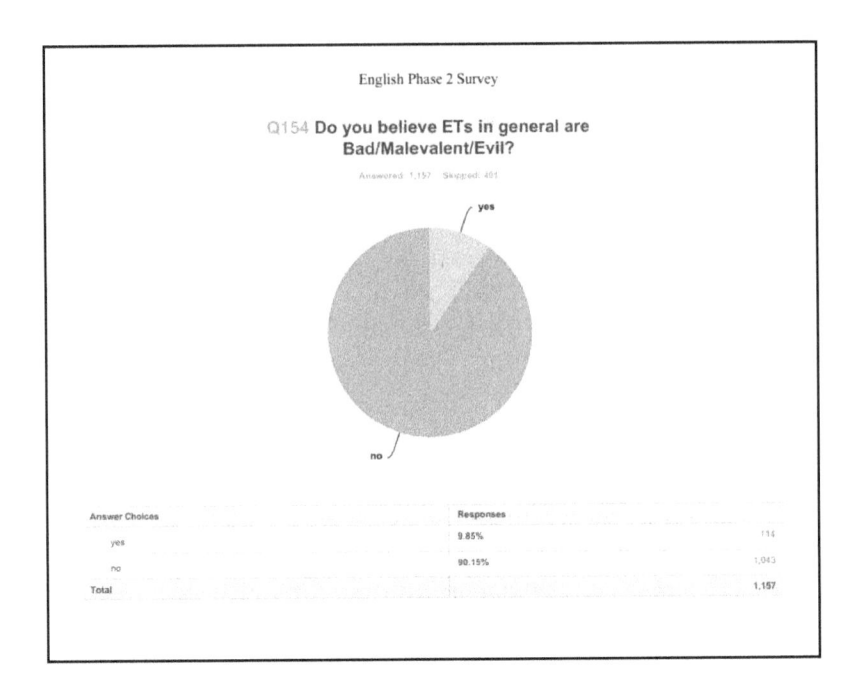

Q154 Do you believe ETs in general are Bad/Malevalent/Evil?

Answered: 1,157   Skipped: 401

Answer Choices	Responses	
yes	9.85%	114
no	90.15%	1,043
Total		1,157

The bottom line to the DeLonge UFO worldview is that the military industrial complex is saving us from the evil aliens, and they should be empowered with every resource we have so they can save us.

This DeLonge claim runs completely contrary to what experiencers report, and they are the ones who are interacting with the aliens. Only 9% of experiencers see the aliens as evil or malevolent. That figure not 0% but it comes pretty close.

The idea that the military might be saving us from evil aliens lacks any history to support it. The question could be asked, "Have the aliens dropped a nuclear bomb yet that killed 100,000 people, or dropped any bomb on anyone?" The clear answer is no.

How then could the US military, which dropped two atom bombs killing over 100,000 innocent men women and children and in 2016 dropped an average of 72 bombs a day around the world in various countries, when there is no declaration of war with anyone, turn around and call the aliens evil? It appears we have met the enemy and it's us.

Following is the evidence DeLonge states supports his claims that the aliens are evil.

Secrets Being Kept from Evil Aliens

....

DeLonge claims the government workers who maintain the UFO secrecy are heroes who did heroic stuff to protect the American people from the evil aliens, who he was told are called "the others."

DeLonge stated that those in charge of the UFO program have been "building a defense system with immense amounts of money for a very long time where if people knew about it they would be in an uproar until they knew the reasons why. Once you understand why they have been keeping their efforts secret, about what they have been doing, you will realize that they need to be empowered and given every bit of resources that they could possibly need for what they are doing." They are "good people doing important work, and thank God they were doing it."[113]

"The UFOs were turning our weapons on," said DeLonge, "just so that Russia could pick up that we are firing our missiles. It was a big chess game. These guys went into complete secrecy a defense system against this phenomenon."[114]

There is a problem with DeLonge's claim based on remote viewing work done at Stanford Research Institute in the 1970s by the CIA (keep in mind that one of the main intelligence officials in DeLonge's group of advisors is a retired high-level CIA officer).

The non-human intelligence behind the UFO phenomena is telepathic, and DeLonge has stated Skunk Works officials confirmed to him that consciousness was an important component of the mystery.

The Foundation for Research into Extraterrestrial Experiences (FREE) supports the idea of telepathic communication, and a survey showed 66% of experiencers reported having received telepathic messages, and of 3,100 participants in another survey, 1,320 claimed to have had telepathic communications with a non-human intelligence.

In another survey, 76.82% answered yes to the following question, "Did your experience involve some type of telepathic or thought transference, or direct knowing, being given you by an ET?"

In a question in phase 2 of the survey there was an even more dramatic reply. When asked, "While in this 'Matrix' type of reality, did you suddenly seem to understand everything?" 36.87% of the respondents replied, "Yes."

If true, this would indicate that with our current technology, nothing can be hidden from the beings the experiencers are encountering, and during their encounter, the experiencers were somehow allowed to tap into that knowledge that the aliens had access to.

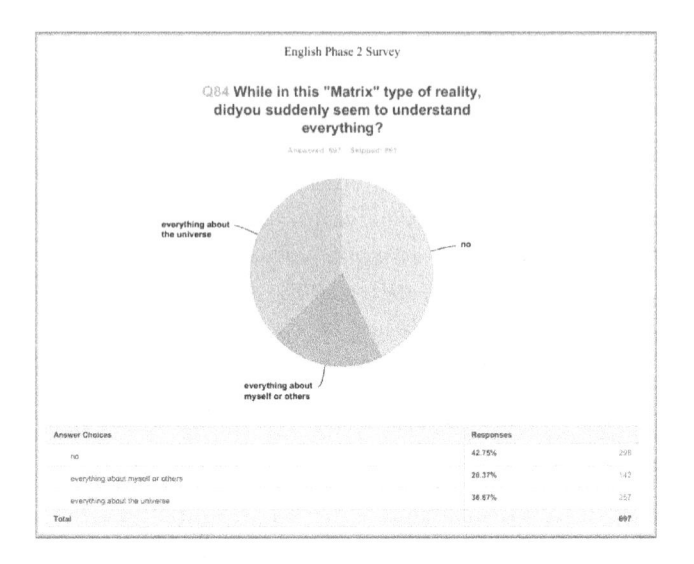

English Phase 2 Survey

Q84 While in this "Matrix" type of reality, didyou suddenly seem to understand everything?

Answer Choices	Responses	
no	42.75%	298
everything about myself or others	20.37%	142
everything about the universe	36.87%	257
Total		697

Therefore, it would also be impossible for the government to "hide" their plans from the aliens, because the aliens are telepathic and way more advanced than we are.

Pat Price, considered the greatest psychic in the CIA remote viewing program, spelled out the principle when he stated, "In psychic space the more you hide something the brighter it shines."

This principle was discovered by the scientists running the CIA remote viewing program at SRI. Price and Ingo Swann, who actually developed the protocols for doing remote viewing, were given a target of a cabin on the east coast of the United States.

When both handed in their results it was apparent that they had both missed the target, but they were both describing exactly the same thing. Both men were describing a facility that looked like an old missile silo. Price was asked for more detail and he read names off of folders on a desk, and folders in filing cabinets along a wall in the facility. He even named the code name for the place – "Hayfork or Haystack."

Asked to find an equivalent facility on the other side of the globe Price immediately began to describe a facility in the Ural Mountains.

Richard Kennet, an officer with the Office of Scientific Investigation at the CIA, decided to go to the site to see what the two men might have been looking for. It was during that trip that Kennet discovered the well concealed facility with the satellite dishes.

When the target was put in for review they suddenly got a visit from CIA and NSA people and everyone endured an intense investigation of how they knew so much about the Top-Secret complex. The details were exact, and the intelligence officers confirmed Price and Swann had identified a well-hidden NSA code facility hidden the West Virginia forests.[115]

This evidence shows that just as CIA and NSA couldn't figure out how Price and Swann were able to know about the hidden stuff, they also, despite what they are telling DeLonge, would not be able to figure out how the aliens know what they know, let alone humans who are having closer experiences with the aliens.

A second piece of evidence that illustrates the inability of humans to hide anything they do from the aliens is the reported inability to capture alien abductions on camera from people's bedrooms. David Jacobs addressed people's inability to hide cameras from the aliens. He spoke about it in his 1998 book *The Threat*:

> *Training a video camera and recorder on an abductee every night has produced limited results. Some abductees report a dramatic decrease in abductions. Most report that the frequency of abductions tends to decrease only a bit.*
>
> *So far, no abductions have been videotaped. Rather, tapes reveal people getting up and inexplicably turning off the VCR, or unusual power outages during which the camera turns off, or the camera simply goes off mysteriously.*[116]

Nuclear Weapons Being Turned on and Off

....

There are major advancements that Russia has, that we have, that China has, based upon technology that has either been given by design or given by accident. I personally think from everything I am hearing… makes it look like it was given by design…to see who is the strongest. That's a scary thought to be given weaponry like that, and then to step back and say, "Now go kill each other, and we will work with the ones that are left over." **Tom DeLonge**

DeLonge states evil aliens are trying to get countries to fight with each other by starting and shutting down nuclear weapons in the United States and Russia. He stated in a 2016 interview:

> *The UFOs were turning our weapons on just so that Russia could pick up that we are firing our missiles. It was a big chess game.*
>
> *These guys went into complete secrecy building a defense system against this phenomenon.*
>
> *36 months ago, (2013) 1/3 of all NATOs weapons were shut down within our oceans by UFOs. They were zipping around and shutting them down. I think what's scary is the mechanism that controls the weapons comes from space and was being shut down as the same time... The way it has been explained to me is that by accident or by design the effect of those crashes is giving greater weapons of war to the people who are fighting each other here on the planet meaning ...what are the effects of it. That's what makes this more scary.*[117]

DeLonge added that turning on the weapons by the aliens was a way to get the Soviets to launch their weapons but it didn't work. He stated that one of his advisors had pointed in his face and said, "There are heroes in Russia, and with grave risk to themselves and their country they did not fire back."

There is a lot of evidence from sources like Robert Hastings and George Knapp that nuclear missiles were indeed shut down as happened in Maelstrom in 1967[118], or turned on the missile to launch, before returning the missile to standby position, as happened in the old Soviet Union.

The problem with this scenario is that the Soviets would not know if our weapons had been turned off or on, and because they were having the same problem they would have realized it probably had nothing to do with the Americans, or a nuclear attack.

Robert Hasting, the foremost expert on the UFOs and nukes, presented his view for the nuclear incidents based on 40 years of interviews with 150 witnesses who have been involved in these nuclear shutdowns and start-ups. Hastings expert opinion does *not* support the evil alien interpretation:

> *UFOs are piloted by visitors from elsewhere in the universe who, for whatever reason, have taken an interest in our long-term survival. He contends that these beings are occasionally disrupting our nukes to send a message to the American and Soviet/Russian governments that their possession and potential large-scale use of nuclear weapons threatens the future of humanity and the environmental integrity of the planet. In short, Washington and Moscow are being warned that they are "playing with fire."[119]*

Cattle Mutilations

....

That's creepy. That's demonic. That's evil weird scientific dark stuff, and it has been going on a long time. I think it scares people that we might be property. **Tom DeLonge speaking on cattle mutilations.**

Another piece of evidence raised by DeLonge to back up his view that we are dealing with evil aliens is the phenomenon of cattle mutilations. This view is also held by others in the UFO community.

The problem with this argument for evil aliens is that it leaves out some key theories as the reason for cattle mutilations.

Most of the cattle found are devoid of blood. In human in-vitro practices, Bovine serum is a key element. For aliens to run their hybridization program (they told experiencer Betty Andreasson Luca that they were doing this to preserve the human species because in the future humankind would become sterile), it makes sense that they would need Bovine blood to make serum. [120]

The part that many may not know is that research by the French into mad cow disease showed that the tissue in cows that reflects the presence of mad cow disease (Bovine Spongiform Encephalopathy) include the eye, the brain and the intestines.[121] And those are often precisely the parts of cows that appear missing in cattle mutilations. Therefore, this would indicate that someone may be monitoring evidence of mad cow disease found when creating Bovine serum. If the aliens are harvesting Bovine serum or blood for use during a future cataclysmic event, why are those precautionary actions evil?

Cows are vegetarians. They eat grass. It is speculated that mad cow disease was created by humans feeding cows animal products, including the remains of other dead cows. We are in essence making cows eat their own people. How is that practice not considered evil?

Further, humans apply flea medicine to their dogs and cats to prevent fleas from eating them alive. Word has it that ranchers have a similar practice with cows, in which they brush them along their spine with insecticide so the cow will retain its weight come slaughter time (they get more for each pound). It does not take a genius that there are probably long term effects of this insecticide on cows, not only to the cows but to the people eating them. If the aliens know about mad cow disease, you can be sure they know about those insecticide effects as well. They are obviously advanced in genetics. So where is the evil? Is it in us or them?

There have been 10,000 mysterious cattle mutilations over the past 50 years in the United States. This amounts to about 200 a year. The number of cows and calves mutilated by the American cattle industry is 41.7 million. That is 2.1 billion cattle mutilations over 50 years. Any intelligent cow voting on 'who is evil' would pick the humans.

People will argue that they are justified in killing cows, but the aliens have no justification for doing so. This argument would not wash with the voting cows because despite what people might think, animals do not like being mutilated and cooked, any more than humans would if they were in the same position.

Further, two cattle mutilation experts, David Perkins and Chris O'Brien, present evidence that would indicate the mutilation phenomena could be a sampling, either by aliens or the government, of radioactive contamination in cows.

The location of the mutilations and the connection to radioactivity was first discovered by Perkins. O'Brien described the connection:

> *David was the first person to notice that the areas of high incidence or repeat where these cases tended to cluster seemed to be all down wind and downstream of where we utilize or mine, weaponize uranium, downstream of power plants, downwind of the Nevada test site.*
>
> *If you look at a map of radiation from 100 above ground nuclear tests, the area where the majority of that fallout occurred tends to be where quite a number of the cases – I would venture to say a majority of the cases are clustered in the upper Midwest Colorado, Wyoming, Montana, Kansas,*

> *Nebraska. These cases, the way the gulfstream works, a lot of that radiation was deposited there.*
>
> *Then if you go down wind and downstream of weapons labs, missile silos, missile fields, places where there are uranium mines. There are exceptions to that of course. This is an east of the Rockies scenario. When you go west of the Rockies the number of mutilations falls off dramatically in number. The vast majority of them are on the front range of the Rockies on the east side of the Rockies and in the Midwest.* [122]

Perkins also made reference to a seventeen-year 1997 National Cancer Institute (NCI) study re the effects on cancer rates of ninety above ground nuclear tests on cancer rates. O'Brien wrote about what Perkins referred to as a theory of "environmental monitoring" as a possibility for the mysterious cattle mutilations.

> *Investigator David Perkins noticed a tantalizing correlation between the NCI map of regions most impacted by radiation and regions suffering continual reports of "cattle mutilations." In Perkins' words, "both maps are almost an exact match!"*[123]

In addition, cattle mutilations generally occur where cattle are raised and kept in quantity on ranges or in pastures. Feed lots are not affected, indicating that cattle in contact with the environment are the focus of the mutilation.

Because the mutilations appear to be linked to government related uranium activities, it would be surprising if government officials didn't see the connection between the two.

One idea for the mutilation is that the cow is a message to the government by the aliens, in the same way that the nuclear weapon shutdowns appear to be a message about radioactive contamination (and about how they will stop it if they have to).

These theories would explain why the cows are left for all to see, otherwise why wouldn't the aliens just take the entire cow and keep it or dispose of it in outer space or another dimension? It makes sense that the cadavers are messages to us (much like toy blocks are put together by someone in kindergarten).

The bizarre nature of some of the mutilations is similar to bizarre things that experiencers find after encounters. Many will report waking up to find their clothes inside out and backwards. One witness recalled how both his shirt and those of his young autistic son (who was wearing a jumper over the shirt) were inside out and backwards.

Yvonne Smith talks about two of her clients who found triangles carved into their penises. A local experiencer in my city reported waking to find a Y shaped cut in the top of his head, his hair covered in blood but no blood on the pillow.

The events seem to be signals to get the person wondering but to also make the experiencer realize that they cannot explain away the events as a normal occurrence. For example, the local man with the Y cut in his head could not explain it as something that may have happened when he was shaving, or caused by bumping his head on the bed post.

Like the very complex crop circles that have appeared in England, some of the cattle mutilations seem to be done to drive home the point that the event was not caused by scavengers, the government, or natural death. Chris O'Brien who has been involved with cattle mutilations for 50 years described one of the most bizarre cases:

> *We had a case. This calf was missing its brain without a break into the skull. The brain case was completely dry. The animal was found in five inches of snow. The lungs were gone. The spine was gone from the back of the skull to where the spine joins the hips. The right front leg was gone. The heart and liver were perfectly excised and left in the bottom of the body cavity. Those are the organs that animals go after first, and it was found in a pristine five inches of snow, and there was only one drop of blood that we found, and it was on the back-left hoof. That in my opinion, and that of the veterinarian, the Sheriff, and the investigators was impossible to pull off.*[124]

Whatever the causes are for cattle mutilations, they don't seem to be happening at the rate at which they used to, if at all. Maybe this points to the aliens having succeeded in their hybridization program to the point where they don't need the Bovine serum anymore.

Alien Souls

....

In an interview with Jimmy Church, DeLonge stated that aliens have a hive mind, potentially don't have souls, and feed off the fear that they create in their abductees. Many assume he was told this by government officials.

The aliens do have a hive mind, working as one and are concerned with the ecosystem of the Earth. Our body also works in this way with the thousands of modules in our brain. The aliens work very much like a collective community such as a commune, or an Israeli kibbutz.

The aliens do not feed off fear, as fear is not a thing unto itself. There is no material thing called fear. Fear is simply negative thinking. We envision the future and put a negative spin on it but it hasn't happened yet and is not real.

"The only thing we have to fear is fear itself," said President Roosevelt.

Fear is an imaginary creation of the left brain, rational analytical mind, as was spelled out by Jill Bolte Taylor,[125] a neuroanatomist from Harvard. Taylor experienced a left-brain hemorrhage that shut down that part of her brain for eight weeks until she had an operation to remove the hemorrhage. During that period she stated there was no fear. It did not exist, and it only returned once her left brain went back on-line.

I do not believe the "aliens have no souls" comment came from officials like DeLonge as it sounds more like a rehash of many experiencers reporting small greys, who can come across as cookie cutter, robotoic beings as compared to taller greys. People are led to believe that they are artificial intelligence creations made by the greys or someone else in order so that they can do the dirty work. Dr. Greer claims that his high-level government sources say that some of these robotic beings are created by the black ops military industry so they can conduct operations that then appear to the public as alien abductions. Greer states that the military create their own craft that look like UFOs but that he can tell the difference between the military craft and the real UFOs. The military craft will have seams, bolts, etc., whereas the UFOs are perfectly smooth because the ships and the aliens are both sentient and alive. The description by Jonathan Van

Weygandt of the downed UFO in Peru would fit with the idea that the ship was alive.[126]

In the end, I predict that full understanding of the UFO mystery will reveal consciousness to be the key. The quantum physics work by Neils Bohr, Erwin Schrodinger, and Werner Heisenberg illustrated that consciousness is the root of all matter and the physical particle does not take a position in time and space until there is an observer.

In a second quantum "entangled particle" experiment proving non-locality, it was shown that the one particle was instantaneously aware of what happened to the spin of its entangled partner despite the amount of distance between the two. This then confirmed that awareness or consciousness is a characteristic of sub-atomic particles and is probably fundamental to everything.

The officials at Lockheed Skunk Works who met with DeLonge confirmed that consciousness was the key, as did Ben Rich, another Skunk Works director.[127] It is almost certain they would not have taken the 17th century Newtonian view that we humans are conscious and everything else is not.

The Three Kings

Eventually DeLonge would bring together three high-level officials for a January 25, 2016 Google Hangout meeting with John Podesta regarding UFO disclosure. The three men were:

1) **Retired USAF Major General Michael Carey**: According to his USAF bio, Carey was the Special Assistant to the Commander, Air Force Space Command, Peterson Air Force Base, which is also the home of NORAD. Petersen is at the base of the famous Cheyenne Mountain.

After Carey's name was revealed, Alejandro Rojas at *Open Minds* pointed out that Carey had posted an Amazon review on DeLonge's first UFO book Sekret Machines.

> *Sekret Machines scratches at the surface of "who do" we trust with our classified technology – certainly our adversaries are aware of our undertakings, as they are doing the same, but what of our citizens, our politicians, even our own military. Tom DeLonge and A.J. Hartley create a convincing narrative describing the "cat and mouse" game that is timeless between strategic adversaries. It has existed under the sea, on the surface of the earth and in its skies, why wouldn't we believe it occurs in space. Our military leaders have been saying space is a contested environment for years now, perhaps we should believe them!*[128]

2) **General William Neil McCasland**: According to his Air Force biography Maj. Gen. William N. McCasland is the Commander, Air Force Research Laboratory, Wright-Patterson Air Force Base, Ohio. He is responsible for managing the Air Force's $2.2 billion science and technology program as well as additional customer funded research and development of $2.2 billion. McCasland is also responsible for a global workforce of approximately 10,800 people in the laboratory's component technology directorates, 711th Human Performance Wing and the Air Force Office of Scientific Research...He previously served at the Pentagon, first as the Director, Space Acquisition, in the Office of the Secretary of the Air Force, and

then as Director of Special Programs, Office of the Under Secretary of Defense for Acquisition, Technology and Logistics. General McCasland holds a doctorate degree in astronautical engineering from the Massachusetts Institute of Technology where he studied under a John and Fannie Hertz Foundation fellowship.

3) **Robert Weiss**: Robert Weiss has been Executive Vice President and General Manager of Aeronautics Advanced Development Programs at Lockheed Martin Corporation since July 29, 2013. Mr. Weiss served as an Executive Vice President of Global Sustainment at Lockheed Martin Aeronautics Co. since October 2008 until July 2010. He served as Vice President of Business Development for Aeronautics since 2005. He also served as Executive Vice President and General Manager of Aeronautics Operations, which included responsibility for Technical Operations, Production Operations, Supply Chain Management, Information Systems & Technology and Quality. He served as Aeronautics Executive Vice President for Global Sustainment, where he was responsible for the $3 billion logistics, maintenance and aircraft modernization lines of business. He is a retired U.S. Naval Reserve Captain who served as an aircraft carrier-based S-3 Viking pilot prior to joining Lockheed Martin. Mr. Weiss is a graduate of the U.S. Naval Academy and holds a master's degree in Systems Management from the University of Southern California.

The Big Meeting

Anything you say on this topic makes headlines. It made its way to me behind the scenes. **Tom DeLonge to John Podesta February 2016**

The biggest story in the Podesta emails was the big UFO disclosure meeting held January 25, 2016. The day before, Podesta's assistant Milia Fisher wrote Podesta spelling out how the meeting would be conducted:

> *12:30 pm Tom DeLonge mtg:* *Tom would like to do the meeting remotely via video conference. I've set one up via Google Hangouts (what we use for all our staff meetings at HQ).* *I'll show you how to get on the Google Hangout from your iPad this afternoon or tomorrow morning.*

The meeting took place as scheduled attended by DeLonge, General Neil McCasland, Major General Michael Carey, Robert Weiss from Lockheed Skunk Works, and John Podesta.

We know McCasland showed up as he emailed Podesta to confirm the time writing, "All - regret my confusion, but am looking to clarify time. 1030 EST or had that been converted to MST for my reception?"

We know Weiss showed up because one month after the meeting DeLonge wrote Podesta stating that Weiss would like an update:

> *Mr. Weiss from Lockheed Skunk Works just emailed me asking if there were any updates. I am not expecting much, but if there is anything I can tell him and the General, however small, I would like to respectfully pass it along.*[129]

This was a significant message as it meant that in the January 25th UFO disclosure meeting, Podesta must have made some promise to do something or provide some information. Now Weiss, who was in charge of the back-engineering of the UFO technology, was sending a message asking for an update from Podesta on the UFO disclosure meeting.

It is particularly significant because when Podesta was the White House Chief of Staff for Bill Clinton, he had done interviews about his interest in the X-Files TV show and UFOs. During one of the interviews, <u>Podesta had confessed to phoning Area 51 for information. Now, two decades later, the head of Area 51 was contacting Podesta for information.</u>

During the meeting, it appeared that McCasland played the role of a skeptic. We know this because later in the day after the meeting had ended, DeLonge emailed Podesta telling him that McCasland was anything but a skeptic:

> *He mentioned he's a "skeptic," he's not. I've been working with him for four months. I just got done giving him a four-hour presentation on the entire project a few weeks ago. Trust me, the advice has already been happening on how to do all this. He just has to say that out loud, but he is very, very aware- as he was in charge of all of the stuff. When Roswell crashed, they shipped it to the laboratory at Wright Patterson Air Force Base. General*

> *McCasland was in charge of that exact laboratory up to a couple of years ago.*[130]

There would be supporting information to show McCasland was just playing the skeptic role during the meeting.

In an earlier email, three months before the big meeting, DeLonge had written Podesta talking about McCasland and sending Podesta information from the General as to what a White House memo on disclosure should contain:

> *I was thinking a bit more about what a White House memo should say. Something like these points to all Federal Agencies: - In light of the President's policy on STEM (citing official policy encouraging the study of science, technology, engineering and math) - some back ground on your project - the Administration encourages a favorable Public Affairs position by all Agencies - appointes NASA to lead (this kind of public outreach is in NASA's job jar, and if no Agency is appointed all will simply note and file the memo and likely do nothing) - and to coordinate with DoD, DNI and NOAA (the other major space actors, putting a bit of light on them)*[131]

In an email, DeLonge sent to Podesta February 23, 2016, DeLonge points out that, General McCasland believes that the DOD would approve the disclosure plan as formulated by DeLonge and discussed at the January 25th meeting with Podesta:

> *The General (from Wright Patt R&D) and I talk every other day. He and I talked on the phone the other night, and he is excited, he really thinks that the DOD is going to embrace my project because I am out to show all the positive things great people have done on this topic. And I am eager to take direction from leadership to do a good and needed public service.*

Podesta Makes a Supporting Statement

A couple of weeks after this big meeting on disclosure, Podesta went public with one of the few interviews he did during the campaign where he talked about UFOs and Hillary's plan to engage in disclosure once she became president.

The interview was done with KLAS-TV in Las Vegas, the station that broke the Area 51 story in 1989. In that interview, Podesta expressed his belief that the UFO subject should be opened up:

> *I've talked to Hillary about that. It's a little bit of a cause of mine, which is, people really want to know what the government knows, and there are still classified files that could be declassified. I think I've convinced her that we need an effort to kind of go look at that and declassify as much as we can so that people have their legitimate questions answered.... More attention and more discussion about unexplained aerial phenomena can happen without people who are in public life, who are serious about this, being ridiculed. I come in for my fair share of people asking questions about whether I am off my rocker, but I've been a long-time advocate of declassification of records.*

Steve Sibelius, the reporter who did the interview, emailed George Knapp who broke the Area 51 story:

> *Had John Podesta in for Hillary Clinton surrogacy, and noticed in my research that he pushed to declassify hundreds of millions of pages of info, including on UFOs. I got him to say he's talked to Hillary about declassifying even more old files, and I told him that I knew a guy who would be very interested in delving into those documents.*[132]

Knapp then wrote DeLonge mentioning his disappointment that he did not get to meet Podesta and hoped DeLonge could mention his name to Podesta:

> *If you are in touch with him, please mention my name. It is possible he will be here in Nevada for the next week since we have a formal presidential caucus coming up in about a week. I'd love to be able to meet him, shake his hand, so he can put a name with a face. It might come in handy some time*

down the road. I don't need to do a story about him or anything but would if he wants....and, like you, he has a permanent invitation to do Coast, even though the conservatives that make up 70% of our audience would shit their pants...[133]

And so, what happened?

The WikiLeaks emails showed evidence that there is a plan to disclose. Four of the most powerful men in the country met together on January 25, 2016, to discuss a plan for revealing the UFO story to the American people.

Reports like Billy Cox and Lee Spiegel wrote to all the participants of the January 25th meeting but did not get a reply. A year later, three New York Times reporters sympathetic to the UFO issue – William Broad, Maureen Dowd, and Amy Choziak were all contacted. They were presented with the story of Podesta meeting with the two Generals and the head of Area 51 about UFO disclosure. They all passed on looking into the story.

In Ufology, the more things change, the more they remain the same.

Additional Tales

Has the President Been Abducted?

UFO Encounters - More complex than we imagine. **Dr. John Alexander**

Could the move to gradually educate/acclimate people have to do with the fact that the story is much more complicated than could ever be believed and the plan is to bring the population up to speed as much as possible just in case the story breaks or the aliens decide to themselves appear and disclose?

What I have been learning as I dig into the account of the White House and their UFO policies is that this is probably the case. The key intelligence figure behind the DeLonge disclosure initiative has said things that lead me to believe that we are not in charge of the events.

What I was told is that at the highest levels, information is scarce, not because they want to keep it secret but because some of the information would be disturbing to people's beliefs, and because only a small portion of the abilities of the ET intelligence is understood.

Many of those in power have strong Christian beliefs or no religious beliefs at all. Both groups appear to avoid the truth about the subject like the plague, because they do not wish to face the truth. When it comes to Christians inside the intelligence agencies, it is one thing to talk about a grandmother coming back as a ghost and saying hi and something entirely different to say aliens are coming through walls at will, shutting down nuclear weapons and possibly abducting high level government officials, including the president.

The idea that the president, who is the most protected person in the world, may have been abducted presents a clear example of how little control we have to what the aliens decide to do. As unbelievable as it seems, the idea is not that farfetched.

There is substantial evidence that the aliens have the power and have indeed abducted many high-level government officials, including the president, and the source is not the *National Enquirer*. The *National Enquirer*, however, does not do UFO stories and hasn't for probably 30 years.

Two sources tell me that high-ranking officials have been taken. One source indicates that the number of senior government experiencers is around 50. The second source does not mention a specific number but confirms part of what the first source said. Both men stated that these people are all sent to a particular person under contract to the CIA (whose name we know), and that person's job is to interview and determine if the person is mentally unstable or actually interacting with the phenomena.

So, who is on the list?

1. <u>Classified</u>. Retired CIA officer Jim Semivan who, in the mid-1990s had a dramatic nighttime encounter along with his wife.

2. <u>United Nations Secretary General, Javier Perez de Cuellar</u>. De Cuellar appears to be an experiencer. In 1989, he was involved in an abduction experience when the aliens appeared to have taken him from a convoy of cars in the middle of the night in Manhattan.

Two key researchers have researched Cuellar's account and have talked about the incident. The first was Dr. Steven Greer who got his information from Prince Hans-Adam of Liechtenstein. Liechtenstein was participating in high-level negotiations involving Presidents Ronald Reagan and George H.W. Bush, Mikhail Gorbachev (Secretary General of the USSR), along with other world leaders. All were meeting with Perez de Cuellar on the night of the abduction. Greer spoke of what Prince Liechtenstein told him:

> *He said what happened was that Perez de Cuellar ... was coming back from a 3 am late night planning session for this event when he was abducted by aliens from his motorcade in Manhattan ... Perez de Cuellar was taken somehow out of the motorcade onto an ET craft where he was threatened by the ETs and told: If you disclose this information, we will abduct every world leader involved, including the President of the United States.[134]*

Greer, who does not believe that aliens abduct people, interpreted the de Cuellar event as a staged abduction, involving highly classified corporate programs using bioengineered "Programmed Life Forms" (PLFs) designed to look like real extraterrestrials. Greer has stated that the power of these corporate entities to abduct people, is the ultimate "trump card" to control the president, or preventing anyone else in authority from revealing the truth about UFOs. In other words, according to Greer, the military is using fake alien scenarios to prevent the people from having contact with benevolent ETs. "It can be made very clear to them," Greer told Art Bell, "that if they don't play along, the trump card can be played."

The second researcher who worked on the case was prominent abduction researcher, Budd Hopkins. His version of the story tells of a November 30, 1989, incident which occurred in New York City involving Linda Napolitano and her son. Under hypnosis, Linda recalled being abducted from the 12th floor of her apartment building on the lower east side of Manhattan.

Budd Hopkins, who had worked with hundreds of abductees, investigated the case. During the investigation, Hopkins learned that Linda had received correspondence from a man who claimed to have witnessed the abduction.

The man claimed his car had stalled two blocks away and that he and two men with him had seen the whole event about 3:30 in the morning. This man, who wrote Linda and Hopkins about the event, turned out to be the United Nations Secretary General Javier Perez de Cuellar. De Cuellar was in New York City at the time traveling from a heliport into the city with his two security men.

After further investigation, Hopkins determined that Perez de Cuellar was not only a witness but was abducted as well. Backup for this fact came from Linda's son who identified the Secretary General from twenty photos of men shown to him by Hopkins, as the man who was with him and comforted him during the abduction. Hopkins contacted Perez de Cuellar in person about the letters he and Linda had received, and de Cuellar didn't deny his involvement or his having sent the letters.

Hopkins declined to name Perez de Cuellar in his book *Witnessed: The True Story of the Brooklyn Bridge UFO Abductions*, detailing the abductions. "I feel a great deal of pity for him," stated Hopkins.

Later in 1996, de Cuellar, under pressure from NOVA to make his account public, and at that time a private citizen denied being abducted.

3. <u>President Bill Clinton and two of his secret service agents</u>. Researcher Yvonne Smith recounted this story in her book *Coronado: The President, The Secret Service, and Alien Abductions*. The book detailed the abduction of a dozen people from a UFO experiencer conference at the Coronado Hotel in San Diego in 1994, the same weekend that President Bill Clinton was speaking there.

In July 2013, Smith was talking to a source on an unrelated topic who reported to her that, "two of the President's men were missing."

She asked, "For what President?" The answer came back, "Clinton." Smith asked where, and got back the answer, "San Diego." Now realizing that the source was referring to the Coronado abduction incident, she asked, "Was Clinton taken with the two secret service men." The source replied, "Yes." If beings are abducting United States presidents, the full extent of the alien plan cannot even be estimated. We may be like nothing more than movie goers eating popcorn at a movie, which we have no control over, which plays on the screen in front of us.

4. <u>Classified</u>. An unnamed president taken from a press conference. This comes from one of the highest-level sources I have ever come across. The entire press corps was frozen while the president was taken and returned. This apparently was done to send a message to everyone about who is in charge.

The MJ-12 Group

A man is having an affair on his wife with Mary. To keep it secret, he decides to tell his wife that he is having an affair with Jane. That way, she will never discover his relationship with Mary. **This represents the UFO community's present belief that the US government is telling UFO stories to throw people off about the fact they are investigating UFOs.**

In the past month, it has become known that Peter Levenda, a co-author on Tom DeLonge's next book, was told about the Top-Secret MAJIC program that has been rumored for three decades to be at the core of the US government UFO program to investigate, control, and exploit the UFO phenomena.

In the past, few years, two articles were written about it, which sum up the general thinking about MAJIC and the elusive group which controls the UFO secrets, Majestic 12 or MJ-12. One article was written by Alejandro Rojas titled *MJ-12: Is this Legendary UFO Conspiracy U.S. Air Force Disinformation?*[135]

The other article was written by researcher Kevin Randle "MJ-12 The Beginning."[136]

In his article, Randle concluded, "I have said for years that MJ-12 should be relegated to a footnote in the history of UFO studies, but it keeps appearing. I know that Alejandro's piece will not end the debate, but, at least, it comes from a different perspective."

I would reply that the reason the MJ-12 story will not die is that there is a lot of evidence to support it. That is why material keeps popping up thirty-five years after MJ-12 was first mentioned.

It is, however, important to make a distinction between the MJ-12 group which is real, and the MJ-12 document, released by Tim Good in England, and Bill Moore, Jaime Shandera, and Stanton Friedman in the United States. Those documents and probably every other MJ-12 set of documents are not the original documents. One set does not rely on the other for its existence.

The main reason most consider the whole concept of MJ-12 to be a hoax is an almost cult-like belief that Bill Moore and Richard Doty were evil and responsible for many of the ills in Ufology.

The evidence relied on supports the evil Moore and Doty theory surrounds a scientist, Paul Bennewitz, who lived on the edge of Kirkland AFB outside Albuquerque, New Mexico.

Bennewitz reported seeing UFOs over the nuclear weapons held underground at the Manzano Weapons Storage area known as Site Able. The sighting of UFOs is not uncommon over nuclear weapons storage areas and silos. UFOs were at Loring AFB, Minot AFB, Maelstrom AFB, Wurtsmith AFB, and RAF Bentwaters AFB.

The large Manzano facility started out as the presidential emergency relocation center until thermonuclear weapons made the site uninhabitable. Its construction began in June 1947, when flying saucers began to invade the skies of the United States and around the world.

At the time of Bennewitz's sightings, Manzano was the biggest repository of nuclear weapons in the United States.

Richard Doty, a low-level agent in the USAF, was involved in the MJ-12 case for a couple of years.

What was missing from the articles above is any discussion of the evidence for MJ-12, which I have presented in two books and in a recent article which is below. It appears that it is time to publish it again. What is even stranger is that although everyone claims they are reviewing all the evidence, it seems that pre-existing beliefs dominate. No one has ever asked for the name of the declassification officer who told us she had seen an MJ-12 type document before Moore ever talked about it, or the name of the archivist inside the vault at the National Archives who reported to me that he believed MJ-12 documents were handled.

What is stranger yet is that almost every piece of evidence I posted in "Is There a UFO Control Group - New Information" was totally ignored.

In my book, *UFOs, Area 51, and Government Informants* I spent a lot of time looking at the evidence that backed the idea of MJ-12. The idea of MJ-12 started to appear in the early 1980s through a researcher known as Bill Moore. Moore had written a book called the *Roswell Incident* which sold many copies and was the forerunner of the modern obsession with the Roswell crash.

The idea of a group controlling UFO secrets goes back to the Canadian Top Secret document on flying saucers where the Canadians were questioning American officials through the Canadian military liaison attached to the Canadian Embassy in Washington.

The report filed, regarding what they learned through classified channels, indicated that there was a group in control. The document stated that American officials said that flying saucers existed and that that knowledge was the most highly classified subject in the United States, with a small group headed up by President Roosevelt's science advisor, Vannevar Bush, looking at the modus operandi of the flying saucers.

Days after Moore released the book, US intelligence contacted him and started to feed him information by both USAF master sergeant Richard Doty and a second person attached to the CIA whom Bill Moore named the Falcon. Later, ten more intelligence sources would come forward to provide information to Moore. Some of these may have been ex-CIA directors (Gates and Helms).

The Moore involvement with the MJ-12 story culminated in a document release made in 1987 by Moore and two other researchers by the names of Jaime Shandera and Stanton Friedman. The paper released and marked "Top Secret Restricted," purported to be a briefing document presented to then President-elect Dwight Eisenhower about the 12-person group made up of high level scientists and military officials who made up the elite Top Secret MJ-12 committee.

In *UFOs, MJ-12 and Government Informants,* I expressed my belief that the leaked document was a mix of real and false material that had been authorized by the present-day MJ-12-type group to desensitize the public about how the White House had handled the flying saucer problem.

I also wrote that although some of the material in the document did not appear to be correct (like the failure to mention that there was a live alien recovered at Roswell), there was lots of evidence indicating this mythical MJ-12 group referred to in the document existed. The reason for altering the document was to avoid breaking the law by leaking classified material, and to protect the overall UFO program that needed to remain classified. The evidence indicating that there was an MJ-12 group included the following items:

• Tim Good received an independent copy of the MJ-12 document in England, and he stated he did not get it from either Bill Moore or Richard Doty. Good had contact with a lot of high level people in the United States, including President Carter's CIA director Stansfield Turner. He talked about many things with Turner including MJ-12. "I corresponded at some length with Admiral Stansfield Turner, Director of the CIA (DCI) from 1977 to 1981, and asked him several times if he was aware of a Majestic-12 group. The MJ-12 question is the only one he refrained from responding to."[137]

• My co-author T. Scott Crain had come across a woman (USAF NCO) who had been on a 1979 declassification team in Okinawa, Japan. While declassifying documents in a general's office, the team came across a report that she told us may not have been the same document but appeared to contain all the same material. This woman was hassled when in 1991 we released the book *UFOs, MJ-12, and the Government*.

• Ann Eller, who worked as an assistant for J. Allen Hynek, the scientific consultant for the USAF investigation into UFOs called Project Blue Book, said that she came across an MJ-12 document in Hynek's files. "In my spare time, I would look through Hynek's UFO files, pull out a case and read it," Eller wrote, "many of the official documents were a disappointment as there would be a title, date, and the rest was redacted. In one file, in the middle, the lines of black ink blotting out the best information, was a list of MJ-12 members."[138] Eller believed that the names included a couple of generals and Brzezinski.

• In conversations with the former President of Penn State University, Dr. Eric Walker, he confirmed the MJ-12 group. His first confirmation came in 1987 just days after Moore made the MJ-12 document public. Walker said, "Yes, I know of MJ-12. I have known of them for 40 years. I believe that you're chasing after and fighting with windmills!!"

• Moya Lear, the wife of Lear Jet inventor Bill Lear, phoned her friend four-star General James Doolittle to ask if the group had existed. Doolittle confirmed the group had existed but said that is all he could say. She was prodded to do this by her son John Lear who had just become aware of the MJ-12 document.

- Edgar Mitchell, the Commander of Apollo 14, is another high-level person who confirmed that the group MJ-12 did exist based on sources he had.
- General Arthur E. Exon, who was at Wright Field in 1947 when the alien bodies arrived following the Roswell crash site, said he "was aware of a UFO controlling committee made up primarily of very high-ranking military officers and intelligence people." He did not know the name of the group but called them the "Unholy Thirteen."
- In July 1989, Bob Oeschler provided some of the most dramatic evidence supporting the existence of a group known as MJ-12. The first material came during a brief meeting in May 1988, with Admiral Bobby Ray Inman, Deputy Director of the CIA (DDCI) from 1981 to 1982, and director of Naval Intelligence as well as of the National Security Agency. The event took place at a ground-breaking ceremony for the National Security Agency's new supercomputer facility for the Institute for Defense Analyses, of which Inman was a former director. It was there that Inman indirectly acknowledged the existence of 'MJ-12.'

Later, in 1989, on behalf of Tim Good, Lord Hill-Norton and myself, Oeschler tape-recorded a conversation on the MJ-12 subject with Bobby Ray Inman. Inman stated that MJ-12 meant something to him, and that "he has been aware of a program to 'indoctrinate the public' in UFO matters prior to his retirement," and that he had "some expertise" in the area of UFOs, but his information was out of date at the time of the conversation.

When asked, "Do you anticipate that any of the recovered vehicles would ever become available for technological research - outside of the military circles?" Admiral Inman responded, "I honestly don't know. Ten years ago the answer would have been no. Whether as time has evolved they are beginning to become more open on it, there's a possibility..."[139]

The subject appeared on the agenda of things to discuss at the UFO Working Group (Advanced Physics Theoretical Working Group) headed up by Dr. John Alexander. The document in my possession did not show anything, indicating it was on the agenda, but had not yet been discussed.

NAME OF FACILITY(IES) TO BE VISITED: BDM McLean Secure Facility 7915 Jonesbrook Rd. McLean, VA 22102		FOR THE INCLUSIVE DATES 20-25 May 1985	DOE Security Officer Verifying DOE Clearance
FOR THE PURPOSE OF: ADVANCE THEORETICAL PHYSICS CONFERENCE (20-25 May 1985)			
TO CONFER WITH THE FOLLOWING PERSON(S): Special Security Officer			
SPECIFIC INFORMATION TO WHICH ACCESS IS REQUESTED: TOP SECRET/RESTRICTED DATA SIGMAS AS REQUIRED			Access requested to: Restricted Data ☐Yes ☐No Other classified info ☐Yes ☐No
Prior arrangements have/have not been made as follows:			

Figure 12 Verification of Top Secret Advance Theoretical Physics Working Group

Finally, in records I recovered at the University of Arizona, I confirmed the story told by Dr. Steven Greer that Goldwater had promised to set up a meeting in 1994 for Greer to talk to Bobby Ray Inman, whom he knew well.

• Another person who gave some confirmation to the existence of MJ-12 was an archivist at the National Archives in College Park, Maryland, who approached me after a lecture in Eureka Springs, Arkansas in 2005. His job was to declassify documents for release, which meant that he worked right inside the classified vault and saw all government documents before their release. He stated that a colleague had reported seeing documents with the MJ-12 designator on them years before doing declassification on Joint Chiefs of Staff documents. I introduced this man to researcher Ryan Wood who flew to Washington to meet with the archivist.

• Harold Stuart, a former member of the Truman administration. He was a member of an advisory committee for MJ-12 in Robert Collins' 2005 book *Exempt from Disclosure*. In replies to a letter from researcher Brian Parks, Stuart stated, "I have a vague recollection of MJ-12, but not significantly specific to make a comment... I was not on the MJ-12 Advisory Board and only have a faint recollection of this project or group. I did know most of the Generals you mentioned in your letter, but sorry I cannot shed any light on your request."

• US Commander Willard Miller, the principal military advisor to Steven Greer, stated that in 1996, he, Greer, and Edgar Mitchell had a meeting with the head of intelligence for the Joint Chiefs of Staff, Admiral Tom Wilson. During that meeting, Greer mentioned MJ-12. When the meeting had ended, an aide to the Admiral stopped Miller as he was leaving the office:

> As I was leaving the Admiral aide turned to me and said, you know the subject of majestic – MJ-12 came up and there has been a lot of debate as to whether that is real or every existed, and he said, "You know.

We know that it exists. We here at the intelligence directorate at the Joint Staff just don't have the need to know what they do."[140]

• Researcher Lee Graham wrote many letters and filed dozens of FOIA requests to try and validate the MJ-12 document. On May 24, 1990, the Defense Investigative Service (DIS) responded to one of Graham's FOIA requests by sending him back a copy of the MJ-12 document, each page of which was stamped "UNCLASSIFIED" across the lower part of the page. This stamp indicated that the document had been declassified. Graham was never able to obtain clarification on who had done the declassification.

• Dr. Steven Greer has made many countless claims that he has sources and documents that confirm the existence of MJ-12. He even claims he was offered an in to the group but turned it down.

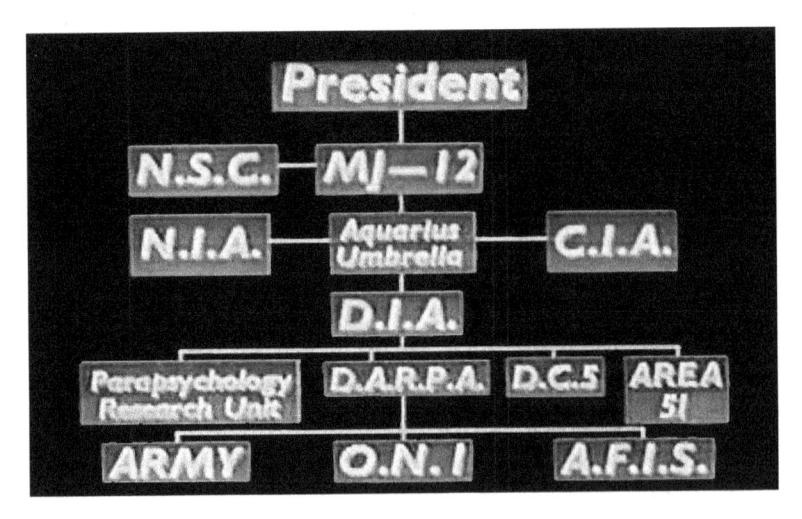

• In a 1987 letter written by John Andrews to his good friend Lockheed Skunk Works President Ben Rich, Andrews stated that he had known of MJ-12 for years "even though officially it didn't exist." In discussions with Lee Graham, he said he had heard of MJ-12 in early 1984, which was almost a year before researchers Moore and Shandera reviewed copies of the MJ-12 briefing documents for President Eisenhower that they received in the mail.

• In October 1988, a couple weeks before the presidential election, a documentary was broadcast by Fox, and produced by Grey Advertising out of New York. In the documentary, a flowchart is shown of the UFO investigation by United States government agencies and MJ-12 is listed.

• Mr. Peter Levenda, co-author with Tom DeLonge on their book *Sekret Machines: Gods: An official investigation of the UFO Phenomenon* was told about MAJIC by a NASA official and provided documentation. Levenda said:

> *"I talked to someone who was deeply embedded in the space program who openly talked to me about a program called MAJIC that existed. It was a real thing. I can't use it yet. I am looking for corroboration because this guy won't let me come out and use his name, and the documentation I got from him."*[141]

Since the release of the book in January 2013, two new pieces of evidence have surfaced confirming the existence of MJ-12.

The first piece of new evidence came from Jesse Marcel Jr., the son of the intelligence officer at the Roswell Army Air Base that handled the remains of the July 1947 UFO crash.

At the May 2013 Citizen's Hearing on Disclosure in Washington, D.C., Marcel stated that some years ago he was called to Washington D.C. by Dick D'Amato for a meeting in a secure room in the Senate Building. D'Amato was chief counsel and chief investigator for Senator Robert Byrd's Senate Appropriations Committee.

When the Area 51 story broke in 1989 in Nevada, Byrd and other Senators on the committee (responsible for all budget spending) wondered if they were in fact financing back-engineering of flying saucers at Area 51 without being told what they were paying for. D'Amato was provided the appropriate security clearances and sent to investigate.

D'Amato confirmed the alien projects but was not able to penetrate them. He told Steven Greer, "I've been asked by Senator Byrd and some others to look into these things, and we've gotten close enough to know that these projects do exist. But I'm telling you that with a Top-Secret clearance and a subpoena power from the Senate Appropriations Committee, I cannot penetrate those projects. You're dealing with the varsity team of all black projects, so watch out. And good luck."[142]

Marcel stated that he and D'Amato met around a huge conference room table. On the table was a book written by Whitley Strieber

243

called *Majestic*, which is about the Roswell crash and MJ-12, the group established to deal with the extraterrestrial appearance on earth. D'Amato said, "I want to tell you something. This (pointing to the book) is not fiction."

Marcel asked, "When are you going to tell the public?"

D'Amato replied, talking about MJ-12, "If it were up to me I'd have done it yesterday, but it is not up to me. I am just here to investigate the cost of keeping it secret. In reality, there is a black government. They have control of the debris. They answer to no one, and they are not elected. They have unlimited money to spend. They are the ones who have control over it."

The second piece of new evidence came from Dr. John Alexander.

In a June 15, 2013, interview with radio show host Nancy Du Tertre, Alexander suddenly announced that the MJ-12 group had existed.[143]

This is the transcript of the interaction:

> ***Alexander:*** *I think that there actually was a group and they have created something known as COG – continuity of government – and it was to prevent nuclear decapitation of the United States. It was really super super sensitive.*
> ***Nancy du Tertre:*** *Well let me ask you this. Does MJ-12 as far as you know exist today?*
> ***Alexander:*** *I don't think so. I had someone whisper to me that it had existed. I didn't think it had existed at all, but when I looked into it and asked if the names were correct, and they said yes and that should tell me what I need to know to figure it out. That's how we came up with this particular occupation because most of them were into nuclear warfare. That was one common thread of all the people on the list, and much more so certainly than with UFOs.*[144]

The continuity of government that Alexander believed was behind the MJ-12 group was located at Mount Weather. Although Alexander has never referred to who it was that whispered in his ear, it appears now that there is a good chance Alexander's source was associated with the continuity of government plan and/or worked at Mount

Weather, and this leads us to Robert Kupperman, who was a friend of Alexander's.

As former Executive Director of the Office of Emergency Preparedness and Transition Director at the FEMA, Kupperman would have been at the center of the Continuity of Government.

The two men had, according to Alexander, discussed UFOs but according to Alexander's book, it was not on the organization's radar.

Alexander repeated his claim during a panel at the 2014 UFO Congress that was moderated by Alejandro Rojas. I asked John Alexander to identify the high-level source who had confirmed the existence of MJ-12 and the names on the MJ-12 documents. Alexander evaded an answer but again confirmed he was told MJ-12 was for real and that the names on the MJ-12 documents released by Good, Friedman, Shandera, and Moore were accurate.

Even though Alexander's opinion differed from that of the group controlling the UFO secrets, the significance of what Alexander said cannot be under emphasized. MJ-12 existed, and the names that appeared in the UFO documents that appeared on a film in the mailbox of Jamie Shandera in 1984 were correct.

To add weight to the story, Alexander being told about the connection of MJ-12 to the continuity of government is important as it relates to the account relayed by Paul Hellyer, former Deputy Prime Minister of Canada, and Minister of National Defense.

At an event in Brantford, Ontario in June 2016, Hellyer stated that one additional person in Ottawa who would know about MJ-12 would be the Chief of Emergency Measures, who heads the Canadian equivalent of Alexander's source at Mount Weather. Hellyer stated:

> The reason I know is that I interviewed the previous one, that the previous one who is now deceased. He went to Langley, and the CIA asked him if he wanted to see one of these craft. They flew him to Area 51 and let him go inside one. He was allowed to make notes and all these sort of things, I guess so he could be in a better position if one of these things crashed here, and he was involved in trying to do something positive about it. Before he was allowed to go, he had to sign an oath of secrecy and not tell anyone, and he didn't in his life tell anyone including his wife. An Air Force buddy phoned me and told me he was dying of Lou

Gehrig's disease, and at that point he thought he should tell someone. I made an appointment with him and my buddy phoned me up and told me "You better get in touch with him right away because he is right on the edge."

I phoned him and he gave me a full report of what he saw and the whole idea of the inside of the craft, and this sort of thing, along with the fact that he had been briefed. He felt that he could now tell, and I would be a good one to tell.

Such is the evidence supporting the existence of MJ-12, which manages or administers the investigation of the UFO phenomena and the technology recovered and reversed-engineered from UFO crashes.

Are all the witnesses I have referred to lying or deluded for believing what seems like the impossible? I think it is safe to say that those who reject all the officials who have talked about this phenomenon suddenly start sounding like they are the ones who are deluded.

Is it possible that the United States government formed a special control group to oversee the biggest discovery of all time following the recovery of extraterrestrial craft and surviving alien(s) at Roswell?

It is possible but not highly likely.

A Plan for Accelerated Acclimatization

It was Ron Pandolfi who told me, in 1991, that the U.S. Government had a phenomenology problem. This was the first time that I had heard this word in that context. And I very distinctly remember telling him that he probably would regret having used that particular word. Feel free to ask him, if he does so regret. **Dan Smith speaking about his CIA official friend Pandolfi.**

You may not be sane, but you certainly are honest. **Ronald Pandolfi to Dan Smith January 18, 2017.**

Although sometimes acting in the capacity of the insane, Mr. Smith is very clever, capable, and well informed. **Ron Pandolfi**

It all started with a January 5, 2017, email from Ron Pandolfi to Robert Collins, a former scientist in engineering physics with the Air Force at Wright Patterson Air Force Base.
In a Facebook post, Collins wrote:

> *From Ron Pandolfi (friend, got me interviewed by the CIA in 1992) at the National Intelligence Directorate on Trump & UFOs.*
>
> *01/05/2017 They may be anticipating some action. I have been waiting for President-Elect Trump to take office before taking more serious actions. He is very "pro-disclosure" and very anti "disinformation."*
>
> *Ronald Pandolfi, Ph.D.*
> *Director, TACP-Network*
> *Kashmir-Robotics, a division of Kashmir World Foundation*

As described in the section 1991, Ron Pandolfi, the head scientist and head of the UFO desk at the CIA, started feeding UFO material to his close friend Dan Smith. It was an arrangement Smith reported to authorities and which became the focus of a six-month internal investigation.

When the investigation was completed, Pandolfi "was able to convince them (government investigators) that his communication with Smith fell within his official purview."[145]

Smith's almost daily conversation with the man seen by many to be the key UFO advice-giver to the White House, places Smith as a key person to watch.

This relationship is especially important because Smith tells it as he sees it. An example of Smith's independence was when he did not hesitate to report Pandolfi to the FBI in Boston when 911 happened. His report to the FBI included the fact that Pandolfi had told him before 911 that the attack would take place.

Researcher Gary Bekkum, who has chased the connection between the intelligence community and the UFO subject, explained the arrangement between the two men:

> *By associating himself with Dan Smith, Pandolfi was able to develop an 'implausible and deniable' means of injecting information onto the Internet. Once released, the information was easily tracked: Persons of interest could be monitored, and when, as was often the case, they interacted with foreign nationals concerning topics of interest to Pandolfi, they could exploit for passive intelligence collection.*[146]

Although Pandolfi openly stated that UFOs are used to collect information, it sounds more like a cover story than the truth. Why would Pandolfi bother deceiving Dan Smith who had only six followers on *Open Minds Forum?*

Smith took what Pandolfi told him and developed an eschatological theory called the best possible world hypothesis (BPWH).

Smith's linking of the UFO material into a religious worldview caused the entire UFO research community to entirely ignore his close 26-year relationship with the top UFO guy at the CIA, and the almost daily reports of what he has learned at the *Open Minds Forum.*

In an interview with Bekkum, Smith talked a bit about the bottom line of what he had learned from Pandolfi:

> *Our present worldview is dominated by modernism or scientific materialism, which has been very inimical to every spiritual tradition. I labor under the impression that not only is the paradigm of scientific materialism vulnerable, but, in fact, there are quite a few individuals, more or less associated with the international intelligence community, who have very specific information concerning ongoing phenomena which, when considered as whole, would shatter what we commonly refer to as the modern scientific worldview. The only problem is how best to disclose the information to the rest of the world ...*
>
> *I am claiming that I have sufficient, semi-privileged information to puncture the very fragile structure that constitutes scientific materialism, and that, were you to care about saving humanity, I could, at the very least, point you in the right direction. Is this an offer that we can afford to refuse? How do we wish to look this gift-horse in the mouth?*[147]

In May 2015, Smith wrote about hints he had gotten from Pandolfi about a lack of leadership and possible players. This revelation is one of the hundreds of posts he has made about what Pandolfi told him about the UFO problem:

> *I'm having a hard time believing that our ship is quite so rudderless, as Ron wishes to make out. Finally, we have the NSC, DNI and MJ12, each, according to Ron, having abdicated, in its own way. And/or he is providing cover for one or more of them. We also may have the ONI as a quasi-independent actor. That gives us four possible actors.*
>
> *He does point to the problem and necessity of compartmenting the information. He suggests that it is mainly a spontaneous process, however.*
>
> *If anyone is left in charge, it would be a handful of independent actors like Ron, no one of whom may have sufficient information to precipitate a pre-emptive Disclosure. How might they get it together,*

and under what auspices? Will it be event driven, finally, or will someone rise to the leadership challenge?

Was Trump Briefed?

....

It is CIA's mission to provide the President with the best intelligence possible and to explain the basis for that intelligence. The CIA does not, has not, and will never hide intelligence from the President, period. **Trump CIA Director Mike Pompeo**

Pandolfi's email to Collins indicated the UFO subject had been raised and Trump's interested in disclosure made no sense based on what was known about Trump at the time. He had never spoken about or showed any interest in the UFO subject.

During his campaign in January 2016, when Trump was in a crowd signing hats and posters, a man is yelling at him for over 30 seconds "What are you going to do about UFOs" "Has anything crossed your desk?" "UFO files - when are you going to disclose?" Trump ignored him.

The other thing that indicated Trump was not interested appeared in a tweet by Maureen Dowd, a reporter for *The New York Times*, in May 2016.

Dowd had an interest in UFOs. She had written an article called "We're Not Alone" in 1997.[148] In that article, she talked about the stupidity of the explanation that the Air Force put out to explain the 1947 Roswell crash:

> *Klaatu Barada Nikto. Or as we say in our galaxy, get a grip. The Roswell report will settle the debate over aliens about as well as the Warren report settled the debate over the single-bullet theory.*

It may have been her straight up article that led John Podesta to copy Dowd on his now famous February 2015 tweet the day he was leaving the Obama White House that his "biggest disappointment of 2014" was once again not getting disclosure on UFOs.

When Hillary Clinton made three mentions of the fact that she would disclose as much of the UFO secret as she could when she became president, *The New York Times* did a straight piece on May 10,

2016, discussing the Hillary UFO disclosure promise and what it might mean.

At the same time, Dowd questioned Trump on Hillary's promise. The answer she got back was not indicative of Trump being the disclosure president. Trump responded to the question by saying he was not interested.

Lastly, Trump seems embedded in a materialistic worldview, which seems opposed to the messages received by experiencers in the UFO field. Dan Smith heard this from Pandolfi:

> *Just looking at Donald. I see no indication that he is contemplating any sort of pivot with respect to scientism. My only source is a professional disinformer.[149]*

It was this list of putdowns made by Trump that made me wonder what had changed as evidenced in the Pandolfi email to Collins.

When Pandolfi sent his January 2017 Trump email to Collins, I contacted a series of people who knew Pandolfi. I wanted to find out if the president-elect had received a UFO briefing, and if Pandolfi was once again seeding the UFO community with information. I wanted to see if there was going to be another gradual disclosure initiative, and how what Pandolfi was doing might be tied into what DeLonge was doing.

Two of the people I talked to had nothing to add. Dan Smith, however, stated that he had been talking about it on *Open Minds Forum* and that I should contact him by phone.

The call to Smith took place on January 19, 2017, the day before the Trump inauguration. Smith was eager to talk.

I mentioned to Smith that based on the history, I was puzzled at the Pandolfi statement regarding Trump being pro-UFO disclosure and that I had written an article on it (see Appendix 7 for Trump and the ETs). I stated that the ideals of the ET intelligence behind the UFO phenomena and Trump's ideals seemed as opposed as black and white. Smith said he was just reading my article.

The Smith Interview

....

The USG (US Government) is obligated to both Gordon (Novel) and me. He and I are part of what Ron (Pandolfi) calls the USG outreach. Is this Operation Outreach? We don't have a need to know that. But, Ron is obliged, officially, to keep us off the streets, from begging. **Dan Smith 2009**

I tell people Ron Pandolfi gets paid to tell us lies. **Dan Smith speaking about Pandolfi.**

Here are the highlights of my January 19, 2017, interview with Smith. Please note that Smith posted much of this on *Open Minds Forum*.

I asked Smith if Trump had received a briefing on the UFO story and he answered yes. In a later conversation, Smith informed me that Stephen Bassett, a UFO lobbyist, had phoned Pandolfi and that Pandolfi had denied doing a briefing on UFOs with President Trump.

I initiated my question after many Smith postings indicating some briefing had taken place.

- Smith had gotten the impression from Pandolfi that Trump had been picked to be the disclosure president. Even when Hillary appeared that she would win, Smith was led to believe there would be a September surprise, which would involve Hillary resigning.
- The material he has received in the last two months is more than the last 26 years of talking to Pandolfi. Smith added that it could all go away tomorrow.
- The best description for the material is unbelievable, and he doubted that any major newspaper would print it.
- He stated that in December 2016, Pandolfi had met with Trump every day. He reminded me that UFOs were not the only thing that Pandolfi was doing for the agency (one figure puts his UFO work at 20% of his daily time).
- Smith stated that during the campaign there had been two briefing teams, one for Clinton and one for Trump.

- Smith told me he believed there were two teams briefing Trump. One team was a hardware team (assumed to be equipment and technology) described by Smith to be more of an MJ-12 type group. On January 16, 2017, Smith also posted this on the *Open Minds Forum* and included the name of former .com executive, Joe Firmage:

    > *Ron and I were able to converse occasionally during the lunch. He spoke of two consulting teams or networks, relative to Trump. I would assume that these could also be viewed as intelligence briefing teams. The larger group is not in favor of disclosure. It was not otherwise discussed. The smaller group that includes him also includes Jim W and Mike P who is formerly of net assessments. Mike is going to visit with Joe Firmage, who has been working on an electrogravitics project, with government sponsorship, for the past ten years. These two are not aware of the portal project, while Jim is.*

- The second team being a software group (assumed to be involved in assessing who the visitors are, the implications, and how to deal with the public – disclosure or cover-up).
- Trump said he was tired and didn't want to talk anymore with the hardware team. The software team was the larger of the two groups.
- The software team included Ron Pandolfi, James Woolsey, and Mike Pillsbury (there may have been others).
- At the same time, a member of the software team, Woolsey (CIA Director for Bill Clinton and intelligence advisor to Trump during the campaign), said he didn't want to be on a briefing team if they weren't doing any actual briefings.
- The software team pulled out as well.
- Asked if they are they still in contact with Trump, Smith replied, "I don't know. Before I went on the cruise (two weeks) through the Panama Canal, he (Pandolfi) said he was talking to Trump every day. He has not repeated that statement since the cruise."
- A plan had been set up by Pandolfi to make the pod public to the media in September 2015, in what Smith described as a September surprise. Smith stated that the announcement wasn't made because

the government wanted more acclimatization as opposed to full disclosure.

DeLonge's Big Man

....

Then came the most important part of the interview where I talked to Smith about another CIA officer in the UFO business. I mentioned the name of the intelligence official who was in charge of DeLonge's disclosure program, Jim Semivan. The man had been referred to as the Big Man.

Smith said he had never heard of the Big Man. He stated that he had only had one source over the years – his buddy Ron.

I asked Smith about his account of talking to Senator Chris Straub on the Senate intelligence committee. They sat in a secure room at the Capitol about the government UFO program, and Smith confirmed he had three meetings with Straub.

Smith confirmed this and that he didn't learn anything other than being told there was a program, and the situation was handled by very qualified people.

I asked Smith if he could mention the Big Man's name to Pandolfi and Smith said he couldn't. He said his method wasn't to ask Ron questions or request details, but that he listened whenever Pandolfi decided to share something with him.

We talked about the CIA official in charge of the team advising DeLonge (the Big Man), and I brought up that the Big Man was an experiencer, with he and his wife having an encounter in their bedroom in the 1990s. The Big Man allegedly went to Pandolfi, who was the CIA expert on such matters and asked him what was going on.

"You are not cleared to know," was allegedly Pandolfi's reply.

It is not clear what the officer did, but his reply to Pandolfi indicated some level of power. "I'm not cleared to know?" was his apparent response.

He did get briefed, and was told that hopefully it was a "one off" -- a one-time experience. If this were the case, he should just let it go. If he wanted to pursue the issue, he got a warning that the move would not be career enhancing.

He apparently decided to continue it, because two decades later the Big Man was in charge of perhaps the biggest UFO disclosure initiative the government would ever try and pull off.

Now Smith was interested in this CIA official and started to ask questions. I had never talked to the Big Man and couldn't answer Smith's questions. I had just heard people talk about him and figured out who he was on my own. Smith saw this as an opportunity to get a second source inside the agency to confirm my account.

True to his word, he posted our conversation on *Open Minds Forum* and included Semivan's name.

Not knowing he was going to do this, I became a bit panicked when I saw the post, and now DeLonge's senior intelligence official was exposed. I did nothing as I figured not many would catch that bit of info, as few people read the *Open Minds Forum.*

However, it was clear that Smith had mentioned our conversation to Pandolfi. Half of the posting about our conversation was gone and in its place, was a message from Pandolfi:

> *Please remove and then stop posting false information about me from loons.*

Smith posted, "...Roger, Wilco]," and removed the offending post. The post about our conversation was edited by Smith five times.

The loon reference didn't mean much as Pandolfi has at one time or another has called every researcher a loon, crazy, or a maniac.

A couple of years back there was a big event in Philadelphia where many of the key UFO and paranormal researchers from around the country gathered. Pandolfi's comment then was that half the wackos from around the country had gathered. Reportedly, when I published my book, *UFOs, MJ-12, and Government Informants* Pandolfi commented that - Grant Cameron, like Dan Smith, makes up stuff.

It was not the first time that Pandolfi had ordered Smith to remove material from the *Open Minds Forum* discussion group. As a matter of fact, only a couple of days before, Smith had posted a letter he had gotten from Pandolfi. That letter "Letter from Gordon to R. James" was from the late Gordon Novel requesting funds for his Replicated Alien Machine RAM project – a back-engineered UFO.

Names mentioned in the letter included James Woolsey and Joe Firmage. Smith took the letter down and on Wed, January 18, 2017, at 9:55 pm, wrote:

> *I'm very sorry, and you may well not believe it, but in my haste to open the document you sent me, below, I actually overlooked your parenthetical*

instructions. I just now noticed them, and quickly removed the offending document, and my references to it.

I'm sure, though, that some damage has already been done. In addition to the blog, I did discuss Gordon's letter with Steve Bassett on the telephone.

I hope I've learned my lesson.... to be more careful in the future.

Dan

After I saw Pandolfi's post on the forum, I talked with Smith who said Pandolfi said there was no truth to anyone pulling rank.

I told Smith that Pandolfi's reaction was likely due to his protecting sources and methods, as he could never confirm an officer, let alone his involvement in UFOs. Smith agreed.

I could have produced a picture of Semivan, and at least one reference that he was CIA, but all it would do is expose him, and that was not my intent. Either the material I had collected was wrong, or it was correct and prompted Pandolfi to request its immediate removal from the forum.

This incident did nothing to move the ball down the field. However, the incident did indicate an apparent disconnect between the DeLonge's government contacts, confirmed in the WikiLeaks emails, and the material Smith was getting from Pandolfi.

It appeared Smith had no idea about the DeLonge disclosure effort. The question arose: How could Smith be so close to the center of the hurricane and not know that the head of Lockheed Skunk Works, an intelligence officer, NASA people, and two generals were involved in UFO disclosure?

Instead of being told about this, Smith was told about a portal and a box of future technology materials Trump had access to, which Smith called a goodie bag. Supposedly he could use items in the box to show to the captains of industry. It now appeared there were two looming disclosure initiatives.

The DeLonge story was many times bigger, and Smith didn't seem to know anything about it. I wrote Smith and asked him why he was not aware of this significant disclosure effort if he was so close to the CIA expert on the subject.

Smith got a second denial from Pandolfi who conveyed that a second officer was not working on a UFO disclosure operation. Smith suggested that I withdraw the story as it evidently was not true.

I replied showing an Instagram that DeLonge had posted saying, "Sometimes, I would be up late at night, sending messages back-and-forth to people within the CIA and DOD, discussing the best way to position certain information within the *Sekret Machines* novel."[150] I asked Smith, "Is DeLonge lying?"

In a second email, I attached another article from *Rolling Stone* where DeLonge stated he is getting help and direction from U.S. intelligence. I notified Smith that I had never talked to DeLonge, which would mean that my three sources to the intelligence connection were independent of his.

The reply from Smith was stunning. It appeared Smith confronted Pandolfi with DeLonge's claim that he was working with the CIA:

> *It appears that the specific encounter of this officer with Ron was a fiction.*

The reply indicated that Pandolfi had denied knowing Semivan, and the story of his experience.

There was suddenly a confirmation that an officer inside the CIA was working with Tom DeLonge on a UFO disclosure project, and it wasn't Pandolfi.

In other conversations, Smith describes the upcoming disclosure as "the mother of all paradigm shifts" where the "hypothesis of scientific materialism is about to collapse."

Smith believes he is playing a role in this latest attempt to get disclosure. If he isn't, Pandolfi certainly wanted him to think he is.

On the evening of January 18, two days before the election, Smith reported about waiting to brief Mike Pillsbury about what he refers to as the Princess and the Pod. This Pandolfi story involved a discovered pod (Stargate) and stated Pandolfi's wife Aliyah "has some control on access to the pod/portal, although the portal itself is government property."[151] According to Smith, Pandolfi had twice traveled through the pod:

> *So, there I was, in my car near the Beltway, awaiting directions from Ron (Pandolfi) as to where to meet with Mike. There was an exchange of communication between various other third parties,*

> *and the consensus was that I should return to home base, which I did.*[152]

It was just like all the other disclosure moves of the last 70 years, a small move forward and then a large unexpected move back.

In a second conversation, after the inauguration, Smith informed me that he received notification that he might be going to the White House on Pandolfi's coattails to talk to Trump. The period mentioned was January 30 to February 3. He also posted this news on *Open Minds Forum*:

> *There is a rumor that I should be expecting a call from south of here... There was no such rumor, previously. Am I to be gratified or wary? There is a political black hole, gaping. Does truth need political support, especially from such partisanship? Can truth look a gift horse in the mouth?... Footmann (Pandolfi) has claimed that at one point he was supporting Bernie. I have no proof of that. I don't have any explanation of why he sees disclosure as such a political issue, in the first place.*[153]

I asked him if he would be briefing Trump on his "Best Possible World" hypothesis and he said: "I guess so." He was afraid to get dragged into a political situation and thought that maybe he should try and talk to Podesta to make it bipartisan. This never happened.

Later, after our call, Smith posted again about the conversations Pandolfi had with Trump and how that compared to other presidents.

> *Ron attempts to reassure me that this is not politics as usual. There is a lot more going on behind the scenes. I have little choice in my new found, strange bedfellows. If anyone wants to be above politics, the best place for that is up in the sky.*
>
> *He claims to have been close with Obama, and at least one of the Georges. I'm speculating that he did not get it on with either of the Clintons. He says that as Donald gradually gets around to charting his own course, the Republicans and Democrats will join in their opposition. And that he is not interested in getting re-elected, and following the polls. Ron's nightmare is that Mike Pence might have to take*

> over (e.g. if Donald gets impeached over disclosure?) And so it goes.... And, yes, they have had lengthy discussions on the deep stuff... if you can believe it... I'm not sure I can.[154]

As March 2017 arrived, Smith was telling me that a disclose date would be no later than August, and that the process was ahead of schedule.

He stated that Aliyah Malik Pandolfi had talked to Trump. She is the wife of magician #13, Ron Pandolfi. All of this briefing had to do with a portal that would play a role in disclosure. Smith wrote on March 3:

> *And about that August deadline........ I suggest that we attempt to bring this sucker in by April Fools Day. Yes?...Could we pull this off without the explicit/public approval/confirmation of the President? That's the challenge. We will try to.*
>
> *We would likely need the private cooperation of the President. Quite likely, he doesn't trust us either. We rely on the Princess (Aliyah) to surmount that hurdle.*
>
> *And the Princess has given her tentative approval to April Fools Day for this...... 'disclosure'.*

Sounds like a crazy idea except for two things.

First, Smith is very close to Pandolfi who is closely tied to whatever the government knows about UFOs, and Smith has reported things from Pandolfi that later turned out to be a lie.

Second, at the same time Smith was saying this, I got an independent Facebook message from Adrian Boniardi in Hollywood who thought there was going to be a gradual disclosure leak of information about UFOs. The leak connected to a new TV show called *Counterpart,* and had to do with a portal. The coincidence and timing were overwhelming. Boniardi wrote:

> *More drip? Keep an eye on this show when it comes up sometime this year. It promises to be very interesting of the kind of 'Fringe'.*
>
> *I've worked on it these last couple of days and the storyline seems interesting.*

> "A U.N (United Nations) employee discovers that in the place where he works at (somewhere in Germany) they're hiding an inter-dimensional portal."

As synchronicity would have it, someone recently brought to my attention that Twin Peaks (2017) features a portal into an alternate dimension, with the portal being kept under guard at a New York City skyscraper owned by a mysterious billionaire.

Trump and the UFO Portal
....

Their separate components have to be assembled to function properly. This function had something to do with a portal. **Dan Smith**

On the evening of January 18, 2017, two days before Trump's inauguration, Smith reported about waiting to brief presidential briefer Mike Pillsbury about what he refers to as the Princess and the Pod. This Pandolfi story involved a discovered pod (Stargate) which Pandolfi's wife Aliyah "has some control on access to the pod/portal, although the portal itself is government property."[155] According to Smith, Pandolfi had twice traveled through the pod, and that it would require people at both ends of the portal to activate it:

> So, there I was, in my car near the Beltway, awaiting directions from Ron (Pandolfi) as to where to meet with Mike. There was an exchange of communication between various of the third parties, and the consensus was that I should return to home base, which I did.[156]

It was just like all the other disclosure moves of the last 70 years, a small move forward and then a large unexpected move back.

In a second conversation, after the inauguration, Smith informed me that he received notification that he might be going to the White House on Pandolfi's coattails to talk to Trump. The period mentioned was January 30 to February 3. He also posted this news on *Open Minds Forum*:

> *There is a rumor that I should be expecting a call from south of here... There was no such rumor, previously. Am I to be gratified or wary? There is a political black hole, gaping. Does truth need political support, especially from such partisanship? Can truth look a gift horse in the mouth?... Footmann (Pandolfi) has claimed that at one point he was supporting Bernie. I have no proof of that. I don't have any explanation of why he sees disclosure as such a political issue, in the first place.* [157]

I asked him if he would be briefing Trump on his "Best Possible World" hypothesis and he said: "I guess so." He was afraid to get dragged into a political situation and thought that maybe he should try and talk to Podesta to make it bipartisan. This never happened.

Later, after our call, Smith posted again about the conversations Pandolfi had with Trump and how that compared to other presidents.

> *Ron attempts to reassure me that this is not politics as usual. There is a lot more going on behind the scenes. I have little choice in my new found, strange bedfellows. If anyone wants to be above politics, the best place for that is up in the sky.*
>
> *He claims to have been close with Obama, and at least one of the Georges. I'm speculating that he did not get it on with either of the Clintons. He says that as Donald gradually gets around to charting his own course, the Republicans and Democrats will join in their opposition. And that he is not interested in getting re-elected, and following the polls. Ron's nightmare is that Mike Pence might have to take over (e.g. if Donald gets impeached over disclosure?) And so it goes.... And, yes, they have had lengthy discussions on the deep stuff... if you can believe it... I'm not sure I can.* [158]

As March 2017 arrived, Smith was telling me that a disclosure date would be no later than August, and that the process was ahead of schedule.

He stated that Ron's wife, Aliyah Malik Pandolfi, had talked to Trump. Ron had apparently delegated some of his disclosure role to his wife. All of Aliyah's briefing had to do with a portal that would play a role in the disclosure. Smith wrote on March 3:

> *And about that August deadline........ I suggest that we attempt to bring this sucker in by April Fools Day. Yes?...Could we pull this off without the explicit/public approval/confirmation of the President? That's the challenge. We will try to.*
>
> *We would likely need the private cooperation of the President. Quite likely, he doesn't trust us either. We rely on the Princess (Aliyah) to surmount that hurdle.*
>
> *And the Princess has given her tentative approval to April Fools Day for this...... 'disclosure'.*

Sounds crazy except for two things. Smith is very close to Pandolfi who is closely tied to whatever the government knows about UFOs, and Smith has reported things from Pandolfi that later turned out to be true.

The April Fools event would happen on St. Catherine's Island on the Georgia coast. Trump would be brought to the island to go through a portal. The event would be supported by Russia, China, GB and the Vatican.

In an advance trip to the island in mid-March Smith reported meeting a young Vance and older Terry who would be with Trump at the portal. Pandolfi gave the men a three-hour instruction on theory, as Smith and Pandolfi's wife made a visit to the island's north beach with Pandolfi's daughter, Kashmir. Smith had never met either man before.

As they left the island, each had an artifact that he carried back to New York City to Trump Tower. Apparently, they worked together. Smith stated that he picked up the one object that was like a small pill box with a knob on it that was almost as big as the box itself. Pandolfi told Smith that he shouldn't play with it so he put it back down on the table.

Smith asked which presidents had been through the portal and he was told that Obama had not. Nixon was mentioned and so was Carter. Smith said Carter had been through it when he was Georgia's governor.

On March 20th, Smith reported that Pandolfi was reporting strange signals from the island, but "not enough data on that to analyze." The plan was still on for what Smith called an April 1st PoNR (point of no return) or TPP (toothpaste point where it could not be put back in the tube.)

The plan was still for Trump to go through the portal, which would encourage him to talk, creating accelerated acclimatization.

Then on March 24th, as this book was being released a UK researcher connected to the Greer's Disclosure Project told me "We are not far off now. All the hard work is starting to pay off. Exciting times." He indicated, however, that Pandolfi had indicated to him that June or July was a more likely timeline.

Strange support for this portal story came from an independent Facebook message I got about the same time from Adrian Boniardi in Hollywood who thought there was going to be gradual disclosure and more information would be leaked about UFOs.

The leak connected to a new TV show called *Counterpart* having to do with a portal. The story is about a "a lowly cog in a bureaucratic UN agency who is turning the last corner of a life filled with regret, when he discovers the agency he works for is guarding a secret: a crossing to a parallel dimension." In other words, a portal.

Trump's Actions

....

When Trump was sworn in, he became the 14th president to have dealt with the UFO issue publicly, and if there was to be full disclosure, it should have occurred at the time he was sworn in. However, he has not revealed any UFO secrets.

Full disclosure would have needed to have taken place at the beginning because with every day he lives with the secrets, he builds a case that he too is covering up those secrets.

Trump could have said something like, "Look what I found when I got to the White House. I told you the system was crooked. The UFO situation is real, and I am making the details public."

Instead, he went with the plan followed by the 13 presidents before him and has thus far remained silent about UFOs. He has also been quiet about all the other secrets he learned in his briefings. Even his favorite new outlet, Fox News, described that he "had become a champion of government secrecy."

Before the election, as leaked Democratic emails flooded the internet, Trump repeatedly told his campaign audience, "I love

WikiLeaks. It's amazing how nothing is secret today when you talk about the Internet."

When the stories broke of the illegality of his national security advisor, Michael Flynn talking to a Russian official before the inauguration, Trump made the same move as every president before him. He went to war against the leaks, tweeting, "The spotlight has finally been put on the low-life leakers! They will be caught!"

One person with a connection to people around Trump told me he believed the intelligence people might not inform the new president on all the secrets. I replied that all of the intelligence officials were now Trump's people and that now he controlled the secrets.

Dan Smith commented on Trump's reference to outer space during his inauguration speech stating, "I was about to say that the speech was so apropos that MJ-12 must have written it."

Before he was elected, the only reference to outer space by Trump was that all the weather satellites in low earth orbit were a waste of time and would no longer get funding. Now he was talking of unlocking "the mysteries of space" and about "American footprints on distant worlds."

During his campaign, he was talking about reviving the coal industries, and suddenly he was talking about harnessing the energies of tomorrow.

However, like prior presidents, Trump within the hour was back to his original position, and his new administration outlined their new energy policy on the White House website, with its focus on gas and oil, a revival of the coal industry, and a scrapping of the 2013 Climate Action Plan. Ignored was the National Oceanic and Atmospheric Administration report two days earlier, where 2016 became the third year in a row where temperatures hit a new high.

Nevertheless, Smith had gotten word that he might visit with Trump to influence his worldview. On January 24, 2017, Smith wrote;

> *Would I have to hold my nose to work with the Don? Hopefully not. His mission was to round up the 'deplorables.' He accomplished that with remarkable aplomb. He has formed his comfort zone around them. Will he now be willing to move beyond that comfort zone?*
>
> *I, for one, have no script for that move. I can only wish him luck. Might he not get cold feet? Maybe I could help with that. Could I hold his*

hand? Maybe, along with Aliyah (Pandolfi's wife), Kashmir (Pandolfi's daughter) and the Footmann (Pandolfi).

After a week's holiday, Smith was back waiting patiently for his meeting with Trump. On February 1, 2017, he posted, "I'm expecting a 'critical update'.... better late than never."

The last piece of evidence indicating Trump might not do anything, despite the stories of the portal, came when Trump did a public signing of the 393 word NASA budget.

Rep. John Culberson (R-Texas) praised Trump saying the president would be remembered as "the father of the interplanetary highway system" the way President Dwight D. Eisenhower is remembered as the father of the interstate highway system.

Trump however brought the story back to Earth saying, "Well, that sounds exciting. First, we want to fix our highways! We're going to fix our highways."

The Future of Disclosure

People make political decisions driven by that 60,000 foot level - people that CIA works for that have other equities involved. We say things and divulge things for certain reasons when it suits certain political equities and vested interests of political leadership, and we don't say other things on other occasions when it doesn't... If decisions are made to release when it serves one kind of interest, then logically decisions are made to withhold when the perception is that it represents another kind of interest. All that kind of stuff is beyond my pay grade. I am not up at the 60,000 foot level (President, Congressional Intelligence Committees, Executive Branch). **Former CIA Liaision to Hollywood Chase Brandon answering the question why the CIA doesn't make a full disclosure on the UFO story.**

As a young child, I was good at playing chess. While in grade 6, I was taken to the high school to play. The UFO events described in this book reminds me of playing chess.

When the opponent is a novice player, and they move a pawn that does not seem to strengthen their board position, it is just probably a random move.

When, however, the opponent is an advanced player, the moving of a pawn or any other piece always means something. There are no random moves. When a piece moves, it fits into a pattern of the next five moves.

So, it was, in February 2015, the day John Podesta was leaving the Obama White House to run Hillary Clinton's 2016 presidential campaign, I realized something was up when Podesta tweeted "my biggest failure of 2014: Once again not securing the #disclosure of the UFO files." I sensed he was not just randomly moving a pawn.

Podesta was perhaps the most influential Democratic operative at the time, having founded and headed the top Democratic think tank. Secondly, he rarely tweeted.

There was suddenly a question that needed answering. Why would Podesta choose this crucial moment in his career to tweet about UFOs? As UFOs are a toxic political issue, my immediate impression was that he was setting up something. His next chess move seemed to support the notion.

On September 29, 2015, as the presidential campaign heated up Podesta tweeted again this time in response to an interview Hillary had just done with actress Lena Dunham. Podesta said, "Great interview, @lenadunham. But Lena, ask her about aliens next time!!"

Podesta seemed to be risking a billion-dollar political campaign on not just the topic of UFOs but of aliens. It was evident this was a related move correlated to his first tweet about not getting disclosure. The events that followed looked like coordinated chess moves setting up some UFO disclosure end game.

November 5, 2015: Based on Podesta emails leaks, we learned that in November 2015, a month after Podesta asked reporters to ask Hillary about the aliens, Hillary was anticipating and hoping for a UFO question during her appearance on the late-night Jimmy Kimmel show. She had even rehearsed her answer for five minutes and was very disappointed when she did not get the question from Kimmel.

November 17, 2015: A couple of days later, Obama took a UFO question from Bill Simmons at *GQ Magazine*. Rather than denying knowledge, Obama seemed to confirm that the Top Secret subjects of UFOs and the Roswell crash are for real, but not that interesting.

"I gotta tell you," Obama said, "it's a little disappointing. People always ask me about Roswell and the aliens and UFOs, and it turns out the stuff going on that's Top Secret isn't nearly as exciting as you expect. In this day and age, it's not as Top Secret as you'd think."

December 30, 2015: A month later Hillary got her wish for a UFO question. New Hampshire reporter Daymond Steer asked her about UFOs after Hillary met with the editors of the *Conway Daily Sun* newspaper. It was in that reply she first mentioned UFO disclosure in public. Hillary told Steer that if elected, she planned to make a disclosure about UFOs. "Yes, I'm going to get to the bottom of it..." Hillary declared, "I think we may have been (visited already). We don't know for sure."

The statement was remarkable on two fronts. First Hillary was promising disclosure about something the government (and her husband) had denied for 70 years. Second, Hillary became the first high-level politician to state that not only did she believe that we would find life in outer space, but that it might already be among us.

February 11, 2016: President Obama moved another chess piece supporting Hillary's UFO disclosure promise. He went on the Ellen DeGeneres Show and took a prearranged UFO question from six-year-old, Macey Hensley.

March 1, 2016: Podesta gave an interview to KLAS TV in Las Vegas where he brought up UFO disclosure again. He revealed to Steve Sebelius, "I've talked to Hillary about that. There are still classified files that could be declassified. I think I've convinced her that we need an effort to kind of go look at that and declassify as much as we can so that people have their legitimate questions answered. More attention and more discussion about unexplained aerial phenomena can happen without people — who are in public life, who are serious about this — being ridiculed."

April 7, 2016: Podesta was adding more fuel to the UFO fire. He told Jack Tapper at CNN, "I think that the US government could do a much better job in answering the legitimate questions people have about what is going on with unidentified aerial phenomena and they should…the American people can handle the truth, so they should just do it."

April 16, 2016: Hillary appeared on The Breakfast Club, 105.1-FM New York City. She reaffirmed her promise that she would disclose as much of the UFO secrets as she could, stating, "I have said I want to open the files as much as we can. I don't know. If there is some huge national security issue, and I can't get agreement to open them, I won't, but I do want to open them because I'm interested. I don't know. I want to see what the information shows, but there are enough stories out there that I don't think people are just sitting out there in their kitchen making them up. People see things. What they see I don't know, but we have to try and get people information."

May 11 and 16, 2016: Josh Earnest, the White House Press Secretary, took three direct questions on the UFO cover-up and did not deny anything. Earnest just replied that he had not been briefed adding, "I know that President Obama has joked publically that one of the benefits of the presidency is having access to that information. I don't know if he availed himself of that opportunity. If we have more on this, I will let you know."

Replying to another question days later, Earnest encouraged the press to go and ask the President about UFOs. "I haven't looked at the documents, so it's unclear to me exactly what the equities might be. So maybe at the next news conference, you can have the opportunity to ask the President that yourself -- which would be interesting."

The press did not take Earnest up on his suggestion.

What most people didn't know was that as Podesta, Hillary, and Obama were openly talking about UFOs and offering disclosure is that there were other UFO disclosure intitiatives going on.

Dan Smith (mentioned above) stated that both Hillary and Trump were being told things about the UFO reality.

More importantly, Tom DeLonge had started his UFO disclosure inititiative. He had received support from Robert Weiss at Lockheed Skunk Works who had sent him to the CIA, and from there he was directed to people in the Pentagon and NASA.

The group of 10 advisors was helping him set up a plan to bring the story of the reality of non-human visitors to the public.

In the **spring of 2015,** DeLonge had contacted Podesta by phone. Two months later, probably after checking with government officials as to what was going on, he agreed to be a part of DeLonge's project to disclose the UFO secret to the public. Podesta told DeLonge UFOs were an important topic and he needed to come to Washington.

In **July 2015** Podesta did an interview with DeLonge on camera on the subject of UFOs. Then in January 2016, Podesta hosted a Google Hangout with DeLonge, two Air Force Generals, and Weiss, regarding DeLonge's UFO disclosure plan.

Introducing the Big Man

....

As an intelligence officer, I was taught that my primary job was to collect information—intelligence—for the president. And that the information I collected had to be well sourced and vetted thoroughly and properly. In other words, the information had to be as accurate and truthful as humanly possible. And this is the same approach I use when discussing the Phenomenon. **Former CIA Senior Intelligence Service Officer Jim Semivan**

The following is the part of the story that was always missing. The missing piece of the puzzle was the existence of the "Big Man," and the fact that the whole disclosure initiative had to have been approved and supported by President Barack Obama.

I can now talk about this because the Big Man, Jim Semivan, has now outed himself by writing the foreword to Tom DeLonge's book, *Sekret Machines: Chasing Shadows.*

Semivan is one of DeLonge's ten advisors. He is, in fact, the head of the initiative. Experiencer Chris Bledsoe, who knew Semivan years before he ever linked up with DeLonge, stated, "Nothing happens without him."

I have known about Semivan for a couple of years after talking to Bledsoe and one other person. I always heard him referred to as the Big Man in Washington. He was one of a number of high-level people I heard about in an August 2015 conversation in Maine and in another meeting involving Bledsoe in 2013, where another high-level official was present.

There were and still are a lot of government people, key UFO researchers, Hollywood producers, and university people, who picked up Bledsoe's UFO story and were taking the time to study him and his family.

Like those people, I knew Bledsoe's story was unique and valuable when I first met him in late 2012. I had two dramatic experiences of my own that tied me to Chris. The second happened in 2013 while visiting Bledsoe where I witnessed two events. The second one, which I won't recount here, involved Chris' dog, Nellie, and was so bizarre that every time I tell it I can see the look of disbelief in the listener's face.

I also knew that Semivan had contact with other researchers because he was generally interested in the subject.

That interest was not just as a curious observer. Semivan is a UFO experiencer himself. He described that encounter which took place in his bedroom along with his wife.

> *As for my formal introduction to the Phenomenon, as we know it in today's context, it came suddenly and unexpectedly. I will not attempt to go into the experience here, but I will say that it was one of life's game changers for both my wife and me. The experience was simultaneously frightening, perplexing, frustrating and absurd. It was also both physical and emotional, although I am undecided as to whether there was any spiritual addendum. Almost thirty years later, I am still not sure what to make of the experience. What I do know, however, is that this event changed my view of what constitutes our collective version of reality.*[159]

Therefore, unlike DeLonge, Semivan had an interest in experiencers and their stories. That is why Semivan had so much interest in Bledsoe and stated, "We know there is no one else in the world as we speak that has the level of contact you do."

In 2007, Semivan retired from 26 years in the CIA. The list of Magicians (Appendix 5) shows that retired intelligence officers seem to be the ones used to run these UFO disclosure programs. This use of contractors provides an arm's length association to the CIA and plausible deniability.

The key thing to know about Semivan is that he has contacts with the White House in this latest UFO disclosure enterprise. I know this for a fact.

Even before I knew of Semivan, I was shown a picture of a mailing envelope from Camp David and a picture of what was in it. I saw a picture of Obama with a young person I did not recognize. I heard of trips to Washington by someone whose only business was UFOs.

I think I was shown these photos to prove that high-level officials were involved. When I saw the Camp David mailing envelope photo on the phone of a man who I trust with my life, there is not much choice but to believe.

Over and over there have been direct indications that the Obama White House was involved.

Tom DeLonge has stated that he phoned and got Obama on the phone. He did not detail the discussion.

DeLonge has posted a few photos of himself in front of the White House and talked about having meetings in Washington for a week.

On July 23, 2015, he posted a Facebook picture of himself interviewing Podesta for an #importantFilmOnSomethingAboutSpace. The caption quoted Podesta as saying, "Yes, the President and I discussed Unidentified Aerial Phenomena."

This association with the Executive Office of the President makes sense as the president is the man in charge of all the UFO data. The CIA has no other job than to provide the best intelligence possible to the president and carry out his directives. The president controls all classified material and security clearances. The president as head of state is the only person authorized to deal with visiting extraterrestrials if that is what they turn out to be.

All intelligence flows up to the president, and all directives flow down to the military, intelligence, and government agencies. The CIA does not operate independently of the White House.

The ten administration officials dealing with DeLonge were dealing with him on authorization by President Obama. They were not rogue officials doing their own thing. They were operating just the way you would expect in a system governed by laws and a constitution. Semivan was merely the official who coordinated everything and would get permissions and directions from the Executive Office.

Once this White House connection is acknowledged, everything else starts to make sense. The DOD, NASA, and intelligence people were part of an orchestrated effort. Hillary's disclosure promise was merely an extension of a disclosure operation which began in the Obama White House. I now know some of the people who are involved and have talked to a few of them. At least one other is an experiencer like Semivan. Many of the names I have heard are officials whom I have identified in past UFO acclimatization efforts. I have chosen to sit silently while they perform their missions.

Obama was sympathetic to the UFO issue. The events listed in this book showed that he never denied or lied about the issue. Obama brought up the issue numerous times when he could have remained silent. He even got the CIA to upload millions of pages on the internet regarding UFOs and remote viewing two days before he left the White House.

The indication from Ron Pandolfi, who is also attached to the Obama White House, is that Trump is open to disclosure and against disinformation, so the leaks will probably continue.

Most of this will come from Hollywood, which has been used by the CIA over the years to direct the public's thinking on various issues.

DeLonge has announced a fictional movie called "Strange Times" about San Diego skateboarders and extraterrestrials, and as stated earlier, he has a non-fiction UFO book out called *Sekret Machines: Gods*.

There are other Hollywood projects which will raise the public consciousness about the reality of non-local visitors. One of these is a massive project which will probably be announced in early May.

I have heard that millions of dollars has been put up by a wealthy American that everyone would know. There is a figure of millions on a system to gather people sightings that can be mined for data.

I have heard about the public acknowledgement of the TR3B and its connection to Roswell. I doubt this story, but what do I know for sure? Over and over the story has been - "This will be big, but not full disclosure." Those that don't believe can still walk away.

These are not my projects and I will leave it up to those who have worked hard to make this a reality. I am just an observer, watching and listening.

Conclusion

I think what you might find is a bunch of men standing around an elephant. **Military general to Tom DeLonge talking about the UFO mystery.**

After decades of work on the disclosure problem I have become much more sympathetic to the position the government has taken, and how they have handled the situation they were handed in the 1940s.

Many in the UFO community will say that full disclosure should be a simple thing and done ASAP. The more I view the evidence, the less I agree with that position and more I see a potential for disaster were that approach to be taken.

In various conversations between Bob Pratt, a prominent reporter for the *National Enquirer* and Donald Keyhoe in 1977, 1978 and 1979, Keyhoe talked about what he had learned about the thinking inside the Pentagon and disclosure of the UFO secret.

The first Keyhoe interview took place just after Jimmy Carter had made his famous promise to release all the UFO files. Keyhoe stated that there were great fears inside the Pentagon that Carter would actually do it:

> *If he does, that would include the Above Top Secret cases. (They) are the ones that scare the hell out of quite a number of people. They're only a relatively small number and the percentage is about less than one percent of the total reports. But some of them in there are disastrous, airplane crashes, mostly pilots pursuing these things and trying to force them down and things like that. But at any rate it would be bad. Some newspapers and TV people would concentrate on that.*
>
> *There are several sources that I know in the Pentagon would like to have everything come out, if it can be done safely and wisely, but they said that if we release all that Carter orders, everything released, the press would immediately seize on these very serious and alarming reports, and they would scare the holy hell out of people. So, I can*

understand why the Air Force over the years burned or destroyed some of those reports. [160]

What Keyhoe was referring to were the early days following 1947, when many planes were lost trying to intercept or shoot down UFOs. According to *The New York Times* one hundred and ninety-two aircraft vanished or were destroyed between the years 1951 and 1956 alone.

The fears expressed by Pentagon insiders just might come to pass with a full disclosure.

What would CNN cover 24/7 for weeks, months or years if the full UFO story broke?

Would they cover the fact that 39% of all experiencers report being healed by the UFO beings, or that 42% have received scientific, mathematical, and technical downloads, or that 85% of these contact experiences with aliens were stated to be "Positive," or that 85% have undergone major transformations for the Positive, and that 71% agreed that: "In my opinion, the widespread occurrence of experiences with unidentified entities is part of a larger plan to promote the evolution of consciousness as a species-wide scale."[161]

Or would they cover the story of planes crashing with dead pilots, cattle mutilations, and stories of eight-foot-tall reptilians whose favorite food is young blue-eyed blond girls?

Studies have shown that bad news far outweighs good news. It's been reported that there are much as seventeen negative news reports for each good one.

It was shown that people have "negativity bias" which is a psychological term for our collective hunger to hear and remember bad news. When given the option to read any story, the results show people gravitate toward negative stories, even though the same people claimed they preferred good news.

A study by the Pew Research Center for People & the Press revealed that since they began their survey in 1986, war, terrorism, inclement weather, and natural or human-made disaster stories consistently ranked highest, with science, technology, foreign news that is not directly related to the U.S. consistently ranked lowest.[162]

A prime example of this effect was the recent 2016 U.S. Presidential election where exits polls showed the two top issues were jobs and the economy. Trump, the professional salesman, able to talk a homeless man out of his shoes, or sell ice to an Antarctic dweller, capitalized on fear.

Even though the unemployment rate had gone down under Obama from 10% to 4.6%, and a record 75 months of job growth, Trump was able to convince voters that most Americans had lost their jobs, and that if they voted for Clinton, everyone else would lose their jobs as well.

GDP had gone from 14,418.74 billion to 18,036.65 but most people believed Trump when he said it was going the other way.

The bottom line is negativity and fear sell. As Daniel Gardner put it in his book *The Science of Fear*, "Fear sells. Fear makes money. The countless companies and consultants in the business of protecting the fearful from whatever they may fear know it only too well. The more fear, the better the sales."

News media outlets would feast on the negative aspects of people's UFO stories knowing that this is what drives up ratings. UFO occupants would become the ultimate poisoned skittles. Trying to stop the negative media frenzy would be like stopping the media's obsession with Trump.

The coverage would go on endlessly based on speculations about worst-case alien scenarios.

Seen in this light the gradual disclosure of the UFO story looks like the only option.

Despite these drawbacks, I know a plan is in place to raise consciousness about the reality of the UFO phenomena. By one account one billion dollars will go into this effort from private sources.

I know eight civilians who have been briefed with various levels of knowledge. As far as I know none have any security clearance or need to know. The briefing included handling wreckage, and offers to meet with beings.

At the same time, I have been told by a reliable source that the United States government blocked three proposed full disclosures by other countries.

I would have more information but I chose not to ask questions. I feared that I would cause the operation to pull back or stop. Worse yet I feared that I would be told I should not tell what I had learned. It is not my story. I am just an observer.

No ETs

....

One of the main objections that will be raised against this gradual disclosure theory is the idea that all of what has been mentioned in this book is nothing more than a government disinformation operation to throw researchers off, or to hide mind control experiments, or other secret military programs.

This government disinformation theory is very strongly held by many researchers. It has become almost like a core myth, held so strongly it has started to resemble a religious cult.

Mark Pilkington spelled out this disinformation model in his book *Mirage Men:*

> *Myth making is a human necessity. It's one of the things we do best. Myths are useful, they guide us and help us make sense of the incomprehensible, those things and events too strange or complex for us to understand. They provide emotionally satisfying answers to difficult questions.*[163]

The problem with the disinformation theory is that it is wacky and illogical at its core. It says that we will hide our greatest secrets by telling people about them.

The disinformation theory proposes that in order to hide the Top-Secret Air Force/CIA research being done at a secret base in the middle of the Nevada desert, military officials told everyone that we have a base in the desert called Area 51 where we back-engineering flying saucers.

Not only did we have flying saucers but at least one live alien who was held at Area 51. The theory goes on to propose that this story of flying saucers and a live alien is the best way to hide what is happening at Area 51 from the American people and the Soviets who send a satellite over the base every day.

Really? If that was the plan to throw everyone off the trail of the existence of Area 51, how did that work out? Within days of leaking the story of a saucer at Area 51 in 1989, there were thousands of people up in the mountains looking down on the now not-so-secret base and pictures of the base flooded the internet.

The word Area 51 became so well known it has probably reached the ears of unknown civilizations deep in the Brazilian rainforest.

In a second example, the disinformation theory asks us to believe that even though the CIA public position was they had no interest in UFOs, they allowed the second most powerful person in the CIA, Chase Brandon, to speak publicly on behalf of the agency, and go on a radio show with millions of listeners. There he stated that 1) the Roswell incident was real, 2) it was extraterrestrial, and 3) there were bodies.

Seriously? That is going to convince people that the CIA is not involved? If I were CIA Director and someone proposed that to me as a way to cover up UFO knowledge or throw the Russians off the scent, I would ask them if they had a headache. I would ask that because it would be evident that the person was either suffering from a hit to their head, or they were having a stroke.

If disinformation has been the plan, how did this plan work with covering up the UFO subject? Again, not so well. UFO information is the topic most requested Freedom of Information Requests in many agencies. These requests have tied up scores of people in government who were then forced to play "hide the files from the inquiring public."

In addition, WikiLeaks recently showed clear backroom disclosure efforts. The Podesta emails strongly indicated there are indeed people in the United States military who have been working on the UFO phenomena, and are feeding that information to musician Tom DeLonge.

Disclosure is Not Yet an Option

....……

The second major objection that will be raised about my claim that gradual disclosure is underway is that gradual disclosure is not disclosure.

The problem with this objection is that it uses a different definition for "disclosure."

When most researchers in the UFO community mention disclosure they are talking about the President of the United States standing up at the podium and formally announcing, "ETs are visiting us."

That may be one version of disclosure, but it is only one version of what the word disclosure means. Disclosure is simply "revealing."

That is what this whole book is about - disclosing or revealing. People since World War II have been revealing elements of the UFO phenomenon that were not previously known.

People will argue that if the government does not address the ET component, it's not really disclosure. That is not true. Announcing ET is big, but it's a limited view of UFOs.

I believe that the final answer to the UFO mystery is going to be something much bigger than ET. The government knows this and that is why the CIA refers to it as a "phenomenology problem" as opposed to a "UFO problem." An announcement of ET would be inaccurate and the government knows it.

Consciousness is the elephant in the room when it comes to full disclosure, and it is a key component of the mystery. Including the role of consciousness in the disclosure announcement will lead to the collapse of scientific materialism in what Dan Smith refers to as the mother of all paradigm shifts (MoAPS).

Consciousness is simply "awareness." Awareness can be seen all the way down to the level of the photon and electron. The entangled particle experiment first proposed by Einstein to disprove non-local entanglement clearly shows that if you have two entangled particles on opposite sides of the universe, when you change the spin on one, the spin of the other will instantly change. The one particle is aware of what you did to its entangled buddy and is, therefore, conscious.

It is this principle that can be used to explain how UFOs get here. In 1993, Ben Rich, the head of Lockheed Skunk Works, which has always been rumored to have back engineered flying saucer technology, implied to engineer Jan Harzen that ESP and all things in time and space are connected. Rich's explanation indicated that UFOs travel in the same way ESP works.

Like an entangled particle, a craft can be aware of another position in space and suddenly be there. The idea is to "be" the ship and then "be" in a new location.

In Raymond Fowler's series of books regarding the experiences of Betty Andreasson Luca, Betty reported in detail the aliens' abilities to manipulate matter and Quaazga, a grey alien, told her at one point that in the future man would once again connect to the science of the spirit.

Many experiencers who remember flying ships or recall being onboard ships, state that they recall being "one with the ship" and that the ships were operated using the minds.

The Disclosure Plan

....

It appears that disclosure will take two forms and will again be gradual. Two different UFO theories will be emerging at the same time.

- Nuts and bolts - good vs. bad aliens representing a Newtonian scientific worldview. The view is supported by the major UFO groups and some defense officials.
- Consciousness phenomenology worldview. This interpretation came from CIA research into UFOs and paranormal phenomena.

DeLonge will represent the nuts and bolts with Cargo Cult theory. He will claim the theory is backed by his Department of Defense advisors. In this worldview, the aliens are a threat or "bad news" and possibly without souls as he spelled out in his first Lockheed Skunkworks meeting.

This reductionist material alien view will be expressed despite the fact that DeLonge knows consciousness is an essential component in the universe. He stated that the Lockheed officials confirmed the importance of conciousness to the UFO mystery. DeLonge pointed out that there was one 45-minute discussion about consciousness and was all the head scientist wanted to talk about.

The statement made by Ron Pandolfi to Dan Smith in 1991 defines the consciousness phenomenology worldview – namely that we have a phenomenology problem. In this view, the UFO is much less physical and more linked to understanding the consciousness nature of reality.

That may be why two days before the election Obama, through the CIA, released not only UFO documents but documents from the parapsychology remote viewing program run by the CIA from 1972-1995. UFOs and remote viewing are connected in an important way. They are part of a bigger phenomenology worldview of reality.

The coming disclosure will come with what has been described by one insider as a war of ideas about whether or not the phenomenon is good or bad.

The reality of the UFO phenomena and 'an intelligence' behind the phenomena will not be at issue. What will be at issue is what the phenomena represents.

There will be tales of evil aliens eating people, inciting wars, and trying to take over the planet. If accepted this will be the false flag the military industrial complex has always dreamed of. They will have a blank check to spend an endless amount of money to take on perceived poisoned Skittles throughout the universe.

Then there will be stories of 'an intelligence' here to guide us through a difficult period in our evolution. One person in the loop said, "Lines are being drawn in the sand and it's plain to see. The truth about life other than us will come quickly, but who and what we are dealing with will be up for debate."

A billion dollars will be spent. I am told names and agencies will allow their names to be associated. Minds will change, and yet those who do not believe will be able to walk away. That is because as big as this is, it is still gradual disclosure. It is an acclimatization of the American people, and maybe the world, as was suggested by various think tanks so many years ago.

The actions and leaks by government officials point to various disclosure plans all playing out at the same time. Dan Smith confirmed this to me saying Pandolfi had told him there were many teams.

There have been many failed disclosure plans in the past like the Gordon Novel Potus Briefing movie, and the Hillary Clinton disclosure initiative, and there will be many more in the future.

At present there appear to be at least **six disclosure efforts** all going at the same time.

Two of them are gradual disclosure plans that are being guided by Jim Semivan, which will represent two different views of the intelligence behind the phenomenon.

1. A gradual acclimatization through media that confirms the reality of a non-human intelligence interacting with the world. This DeLonge version will emphasize what is believed are the dark side of the encounters with the "bugs." It will place the defense department heroes who struggle daily to develop a defense against an evil UFO force. At the same time, people will be made aware of the fact that consciousness is a major component necessary for understanding the phenomenon and in turn the entire universe.
2. A gradual acclimatization through media that confirms the reality of a non-human intelligence interacting with the world. This version however will emphasize the experiencer story of

Chris Bledsoe that broke off from the DeLonge camp. It will present the phenomena in a more positive light.

There will be an emphasis on the message that the intelligence seems to be delivering in order to guide and help us. It places the defense department as good guys just looking for answers and views most of the aliens as good guys. As with disclosure 1, people will be made aware of the fact that consciousness is a major component necessary for understanding the phenomenon and the entire universe. One expression used by a government official was "if you're a negative person you get negative in return, if you're positive you get Angels in return."

This gradual disclosure plan, which will probably be announced in May 2017, does not involve evil aliens here to eat us or an evil government that has a one-hour meeting each morning before breakfast to plan how to mess up the world of UFO research.

This is a position that has supports among a number of academics at various universities who have interacted with the DeLonge disclosure effort. Whether or not they speak out on this remains to be seen.
3. A third disclosure is the full disclosure effort that Dan Smith has been talking about for years and which it is believed will take place under the Trump administration. It appears to take a neutral attitude to the intelligence behind the phenomena, focusing more on the connection to other paranormal phenomenology and the hardware aspects of the UFO technology.
4. The fourth effort is the continuing Steven Greer effort to force the American government to disclose. He is due to release a crowd-funded documentary called *Unacknowledged: An Expose of the Greatest Secret in Human History*. "Unacknowledged" is named after the super-secret and illegal Unacknowledged Special Access Projects (USAPs) that deal with the UFO/ET issue.
5. After I did a webinar on the disclosure plan, I received word of two new possible disclosures. One was from a producer who had been involved in the Gordon Novel Potus Briefing (see March 2009). He stated that he was now working on a project talking about the infamous Bill Moore aviary of 24 sources providing UFO information. The help according to the

producer was coming from the CIA, and they had actually introduced him to many of the aviary members. The CIA official stated that I was one of the people the producer might get help from.
6. Then I got another Facebook message from a producer that I mentioned in the webinar who sent a picture of himself interviewing John Podesta. This would make two Podesta interviews that have yet to surface. The other one was done by Tom DeLonge. Earlier this producer had asked me what questions I would have for Bill Clinton if I were to interview him, indicating to me that perhaps he had gotten Clinton to agree to a UFO interview.

There is also an initiative described by 1980 Rendlesham Forest witness John Burroughs. He sees the government following the pattern of the movie *Contact*. He believes that there will be confirmation rather than disclosure as described by businessman Bob Bigalow. This plan is working toward an announcement based on discoveries, such as the seven planets around the star Trappist 1, that we are not alone. Burroughs has heard the date of July 17, 2017 which would line up with the 20th anniversary of the *Contact* movie.

My view of all of these disclosure efforts is that everyone, no matter what team they are on, is trying in their own way to save the world, or do the best for themselves, their children, and grandchildren.

Some of the officials who are involved may be deluded, or psychotic, but they still believe they are within the law, and upholding the U.S. Constitution. I have met some of these people and they are just ordinary people who have the same questions and desire to get answers like any man on the street. The evil seems to evaporate when there are face to face conversations.

In this view, government people go to work like any other employee and put out their best efforts. All the government people that I have met have fit this model.

There is a clear pattern of officials releasing the UFO story to the public, and at the same time distorting the message with disinformation. This approach puts out the core truths and at the same time stops the story from getting out of control. It also protects the classified information related to technologies that have strong national security implications. It allows the story to be investigated in secret, and yet brings the pubic up to speed in case full disclosure is forced on them.

The general rule seems to be that officials in charge of the UFO problem will take every offer of help they get to reveal the true story as long as 3 conditions are met;
1. The officials lead the dance. They will not deal with people who will not do as they are told. DeLonge defined this condition saying that he keeps their names secret, he is respectful, and he gets permission for everything he does.
2. The officials will avoid people who are into conspiracies theories.
3. At no time will they accept a plan where the president stands up and does full disclosure.

What has changed in the last couple years is the intensity of the effort to get out the story. I have been told for a couple years that this UFO disclosure is not something the government is considering or dabbling with. There is a definite plan and it is now being carried out.

The best explanation for what the government is doing was hinted at by neuroscientist Dr. Kit Green, who in my opinion is regarded as one of the most trusted government people regarding UFO phenomena.

Green is the man the government sends high-level people to when they report abduction-type symptoms. One source says Green has seen 50 people and Green claims to have talked to more than one president about UFOs. It is rumoured that he used to run the weird desk at the CIA that dealt with UFOs.

In 1986, Green, Jacques Vallee and Hal Puthoff came up with a theory referred to as "core story." In the late 1980s, Green in a case I was in charge of attempted to talk with Dr. Eric Walker at Penn State University about UFOs. Walker, however, wouldn't engage him and stated his only duty was to answer to the president, and Green was not the president. In the 1970s and 1980s, Green was also the CIA control officer in connection with Sanford University and remote viewing.

Green has been part of almost every major UFO disclosure initiative mentioned in this book. He was known as Blue Jay in Bill Moore's UFO aviary.

He attended at least one meeting held by the UFO working group as recounted by Howard Blum at *The New York Times*. He was one of the consultants brought in by billionaire, and aerospace businessman, Bob Bigelow. It appears Green is still contracted by the CIA to do things in the UFO field. When Green talks, many listen.

In the book, *Mirage Men*, Green is quoted talking about how the government deals with the UFO phenomenon:

This applies to the UFO problem. If something really strange in the area of UFOs is true, then what do we do about conveying that information to the public? First, we consider what may be the basic facts; maybe there are civilized life forms elsewhere in the universe; maybe they visited us in their spacecrafts a couple of times and then went back home; perhaps they left a vehicle or some technology behind, and we have spent a lot of money trying to figure out how to use it. And then there may be people in government who believe that this did happen, and believe that the information needs to be public knowledge, because perhaps someone outside government will be able to make sense of their technology. But then there's another group of people in power who say," No, it will make them sick to know all this, we can't let the story out, it's too dangerous."

So, what do we do? There are studies on both sides of the problem. Some show that people will go crazy and jump off bridges when they are presented with this information. Others, however, say that if you don't want them to go crazy, what you do is systematically desensitize their fears.

If you are a psychiatrist with a patient, you can do that in a very methodical way. If you are a sociologist working with a group of students at a university you can also do this is in a very structured and experimental way. But if you are a government working with a population it's a lot more complicated. Sure, there are those who are going to shrug and say, "I always knew the aliens were real, it's no big deal." But you also know that some of them are nuttier than a fruitcake and could cause a lot of trouble. So, we have to ask ourselves how we can tell the people what they deserve to know, and, maybe what they need to know?

The way to do it is to construct a framework whereby they can parse out things they have heard that are not true, and you whittle it down to a manageable story. A story like this; There were three spacecraft that came here over 30 years ago, and we've got one of them. We can't figure out how it works, we've crashed it because there is still a lot of physics that we need to learn. We do have something that is like a magnetohydrodynamic toroid, and it really did get a craft off the ground, but it smelled bad and killed a couple of pilots. We're really sorry about that, but we did it because we've got this machine that came from another planet, and we need to know how it works.

How do you tell people that story? If it's true?

If you were to give them the core story right off the bat, they'd get sick, so you do it slowly over ten or twenty years. You put out a series of movies, a bunch of books, a bunch of stories, a bunch of Internet memes about Reptilian aliens eating our children, about all the crazy stuff we have seen lately in SERPO. Then one day you say, "Hey, all that stuff is nonsense, relax, it's not that bad, you don't have to worry, it really is this," – and then you give them the real story.

Now that is the tried and true desensitization model. And to the extent that there is a core story that is true, and to the extent that the people who want to get that core story out want to do it in a way that will not hurt the people, that's what they do- they come up with a bunch of nonsense, and then they get rid of it, gradually making the people more comfortable so that when they are finally presented with the truth, it is not as frightening as they originally feared. "I can't believe that," they will say. "I didn't believe the crazy reptile stuff. I really didn't believe that they were abducting babies from wombs on beams of light. But I did believe the part about the spaceship and the back-engineering technology."[164]

Another similar statement was made by Bill Moore who spent years dealing with some of the most powerful government players. I defer to him for the last word on the disclosure games I have described in this book. Moore has so accurately described what I think is going on:

> *Whatever is going on, it seems clear that certain elements within our government know enough about it to cause them to play their own kind of games – games that are either designed to condition the public in preparation for a final day of reckoning when the truth can finally be told, or to bury the public interest in UFOs by confounding the curious with an array of increasingly outrageous and incredible tales which sap their interest, drain their resources, and strain their reputations to the point where they will either stop digging or dig in only carefully fenced-off, perfectly harmless places.*
>
> *Even with the extensive work we have already done, much of it still unpublished, we still cannot say with any degree of certainty where this path will lead us...UFOs are not just lights in the sky to be chased by fun-seeking "investigators" bent on discovering evidence of other-worldly visitation. Neither are we dealing with "take-me-to-your-leader" type extraterrestrials who have come to bestow upon us all of the secrets of their ultra-advanced civilization. UFOs are not a simple phenomenon to be explained away in simplistic terms. Rather we are dealing with something which has been a silent partner to civilization for a long time, and which will continue in that role until we, as conscious beings, ultimately "discover" them and are able to say "thank you—we now understand who you are and what your purpose is" Whether that day lies just around the corner or many years in the future, we cannot say. We can only hope that our continued efforts will somehow hasten its coming.*[165]

Final Word

The final word on disclosure goes to discussing the intelligence behind the UFO phenomena. Where do the aliens stand on this important issue of disclosure? It is a question UFO disclosure advocates rarely consider.

One of the 64 reasons that the government has not made a full disclosure about UFOs is the fact that the intelligence behind the phenomenon is also not disclosing. It is like the government is up against some secret foreign power that is operating in secret, and thus must be considered a threat. The secrecy of the aliens is an important factor in disclosure.

Like the government, the aliens are not disclosing. However, they are not covering up because we know they can cloak their actions as when they perform abductions and they are not, and yet no one sees anything. The aliens are doing something in between. They are doing a gradual disclosure of their presence and why they are here.

Many people are expecting the aliens to make themselves visible and end the cover-up. Even though some contactees have claimed to have received messages from the aliens that they will do this, it hasn't happened, and it would be a safe bet to assume it will not happen. There must be a reason for this.

The aliens have not come like Santa Claus to give us the answers to the UFO mystery test. Instead, they have done things that make us realize there are many more questions regarding what is happening than when we first began the test.

They have not come to feed our poor, provide us with cheap energy, or stop our constant wars.

The aliens have given us glimpses of themselves. There have been many sightings by people, encounters with beings appearing in bedrooms, or on board ships. These, however, are just glimpses. They are short and come with no explanation as to what is going on.

They have stalled cars, left ground traces, talked in people's heads, and left marks on experiencers' bodies as a calling card to say, "yes this really happened."

The process is almost like the one used by the UFO officials of putting out a tantalizing story, and then pulling it back when we reach for it.

Both the government and the aliens seem to be leaving a trail of bread crumbs for people to follow, meant to slowly release the truth of what is happening. It also makes one wonder if the government is imitating what the aliens are doing.

The situation might be very simple. Knowing everything is not a part of existing in the physical world. Perhaps we and the government are not meant to know, or maybe they are trying to tell us that the key part of life is figuring things out.

This would mean that the aliens are not here to do our homework, or give us technology that we did not work hard to create. The whole process might be that for us to become strong we have to go into the gym and do the lifting.

This philosophy has been described often by scholars but seems to be forgotten when we make demands for disclosure.

We forget the constant reminder by contactees and channelers of the "prime directive." They cannot interfere with evolutionary learning any more than we can help our children by going to schools for them and writing their exams. This message was clearly given to Wilbert Smith, who ran the Canadian government flying saucer investigation from 1950- 1954.

Smith was an experiencer and he gathered together material from other experiencers to compare notes with. The message he got from the alien named AFFA was that the only time they would step in and interfere with the world is if there was a nuclear war (and yet cases like Castle Bravo show that there was a warning but ultimately many died without the beings who gave the warning having stopped it). Indeed, AFFA's message to Smith was "We will allow the people of Earth to stew in their own juices."

If we assume that reincarnation, rather than one life, is part of reality, then a person would know everything before birth, pass through the river of forgetfulness, live their life trying to figure out what is going on, and then become totally aware again after death.

Therefore, the government is also in the dark about much of the UFO mystery. They are also seeking full disclosure but know only bits and pieces. This is backed up by Jim Semivan who says the phenomenon is not something that can be scientifically quantified:

> *I am very much aware, particularly in regard to the Phenomenon, that this measured and linear approach is arguably laughable. How do you make sense of any of it when there does not appear to be*

> *any apparent "there" there? The Phenomenon seems to work on another level (consciousness, dimensions?) unknown to our science.*

Another example comes from the 13% of experiencers who have reported being allowed to fly the ships. What they describe is a process where they put their hand on a pad or a ball type object which allows them to become one with the ship. The entire ship starts to change in structure and size, and they are able to just move the craft around just by thinking.

The whole process shows that the technology involved is light years ahead of what we now possess and is intimately tied to consciousness. This is backed up by Chris Bledsoe who told me that a General in the USAF wanted to talk to him about the process.

This points to a situation where the military is in reality seeking enlightenment about the process by talking to a civilian who is an experiencer. Chris has been approached by many government people looking to him for answers as to what is going on. Because he has such a high level of contact, he is seen as a way to communicate with the UFO intelligence, and find out what is really going on.

Asking the government to disclose might be equivalent to demanding that the aliens land and disclose. This would be like saying I will not play by the limitations of the "river of forgetfulness" and demand the answers to all the questions.

The answers appear to be there but it is part of the game to find them for ourselves. We know from the FREE survey that 37% of all experiencers report that at some point during their experience they knew the answer to "everything in the universe."

All that information was forgotten as the abduction/encounter ended and the person was returned to their everyday nuts and bolts 3-D world. Experiencers are often told that Earth is a school.

Information is available to experiencers but the process seems to indicate that it is not intended that they have the unlimited knowledge (at least for the time being) so it was taken back like a dream dissolving upon waking. Betty Andreasson Luca was told that people have secrets locked in their minds and that the will remember when the time is right.

The same knowledge of "everything" is reported by people who have near death experiences, or people who are taken into deep states of hypnosis like the technique perfected by Delores Cannon, called Quantum Healing Hypnosis Technique (QHHT).

Appendix 1 - The Illusion of Deaths by Religion

When people make the argument about religions causing deaths they usually refer to the genocide during the Crusades, which took place between the 11th and 14th century, where between 1,000,000 and 9,000,000 people died. What the argument leaves out is that this genocide over 300 years is nothing compared the genocides in the 20th century, and the fact that these deaths were not motivated by religious beliefs but other cultural philosophies and views.

Following is list of all the major genocides of the 20th century and the biggest war in the United States. It clearly shows that religion had nothing to do with people dying. A close look shows that the cause of the deaths was the belief in some sort of separation, whether it be us versus them, good people versus bad people, survival of the fittest (strong versus the weak).

Civil War- 620,000 soldiers died - The deaths had nothing to do with religion, but by the belief in separation. Pulitzer Prize-winning author James McPherson writes that, "The Civil War started because of uncompromising differences between the free and slave states over the power of the national government to prohibit slavery in the territories that had not yet become states."

Congo Free State (1886-1908): **8,000,000** people died in this situation and it had nothing to do with religion. The deaths arose after Leopold II and the formation of the Congo Free State. Leopold exploited the indigenous population and imposed a forced labor system in a private venture to extract ivory, rubber, and minerals in the upper Congo basin which led to the death of 20% of the population.

South Africa Apartheid - The deaths had nothing to do with religion, but by the belief in separation. **21,000** people died in political violence. 14,000 of them died during the six-year transition process from 1990 to 1994. A separatist belief existed where whites were believed to be better than blacks. If everyone had believed in oneness, these deaths would not have occurred.

Soviet Union - The Soviet Union was a secular atheist state where religion was not even allowed. The deaths were caused by separation and a belief of two separate political classes. It was believed that the proletariat (rank and file workers) had to kill the evil bourgeoisie (the capitalist class who own most of society's wealth and means of production) elements of society. The battle involved the oppressed fighting their oppressors. The second group to lose their lives involved the World War II against Germany where religion once again was not an issue. When Lenin took over, **9,000,000** people died in the next eight years in what was called a civil war. In the years of Stalin (1924-1953) another **20,000,000** died.[166]

China – The deaths also had nothing to do with religion, but a belief in separation. China was a secular atheist state where religion was not allowed – the belief that the proletariat had to eradicate evil bourgeois elements prevailed. Conservative estimates place the number of dead at **40,000,000**.[167]

Cambodia – 1975-1979 – Once again, this was a secular atheist regime that killed **2.0 to 2.5 million** people after taking power. The Communist Khmer Rouge "executed almost everyone suspected of connections with the former government or with foreign governments, as well as professionals and intellectuals." It was a straight belief in separation where anyone seen as opposition to the government was executed. The separatist belief was so fanatical that anyone with eyeglasses was executed under the belief that if they could read, they were evil intellectuals that needed to die.

North Korea – Once again, we have a secular government where religion did not play a role and it is estimated that up to **3,500,000** people have died over the last few decades. The anti-religious movement in the country is so severe that a person can be executed for professing a religion, which is viewed as being in opposition to the government. Executions of Christians have included public execution by running over them with steamrollers, being hung on a cross over a fire, herded off bridges, and trampled underfoot. The separation here is the government versus people's religious beliefs, which are seen as a threat to government.

Appendix 2 - MJ-12 Document Leaks

This is a list of the MJ-12 documents supplied by Dr. Bob Wood that show the scope of document leaks. A quick look over the list makes the theory that one person like Richard Doty or Bill Moore created all these documents on their typewriter is pretty far-fetched.

There were many sources and pages

Source	When	Docs.	Pages	Classification.
Jaime Shandera	1984	2	8	TSMEO
Bill Moore	1985	1	11	TSR
Legionnaire via TC	1992	1	4	TS
CIA archivist via TC	1992	1	1	TS
Cantwell via TC	93-96	16	42	TS
Quillin via D. Berliner	1994	1	23	TSRMEO
Tim Cooper/FOIA	1994	1	1	MJ-12ref
Salina via TC mailbox	1996	14	38	TSMEO
S-2 (mail plus to TC)	1999	48	3132	S, uncl
Ft. Meade Army FOIA	1999	1	335	TSM, conf
S-1 (mailed to TC)	2000	10	150	TSM
S-3 (mailed to TC)	2000	3	4	TS, x2
S-4 (mailed to TC)	2001		4	TSOmega
	Totals	103	3766	

Appendix 3 - The Five Messiahs

....

Many whistleblowers in the UFO community have come forward over the last 70 years willing to violate their security clearances, and claiming they are prepared to reveal the details of the most highly classified subject in the United States. Each whistleblower cites different reasons justifying why. They state they were participants in the government/military lies, but we should believe them because they are now telling the truth.

Instead of dealing with all of the whistleblowers in this conclusion, I have chosen to deal with the five most famous "messiahs" whom the government chose to reveal the truth to the public.

The five are Bill Moore, Steven Greer, Timothy Cooper, Tom DeLonge, and Dan Smith. They differ from other whistleblowers in that they are leaders of groups, comprised of civilian and military witnesses, who are feeding them information to share with the public.

The five messiahs are not lone rangers. Each (except for Smith) claimed to have more than a few high-level government officials who have chosen them to get the message out. That makes them more valuable than a single lone whistleblower who professes to know all the secrets, and is willing violate his or her security oath to tell all.

After considerable time studying these five messiahs, I have concluded that they do have the sources they say they have, and none of them are lying. More importantly, it does appear that someone has "green-lighted" them to reveal data regarding the UFO phenomenon, and they have been receiving inside information from these sources on what the government knows about UFOs.

Each Messiah is a witness having some flaw that provides plausible deniability to his documents.

DeLonge, for example, wrote a song about having sex with a dog, and also posted stories that he knew probably weren't true on a conspiracy website he had. In some cases, like Timothy Cooper, one of Cooper's documents pointed back to his typewriter. |

Some like Moore and Greer exhibited big egos which turned other researchers off.

None of the five, except possibly Moore, had any "need-to-know" for classified information. Bill Moore had worked with the CIA, but claimed that during his time working with high-level officials on the

UFO subject he was not working for the government and was not getting paid. [168]

Each of the five felt that the officials he was dealing with were his friends, and each believed that his sources were giving him the truth.[169] Smith conceded that his source, Pandolfi, was paid to lie, but was still providing him the truth.

The information each got was being allowed for release by someone giving the green light. None of these individuals were arrested or punished in any way for their massive leaks of information.

Messiah	Beliefs	Contacts
Bill Moore 1980-1994	Believed he was the only one who knew what was going on.	<ul><li>CIA directors Robert Gates and Richard Helms</li><li>Richard Doty</li><li>Col. Lane and others in the military.</li><li>20 other contacts</li></ul>
Steven Greer 1990-Present	Believes he had been given answers by aliens. Believes he is the only one, aside of the cabal, who knows what is going on.	<ul><li>John Petersen</li><li>Commander Will Miller</li><li>Military contacts</li></ul>
Tom DeLonge 2014-Present	Believes his Cargo Cult theory explains everything, and that he is being given information rather than disinformation.	<ul><li>Retired USAF Major General Michael Carey</li><li>General William Neil McCasland</li><li>Robert Weiss</li><li>Jim Semivan</li><li>Six other advisors</li></ul>
Timothy Cooper 1993-1999	Believed he had been sent documents because of his father's government UFO involvement.	<ul><li>Cantwheel</li><li>Cantwheel's daughter</li><li>A CIA archivist</li><li>Legionnaire</li><li>Alleged CIA FOIA release</li></ul>
Dan Smith	Believes the CIA chose him to announce a	Only one source. 26 years of almost daily

Messiah	Beliefs	Contacts
	UFO phenomenology problem. Believed like DeLonge that he might be a Messiah.	conversations with the CIA man in charge of the UFO situation.

Moore: Moore thought that the military and government officials chose him. He received his first contact in 1980, days after publishing *The Roswell Incident*. Moore was told, in two initial phone calls, that he was the "only one" who knew what was going on. According to Moore, his primary contact said he wanted to help him. The hook was set, and the operation to use Moore to get out a message began.

He believed there were attempts to monitor and possibly sidetrack his efforts. Much of his beliefs came from officials talking to him and his partner Shandera using codes and postcards. These had him flying around the country for secret meetings.

To deal with this, Moore created bird names for all his sources because he believed he was being watched and by using bird names he and Shandera could talk on the phone about people without using their names. Moore felt high-level officials were doing the best they could to handle the UFO situation that they were facing.

Moore claimed 24 sources.

DeLonge: Like Moore, DeLonge thinks he was chosen to get the message to the young people of America. Those who had released material before him, according to DeLonge, had been the victims of "effective disinformation." DeLonge differs from the others in that he got advisors to help him after he requested them. So, he believes he put the group of advisors together.

DeLonge claims to have ten high-level sources.

Greer: Like Moore and DeLonge, Greer thinks he was chosen to bring UFO disclosure to the world. Like Moore and DeLonge he believes he knows more than anyone in the field. He even feels he knows more than the President of the United States, which inspired him to send disclosure briefing materials to Clinton, Bush, Obama, and Trump.

Greer claims 540 high-level sources.

Cooper: Cooper got documents through filing FOIAs to twelve government agencies. Many researchers accused him of hoaxing all the new Majestic documents from the 1990s because of one document typed on a similar typewriter to his.

The defense that there were 3700 pages of documents produced by one man, on many typewriters, mailed from other points in the country such as the post office box of the CIA, is not believable. The fact that only one document pointed to Cooper, when all of the documents should have pointed his way was ignored. The single document pointing back should have been viewed as a red flag that plausible deniability was being set up, but it was not even considered.

The fact that he produced 150 photographs from the early history of the modern UFO mystery, and a manuscript that was actually tracked back to its 1950s author was also ignored.

Smith: Smith has only one source but there is no question as to who he is and the important role he plays in controlling what the United States government knows about UFOs.

Smith believes he was chosen and calls himself the CIA eschatologist, as he believes the CIA knows the UFO mystery may involve the final destiny of the soul and of humankind.

Appendix 4 - The Fourteen Magicians

Something does not make much sense here. Why would someone in Washington mount a disinformation effort if the only result is to confuse members of the UFO research community, which is a very small group without much influence over the public at large? **Researcher and author Jacques Vallee**

I'm certainly not going to jump to any conclusions because I still place considerable trust in the other parties. My opinion is the same---those other people are solid. If they are up to something, there are good reasons, although I sure as hell don't understand what they are at this point and probably never will… All I'm saying is, those other people still have my trust until someone proves otherwise. The rest of us only dabble in the UFO subject. Those guys walk on a high tightrope without a net, and it might be tough for non-spooks like us to figure out what the hell they are doing and where their loyalties lie. **George Knapp**

The following is a list of key people who have played a role in disclosing bits and pieces of the UFO story to the American population. There are lesser figures that could be included but weren't, as my knowledge of their role is less clear. These names would include Henry Kissinger, Jack Verona, Ernie Kellerstrass, and Dale Graff.

Those who believe that the CIA has done everything it can to cover up the story, or that the CIA is not involved as is defined by the official CIA position, have to explain why these CIA personnel made obvious moves to help let the UFO story get out.

Another key thing to remember is, as Rositzke (below) pointed out in his writings, that the CIA does not operate as a separate and independent entity. It takes its instruction from the President of the United States, in the forms of secret directives and executive orders.

Therefore, stories that the CIA went out and did this or that cannot be right. They have only one role, and that is to provide the best intelligence possible to the people at 60,000 feet and carry out orders from the president. Therefore, if the CIA does something related to UFOs, the president is behind it.

1. Roscoe H. Hillenkoetter

Admiral Roscoe Hillenkoetter was the first CIA Director from 1947–1950. According to researcher Todd Zechel, Hillenkoetter "was very vociferous about the dangers of accidental nuclear war triggered by UFO intrusions and overflights, either in the Soviet Union or America. This was to the point he allowed NICAP Director Don Keyhoe to publicly quote him warning as such while he served on Keyhoe's NICAP Board of Governors."

His appearance on the UFO board gave support to the fact that the phenomena were real and not fictional as the CIA was still maintaining. Hillenkoetter stated, "It is time for the truth to be brought out in open Congressional hearings. Behind the scenes, high-ranking Air Force officers are soberly concerned about UFOs. But through official secrecy and ridicule, many citizens are led to believe the unknown flying objects are nonsense. To hide the facts, the Air Force has silenced its personnel through the issuance of a regulation."[170]

2. Arthur Lundahl

Arthur Lundahl was a key CIA official who seemed to support some UFO disclosure. He headed up a Navy photographic laboratory that did the analysis of the films for the CIA sponsored Robertson Panel report on UFOs in 1953.

He received a promotion to run the new CIA lab that did an analysis of all the U-2, SR-71, and spy satellite photographs. It was Lundahl that discovered the Soviet missile in Cuba, and who briefed President Kennedy during the Cuban missile crisis.

It was also Lundahl that channeled an alien (AFFA) in 1959 at his NPIC facility in Washington. He allowed the story's broadcast in a 1974 documentary called *UFOs: Past, Present, and Future*, but refused to appear on camera talking about the incident.

He interacted with some UFO researchers such as Army Security Agency employee Todd Zechel. Zechel reported that Lundahl has told him, "in February 1969 a high-ranking Soviet KGB official flew to Washington, DC, to meet with the CIA hierarchy and work out a sort of non-aggression pact on UFOs whereby each side would pledge not to falsely claim the UFOs, hovering over the other's sensitive military installations, were secret devices which belonged to them...."

> April 9, 1970
> Bethesda, Md.
>
> Dear Jim —
>
> Just returned from a trip to Midwest to discover your letter of 4/1. Would like very much to see you while you are here in the D.C. Area. Right now, April 28 at noon - for lunch, or later in the afternoon looks best from my schedule. Don't expect to be in town on the 26th. How about calling me when you can on Monday April 27th. Then we can confirm lunch on the 28th or reschedule to some other time of mutual agreement.
>
> My home phone: OLIVER 4 5946
> My office phone: 351 - 2170
>
> Will look forward to seeing you and engaging in more discussion of a most important subject - the UFO's. Cheerio
> Curt Lundahl

"This pact was put in place in order to try to prevent an accidental nuclear exchange or war triggered by UFO intrusions and overflights. He also told Zechel that he had briefed four presidents on the subject of UFOs."[171]

He was fascinated with the UFO subject as is shown in the letter pictured here, which he wrote to James McDonald, at the University of Arizona – Tucson– who was a high-profile contributor to scientific UFO research, beginning in the Spring of 1966 and continuing until his death in June 1971.

I have a whole collection of correspondence by Lundahl on UFOs. This file is significant because an FOIA filed with the FBI stated there has no file on Lundahl.

3. Richard M. Helms

Richard Helms was the CIA director from 1966–1973. He was Kit Green's (see below) boss. One of the key stories related to the Aviary was that Helms was a key player and may have been one of the key powerful birds supplying Bill Moore (a former CIA employee) with UFO information. Apparently joins group in 1988-1989. Called Mr. R by Doty, also called "Raven."

Helms was CIA director when Emenegger and Sandler were given access to high level officials for their 1974 documentary *UFOs: Past, Present, and Future*. After it was over Linda Howe stated that Emenegger showed her a letter from President Nixon thanking him. Helms would, therefore, have been carrying out the president's directive.

Gary Bekkum at Starstream Research group adds a Helm's disclosure story from what Bekkum considered a reliable source. The person in question was part of a three-man team. He wrote about his encounters with Helms and UFOs, describing being contacted almost the same way that Moore was contacted by Falcon. Helms had contacted the team of three to discuss how to best promote government disclosure of the alleged extraterrestrial Core Story.

"Why he contacted me," the one team member wrote, "and wanted to meet with me privately at the National Research Council, and was so unambiguous, confuses me. I did not get the impression he did so because he was using me. Indeed, he was insistent on privacy... I am not prepared to repeat what he said to me before that, because I am uncertain as to his mental state -- he seemed intact, but the subject was, after all quite crazy -- he required secrecy, and he never said I would be released from it - the Core Story (explained later in the article) he claimed was true is the same we have heard."[172]

4. William Colby

Colby was the CIA Director from 1973-1976. According to Steve Greer Colby had reached out through his best friend, a colonel, to the Disclosure Project to help just before he died in a mysterious canoeing "accident" where he suddenly left the canoe at night with the cabin unlocked, and with the computer and coffee maker still on. Greer had told the story many times including early on when he told radio host Art Bell in 2004:

> *CIA Director Bill Colby, whose very dearest friend approached us in the mid-90s. And the week that we were going to have a meeting - listen carefully -- the week we were going to have a meeting with this former CIA Director who had been on the inside of these covert operations, where he was going to transfer to our group $50 million in funding... as well as existing extraterrestrial energy devices that were functional.*[173]

Colby was also the CIA director at the time that Emenegger and Sandler were given access to high level officials in producing their UFO documentary *UFOs: Past, Present, and Future*.

5. Kit Green

Kit Green was reported to have run the UFO parapsychology desk at the CIA from 1969-1983. Although he only spent 10% of his time on the task, he stated: "it has resulted in 90% of what is thought to be known about me!"

He probably took over the task from Arthur Lundahl. He remains employed under contract to the CIA. Green recieved the President's National Intelligence Medal in 1985.

Until 1983, when he left the CIA, Green was one of six or eight analysts who was involved and familiar with the remote viewing program being run by the CIA at Stanford Research Institute in the 1970s.

One of his reported contract jobs as an expert in forensic medicine is to investigate any high-level government officials who are exhibiting "abduction" symptoms. Green's job is to determine what is going on. The story is that 50 people fall into that category.

Green was rumored to be the man who briefed the president on UFOs and in an interview with reporter Gus Russo stated he had discussed UFOs with four presidents.[174] According to researcher Todd Zechel, "Green issued an order in 1979 to take UFOs 'off the record' within the CIA to prevent CIA's interest in UFOs from being disclosed."

Green has been part of many UFO stories such as John Alexander's UFO Working Group, Bob Bigalow's NIDS program, Bill Moore's aviary, the Serpo story, and a friendship with Richard Doty. Green was given the name Blue Jay in the aviary group used by Bill Moore to gather UFO information.

According to Robert Collins, Green was also present in an Albuquerque hotel meeting that was a follow-up to the 1988 "UFO Cover-up? Live" documentary. Others in the meeting included Hal Puthoff, Rick Doty, Bill Moore and Jaime Shandera and Collins. Collins wrote about the meeting stating, "Kit Green took center stage by proposing several lines of attack involving disclosure strategies."[175]

Green helped out trying to resolve some of the mysterious rumors in the UFO community after he left the CIA in 1983.

Kit Green was the Blue Jay in Bill Moore's disclosure initiative. Moore gave Green a series of things to do. On one occasion he approached Dr. Eric Walker at Penn State University to determine his knowledge about UFOs and the control group known as MJ-12. On another occasion, Moore sent Green for a secret rendezvous with Robert Gates who Moore believed was part of the modern-day MJ-12 group. Green was to approach Gates with a specific code word which he apparently "messed up" and the meeting never took place.

Lastly, Green is the magician who came up with the idea of the Core Story, which he developed with Hal Puthoff and Jacques Vallee. Green described the Core Story this way, "Simply put, the core story is this: 'The ETs came here, maybe once, maybe a few times. Either through accident or by design, the US government acquired one of their craft. The only problem was that the physics that powered the craft were so advanced that for decades, we humans have struggled to understand it or replicate it."

6. Harry Rositzke

Rositzke was an agency official from 1946-1970 involved in espionage, counterespionage, and covert operations. He headed up military intelligence in London, Paris, and Germany during World War Two. Rositzke was the first chief of the CIA's Soviet division.

He wrote a book called *The CIA's Secret Operations: Espionage, Counterespionage, and Covert Action*. He described CIA policy as "an all-purpose action instrument for secretly executing presidential policies." Rositzke simply dismissed the spate of recent charges against the CIA (involvement in JFK's assassination, involvement with domestic police, etc.) as an "exercise in absurdity" which in his opinion only aided the Soviet KGB; he also insisted that, since the CIA always follows executive orders, the CIA was being made a "fall guy." He died in 2002.

According to Bill Moore, Rositzke was pulled out of retirement to leak the MJ-12 document, and introduce the concepts of Project Aquarius and the live alien into the public consciousness. Rositzke contacted Moore days after Moore started a tour for his book *The Roswell Incident*.

Moore described the disclosure plan, stating, "In early September, 1980, I was approached by a well- placed individual within the intelligence community who claimed to be directly connected to a high-level project dealing with UFOs. This person told me that he spoke to a small group of similar people who were uncomfortable with the government's continuing cover-up of the truth and indicated that he and his group would like to help me with my research into the subject in the hope and expectation that I might be able to help them find a way to change the prevailing policy and get the facts to the public without breaking any laws in the process."

7. Robert Gates

Robert Gates served as CIA Director under George Bush from 1991-1993.

According to Robert Collins, "Robert Gates (today, Bob Gates will lie about this) and Henry Kissinger were behind the Reagan Disclosure Program which failed in 1991. Rick Doty, Bill Moore, and Jaime Shandera were key players, as I, Robert Collins, was."

When Gates was confronted about the story that Chase Brandon was putting out about Roswell being real and involving extraterrestrials and bodies, Gates had a chance to kill the story but didn't, stating, "I've known Chase as a martial arts instructor for the Agency....So, I'm not going to question Chase. I'm just telling you what I said."[176]

Confronted again back stage, Gates stated he had not heard Brandon's claims about the extraterrestrial craft and bodies at Roswell but told Cox, "I'll respond in this way. As director of the CIA and Secretary of Defense, I think I have had every security clearance that there is available in the United States government. I first joined the government 46 years ago, and I have never seen one shred of evidence or one report of any UFO or remains or cadavers or anything."

Cox asked him, "Is there a way to reconcile that story?" Gates replied, "No."

8. Walter Ferguson

Not much is known about Ferguson. He may have been the Raven who in 1995 showed Jamie Shandera a secret apartment the EBE3 was being kept in DC. Walter Ferguson was with the CIA. Only Moore and Shandera dealt with him.

9. Thomas Cantwheel

The Cantwheel document leaks were the biggest in history. Thomas Cryll "Cy" Cantwheel claimed to be part the Counter Intelligence Corps (CIC), Scientific and Technical Branch, Interplanetary Phenomenon Unit (IPU) from 1942-1958.

The pages of documents that were leaked between 1992 and 1999 through researcher Timothy Cooper were actually a collection of material received from 1) CIA counterintelligence officer Thomas Cantwheel, 2) Cantwheel's daughter Salina, 3) a Legionnaire, formerly Air Force counterintelligence, and 4) a former CIA archivist.

Cooper had been requesting FOIA material from 12 different agencies on the Kennedy assassination and UFOs when he started to receive UFO documents from the various agencies. Of significance was one commendation document he received showing that his father had worked analyzing UFO photos at the National Photographic Interpretation Center run by Magician #2 above - Arthur Lundahl.

Although there was a lot of controversy over some of the documents and writing, the amount of material released was absolutely enormous. It included the June 1999 receipt of a 339-page UFO manuscript titled, *An Encyclopedia of Flying Saucers*. It was written between 1957 and 1961 by author Vernon Bowen on original watermarked paper. He sent it to the USAF for fact checking and it disappeared. Bob and Ryan Wood were able to confirm the date of the paper and various inks used on the manuscript by government reviewers.

The material received by Cantwheel also included 150 photographs, and over 3,000 pages of documents. Some of these documents were photocopies but some were on original paper with traceable water marks.

The documents and Cantwheel's writings also introduced many concepts that have now shown up in the Foundation for Research into Extraterrestrial Encounters survey of 3,000 people who claim to have had contact with the intelligence behind the UFO phenomena. Those concepts include the idea of a key spiritual component to the phenomena, the idea that the UFO craft is actually alive, and the connection to nuclear weapons.

10. John Gannon

Gannon was a mentor to the present UFO man at the CIA, Ron Pandolfi. The company BAE whom Gannon worked for described his background as follows:

> *Gannon served in the most senior analytic positions at the Central Intelligence Agency and in the intelligence community, including as deputy director of intelligence at the CIA, chairman of the National Intelligence Council and assistant director of Central Intelligence for Analysis and Production. In 2004, President George W. Bush awarded him the National Security Medal, the nation's highest intelligence award.*

Of interest to ufologists is the fact that when the SERPO story (astronauts visiting another planet and an alien being the guest of the US government) broke, many key people connected to the CIA such as Pandolfi, Green, and Hal Puthoff, all seemed to pay attention to the bizarre tale (Green references the importance of the Serpo material in conclusion to this book). I, on the other hand, never read it seeing it as just unbelievable fiction.

It came close to figuring out where the *Close Encounters of the Third Kind* story originated. Some placed its beginning in the office of John Gannon.[177]

The story gained steam in 2005, when Pandolfi leaked a series of e-mails between himself and Kit Green. In the leak, Pandolfi was trying to pin the SERPO postings to former Air Force officer Richard Doty, and move it away from Gannon.

Doty was a close friend of Green, and Green had defended him in a CIA meeting in 2008 wherein he presented an FBI lie detector test during a discussion in the office of the head of counterintelligence showing that Doty was, in fact, telling the truth.

11. James Woolsey

James Woolsey and his wife Susan had a daylight UFO sighting in the late 1960s in New Hampshire. He is, therefore, an experiencer because when someone sees a UFO (as is clearly shown by abduction reports are not seen when they are operating), they are a part of what the UFO intelligence is doing. The sighting, therefore, was probably not random but intended, and Woolsey may have a mission.

Woolsey is a very powerful force connected to the government. The Institute for the Study of Globalization and Covert Politics ranks Woolsey as #2 behind Henry Kissinger. They had him sitting on 89 Non Government Agencies funded by corporations, foundations, membership fees, fund raisers, and occasional government grants.[178]

Woolsey asked for a meeting with Dr. Steven Greer in 1993 to discuss the UFO situation. After a three-hour conversation in December on the subject, Woolsey initiated both an unclassified and a classified review of CIA files on UFOs. The unclassified files ended up being summarized in an article titled "CIA's Role in the Study of UFOs, 1947-90: A Die-Hard Issue" published in the CIA's *Studies in Intelligence*.

Although Woolsey denied any interest in what Greer was saying, his wife attended a special briefing that Greer set up for members of Congress in the spring of 1997, where he gathered together about a dozen military witnesses of UFO events.

Woolsey was also part of a disclosure initiative in 1998 where the population would get prepared for a world "where it was known that aliens were among us." (See 1998 for full story)

Woolsey, it is believed, was involved in the briefing of George Bush. Although the media reports that he has left the Trump intelligence team, I am told he is still active and is helping to brief Trump on the UFO issue.

12. Chase Brandon

The Chase Brandon story can be found in the section of this book called "2012." Brandon informed radio host John Wells that his book *Cryptos Conundrum* had been heavy reviewed and that many changes were requested. The book was a fictionalized version of how the intelligence community handled the Roswell UFO crash.

Brandon told Wells, "It was a craft that clearly did not come from this planet, it crashed, and I don't doubt for a second that the use of the word 'remains' and 'cadavers' was exactly what people were talking about."

Brandon made his controversial statements about Roswell and then disappeared into the darkness. The media did not pursue him. He stated that he had another fictionalized book on UFOs that would be out in a year, but that book has not yet appeared.

9. Ron Pandolfi

Pandolfi is the most well-known magician among the twelve. He was described by researcher Gary Bekkum, "One man, and one man alone appears to occupy the best possible position to probe into the facts, fantasies, and fallacies behind the real-life 'X-Files' of UFOs, alien visitors, spies, lies, and polygraph tape."

He is a physicist who joined the CIA in 1983. Pandolfi seemed to take over the phenomenology (UFO and paranormal) desk from Kit Green and has run it ever since. In recent years, he appears to have moved up to a position in the office of the Director of National Intelligence above the CIA.

Pandolfi is the man who is rumored to talk to the president about UFOs. During the Clinton administration, Dr. Jack Gibbons, Clinton's science advisor, asked for a UFO briefing to prepare for a meeting with billionaire Laurance Rockefeller, who was coming to the White House to talk UFO disclosure.

The records show that Pandolfi at the CIA was given the job and that he handed the job to a civilian named Bruce Maccabee. This happened because this was a public event and the CIA, which has always claimed they don't do UFOs, could not be seen giving a UFO briefing to the White House.

Pandolfi has always been identified as part of a group of former and present intelligence and government officials who have looked into the UFO phenomena. The bird idea came from film producer Jamie Shandera who worked with Bill Moore on a disclosure initiative initiated at the CIA. There were 24 birds according to Shandera:

> We wanted the information but didn't want to reveal where we got our clues. To maintain anonymity, I gave Bill's source the name "Falcon," the next source we used we called "Condor" and so on until

we had 24 contacts from all levels of the government. It was my idea to use bird names.

One of the key things Pandolfi has done on the UFO disclosure front is to leak various ideas and names for 26 years to his good friend Dan Smith, who in turn posts the material on various UFO discussion boards where researchers hang out. When things get out of control, and Pandolfi is forced to answer for what he says, he usually refers to Smith as being crazy, drinking too much, or being a maniac.

Pandolfi was responsible for forcing transfer of the remote viewing program from the DIA to the CIA in 1995. Shortly thereafter, it was shut down with the public statement that it did not work. It appeared to be an effort to get the program out of the classified world with congressional insight and a document trail, to a super black budget program where research could continue without accountability.

Pandolfi is the man responsible for briefing President-elect Trump on UFOs and foreign government technology issues.

The researchers and producers Pandolfi would have managed through a quid pro quo include Bill Moore, Dan Smith, Gordon Novel, Steve Greer, Gary Bekkum, Bruce Maccabee, Ed Komarek, and Kevin Alber.

10. Jim Semivan

Jim Semivan, according to Simon & Schuster, "retired in 2007 after a 25-year career in the Central Intelligence Agency's Directorate of Operations. At the time of his retirement he was a member of the CIA's Senior Intelligence Service. Jim served both overseas and domestically and is the recipient of the Agency's Career Intelligence Medal."

Semivan is referred to by some as the Big Man. He stated that he became involved with DeLonge in April 2016 after DeLonge contacted the military to get the UFO message to the young people of America and is an experiencer who had a dramatic night-time experience in his bedroom. One Swedish UFO group described Semivan as having a "long-standing interest in UFOs and the paranormal with several intriguing personal experiences."[179]

He has an interest in the holographic brain concept so his UFO view would probably fall into the Edgar Mitchell holographic universe worldview, or the phenomenological problem as described by Pandolfi.

Being an experiencer, Semivan was focused in part on experiencers. This would separate him from the other magicians (except Woolsey who is also an experiencer) who were more into the nuts and bolts or political angle to the UFO mystery.

When the Big Man heard that DeLonge had made a connection inside Lockheed Skunk Works and offered to help disclose the UFO story through his media empire, he decided to investigate and become involved.

He is now running the DeLonge disclosure operation, and as CIA takes instruction from the Executive Order of the President, the President became involved as well.

The final story of interest with the Big Man is that he provided a consultation with Col. John Alexander about the reality of the UFO situation.

Alexander had talked to top officials in all the alphabet agencies and wrote in his book *UFOS, Myths, Conspiracies, and Realities* that he had spoken to the head or the deputy of all the lettered agencies and could find no one working on the UFO problem.

Therefore, when Semivan told him it was for real, and people were, in fact, working on the problem, Alexander apparently asked, "Who's in charge?"

Semivan replied with two words, "They are."

I heard that Alexander had received the green light to talk. We will see what he says. In a February 2017 lecture at UFO Congress, he stated that "UFOs are real" and they aren't a risk as they have not attacked us.

The researchers and producers he would have managed through a quid pro quo include Tom DeLonge and Chris Bledsoe.

Appendix 5 - The Defense Intelligence Agency Connection

DIA Links Mentioned by Howard Blum

Blum in his book about the Top-Secret UFO Working Group mentions DIA's Directorate for Management and Operations as being the main office involved. He also claims they have a Project Aquarius. (p.33)

Blum says he phoned the DIA office in the Pentagon and talked to Phillips. (p.50)

Blum states that the FBI went to the DIA headquarters in Pentagon room 3E258 to ask questions about the leaked 1987 Top-secret MJ-12 document. (p.209)

Blum states that Col. Harold E. Phillips, (Col. John Alexander) U.S. Army was transferred to the DIA in June 1985. Blum states that he entered the Army as first Lieutenant, has a graduate degree in electrical engineering.

In 1986 Blum claims that Phillips became "Associate Coordinator of Space Reconnaissance Activities," inside the DIA. This made him an assistant to the DIA's representative to the National Foreign Intelligence Board's Committee on Imagery requirements and Exploitation (COMIREX) – one of the most sensitive and powerful jobs in the intelligence community.

DIA is persuaded to convene a top-secret working group to investigate UFOs (p.40)

Mentions arrivals at the Pentagon DIA Directorate for Management and Operations by various high-level scientists and intelligence people invited for the first meeting of the UFO Working Group. (p.41)

DIA - UFO Links

....

Blum mentions that in the fall of 1983 researcher Bill Moore got a call telling him that Korean Flight 007 "had been shot down over the

Soviet Union – before the story hit the press." (p.237) The agency in charge of the investigation of the Korean incident was DIA. At the point hours before the story had hit the press, it would be safe to assume the only people who would know would be people at DIA headquarters.

Bill Moore produced a flow chart showing the hierarchy of government agencies involved in the UFO cover-up. This chart was composed based on information he had discovered from people on "the inside." The DIA is given a key role in the chart.

It is generally believed that Bill Moore's top contact, Falcon, who was the main source of most of the material he received was with the DIA. The Blum encounter with the DIA UFO Working Group oddly occurs at the same time as the two-hour UFO Cover-up Live documentary which was filmed in Washington DC, home of DIA headquarters. All evidence pointed to Falcon as the initiator of the UFO documentary and source of much of the information used on the show.

In Phil Klass's January 8, 1988, phone interview with Richard Doty, Doty made a statement, which also pointed to the Falcon as being in Washington. Doty told Klass that he had retained a lawyer to "take action" concerning the story he had leaked on the document. He then claimed that Moore had named the man he had gotten the documents from. (MJ-12)

"He gave the person's name in the affidavit that he received the documents from, and this person – I don't know him – this person in Washington D.C. My attorney went to Washington D.C. and spoke to this person and he denied ever giving Bill Moore anything although he said that he had regular contact with Bill Moore."

More importantly, in the same interview Doty states that the FBI investigated the MJ-12 document and interviewed the same person in Washington about the document. In a question from Klass as to who produced the documents Doty stated:

> "Well, the FBI knows that. The FBI knows who did it. That information was provided to the FBI. The FBI interviewed this person and of course this person denied that he gave them to Moore . . The FBI never pursued it, I don't know why, unless they couldn't. I don't know if there was any law that this person broke. I don't know if it is public record or not, but you'll have to go to the FBI to find out. But I

know for a fact they interviewed him – this person in Washington, D.C."

Now Blum, in his book "Out There" tells a story that closely matches what Doty told Klass about going to Washington to interview people about the MJ-12 document.

The two foreign counterintelligence FBI agents, according to Blum, go to room 3E258 in the Pentagon. This is the office of the Director of the Defense Intelligence Agency, as the agents had learned the DIA was "covertly investigating UFOs." They were there asking for help in their investigation of the MJ-12 document. Blum writes:

It was the FBI's undisputed responsibility to investigate thefts of classified documents. And that was why I finally learned, the two agents had come to the DIA looking for guidance. They were trying to determine whether an incredible UFO document had been stolen from the government of the United States. And, more perplexing, whether the document was genuine.[180]

Blum even states that the UFO Working group discussed the document, and that Colonel Phillips confirmed the fact that the FBI was asking questions about the legitimacy of the MJ-12 document as if he had been interviewed.

The FBI did investigate the MJ-12 document. In the 22 pages that make up FBI file 65-81170 they refer to an investigation by INTD, Section CI-2." A note made related to A COPY OF THE MJ-12 document, which appeared in Dallas stated, "attempt should be made to determine any DOD interest in the enclosed document." There is no record of any visit to DIA headquarters at the Pentagon in the fall of 1988, and all the FBI documents are dated in 1991 almost 4 years after the report was first made public.

The DIA Falcon Link

....

If Doty's story about Moore identifying the man behind the MJ-12 documents to the FBI is true, the trip of the counterintelligence agents to the DIA Headquarters in the Pentagon, mentioned by Blum, indicates the man Moore identified was in that office. As Coleman said he knew him and that he had a definite need to know, all point to one of the upper echelon persons in DIA headquarters in 1988 when the FBI made their trip.

Bill Coleman told Billy Cox that Falcon, who was in the audience at "UFO Cover-up...Live" was definitely with "the agency" and that he had "need-to-know security credentials." Cox stated:

> "Coleman said he was totally surprised by the Falcon's testimony, and didn't know what to make of it. But Coleman was an Air Force censor and knows a lot more than he lets on. But he tends to be skeptical about government cover-up stories, or at least that's the face he wears around me. Anyway, he said that the show had gotten his curiosity ignited and he was going to make a concerted effort to "get to the bottom" of the Roswell thing. Unless, of course, the government decided that his curiosity wasn't in the best interests of national security, in which case he would get a debriefing. I said, 'Bill if that happens, will you at least let me know about it?' Coleman says, 'No.'"

Doty was not with an "agency" and Coleman would be more likely to know people in the DIA than the CIA.

Appendix 6 - Revision of "True" Article on Flying Saucers

This article shows the openness that existed about flying saucers in the early 1950s in the public domain. It also shows that American officials were open to working with other countries such as Canada on the flying saucer problem.

In November 1950, Major Donald Keyhoe sent a six-page draft paper on flying saucers to the Canadian Defense Research Board (DRB), and Wilbert Smith, through the Canadian Embassy in Washington, D.C. The DRB was a Canadian defense group responsible for all weapons development in Canada, and a group, which provided "full cooperation" to the Canadian government official flying saucer investigation, which became known as "Project Magnet."

Keyhoe's intention was to publish the article in "True" magazine. It was an article that dealt with the Canadian government effort to investigate flying saucers, and was based on an earlier interview that Keyhoe had done with Wilbert Smith, who would go on to head the Canadian Government saucer study. Dr. Omond Solandt, then the Chairman of the DRB realized that the article was going to present problems, so he forwarded the article on to Smith.

In a reply letter to Keyhoe, written on November 24, 1950, Smith thanked Keyhoe for "letting us see this advance document and to comment upon it." He stated, however, that he felt "the presentation might cause considerable embarrassment to the Canadian Government since they would be required to make some sort of official statement shortly after the release of the article, which they are not, at the present time, in a position to do."

On the same day, Smith wrote back to Dr. Solandt notifying him that he had sent a five-page revision of the flying saucer paper to Keyhoe along with a letter explaining the Canadian position.

In his memo to Solandt, Smith also suggested that "the article, as revised, be scrutinized by others in the group" for any further revisions they might suggest.

Most importantly, it should be noted that the following five-page draft was sent not only to the Research and Development Board, but to a key member of the board Vannevar Bush, who Smith had identified in a Top-Secret memo as the head of a small group which was making a concentrated effort on the modus operandi of the saucers. This Bush role in the article was described in January 1951 correspondence between Wilbert Smith and the Canadian Embassy in Washington, D.C.

No document has yet surfaced as to exactly what Bush's opinion of the article was. We do know that it was cleared for public distribution though. The Canadian military liaison to the Research and Development Board, Arnauld Wright, got the article from Vannevar Bush and returned it to Keyhoe. It did not make the 1950 issue of "True" as intended, but was published in Major Keyhoe's `1954 book "Flying Saucers from Outer Space" pp. 133-136.

The Smith revision of the Keyhoe article forwarded to Vannevar Bush "for clearance" was found in Smith's files at the University of Ottawa. It reads as follows.

Proposed Revision of "True" Article on Flying Saucers

A group of Canadian Scientists has been working for some time on certain problems connected with the earth's magnetic field. These investigations appear to point the way to new technology in magnetics, and if the initial conclusions are correct, they offer a ready-made explanation for many of the striking features, which have been reported in connection with the sighting of flying saucers. The basic promise is that it is possible to produce a magnetic "sink" within the earth's field; that is, a region into which the magnetic flux will flow at a controlled rate, giving some of its potential energy in the process. Such a sink would have many interesting properties, such as the following;

1. Electrical power could be obtained from the collapse of the earth's magnetic field into the sink.
2. Powerful reaction forces could be developed into a conducting ring surrounding the sink and offset from it, sufficient to support a suitably designed ship and to propel it.
3. If the rate of flow of magnetic flux is modulated the resulting magnetic disturbance could be used for communication purposes.

It is curious to note that most of the descriptions of flying saucers are in accordance with the design, which would be necessary to exploit the properties of a magnetic sink. For example, the saucers are described as consisting of a large circular disc, slightly dished, with a small central cabin. In this sense, the sink could be located in the upper central part of the cabin, and the collapsing field in cutting through the surrounding magnetic ring would induce in it an electric current, which would react with the magnetic field that induced it, producing a force, which would have a substantial vertical component. Support and propulsion of the ship would then be a combination of this resultant force, the airfoil action of the disc, and the interaction between currents in the disc by its rotation and the main field.

Rotation of the disc may be either deliberate, for induction of eddy currents or may be incidentally caused by the electronic drag of the very large current circulating around the disc. In any case, there is good observational evidence that the disc appears to rotate.

Since the lift on the saucer will be proportional to the product of the earth's magnetic field and the field produced by the current induced by the disc, it follows that when the saucer is accelerating upwards, a greater force is required and hence a greater circulating current. If the circulating current is sufficiently large and the cooling of the disc is inadequate, it may become red or even white hot, which is in line with several reported observations. Also, under certain conditions of operation a very high voltage may be built up between the center and the rim of the disc, which would result in corona discharge through the surrounding air if the saucer were at a sufficiently high altitude. Such a discharge would resemble the northern lights but would be very much more intense. This also seems to be confirmed by observations.

Navigation of such a flying saucer would be a very complex process indeed. In the first place the earth's magnetic field makes all sorts of angles with the horizontal, depending upon geographical latitude, and upon peculiar local conditions. Thus, the direction of the force, which results from the interaction of the earth's field and the field of the disc, may be in almost any direction.

Furthermore, the tilt of the saucer to get the reaction force in the wanted direction most probably will result in aerodynamic forces in some other direction. Navigation therefore would resolve into a determination of the field direction, comparison with the direction in which it is desired to move, and an analysis of the aerodynamic forces, which would result from such a motion, and the suitable correction in the initial tilt of the saucer and the flow of magnetic flux. It is doubtful if a human pilot could manage to do all this at the speed that which would be necessary to maneuver a saucer at the speeds and through the intricate motions, which have been observed. It is therefore highly probable that the saucer control systems are semi if not totally automatic, and most likely a push button effort.

There are many reports of saucers hovering in one spot for some time. For a saucer designed to operate as described, this would probably be its easiest maneuver, as it would be necessary merely to adjust the flux flow and tilt until the resultant force exactly balanced the weight of the saucer. There would be little or no aerodynamic problem in this case.

The only sound, which would be expected from such a saucer, would be a swish as of any object passing through the air, plus any incidental noises, which might originate with the internal machinery of the saucer. There would be no roar of engine exhaust or jets, or beat of propellers, or any other noises usually associated with aircraft.

It would be quite possible for a saucer such as has been described to leave vapor trails if it happened to pass through a region of supersaturated air, with a sufficient voltage on the disc to produce a corona discharge. The ions produced by the discharge would form nuclei for the condensation of droplets of water or crystals of frost, and the path of the saucer would be marked by the resulting visible cloud.

There is no indication that accelerations to which a saucer crew would be subjected would be any different from the accelerations going on through the same maneuvers. Those authorities that have been consulted say that gravity can be neutralized or the inertia of matter overcome. Where saucers have been observed to execute close turns and other maneuvers which would result in large accelerations, it is most probable that such saucers are remotely controlled and do not contain living matter as we know it.

Appendix 7 - Donald Trump and the ETs

Now that Hillary Clinton has lost the election, her promise to get to the bottom of the government secrecy on UFOs has ended. The stories of some imminent revolution in government regarding ET awareness did not happen.

As soon as Hillary left the scene, there was a message to Steve Bassett from a person inside the Pentagon who said people were working on the problem and were willing to come forward if they were given the green light by those in the government who control the issue.

That went nowhere, as apparently, no one in charge was willing to give the green light necessary.

There was also an effort to get Hillary to elaborate on her knowledge of what happened with UFOs during the Clinton administration. The plan was she would tell reporter Maureen Dowd how the system had kept the secret, and that that might stir enough controversy to turn on the light green.

There was also another planned move to get the government to open up and rocker Tom DeLonge is a big part of this, supported by those controlling the secret who favor gradual disclosure.

I have an inside source who is among the large number of people supporting DeLonge's disclosure effort, and I am aware of the person in Washington heading his effort.

When the presidential election was over, I asked if the light was still green or whether it had turned red and was told it was green and that the disclosure project was bigger than ever. I was told there would be big names and big money behind what was about to happen.

I was pointed to a big event in January. Those who didn't believe could still walk away.

In the end, there seems to be no clear intent by any reporter to go down the road of pressing for answers, so we may just be heading back into the dark ages of knowledge about the UFO subject, or perhaps into the world where Hollywood will play a bigger role in getting the masses ready for contact.

As the researcher who has invested 30 years of research into the relationship between United States Presidents and UFOs, I looked to see how Trump now fits in and now that he has won the election, the time has come to write about what I have found.

The first thing to mention is that Trump was told about the secret by at least one team of intelligence briefers led by Ron Pandolfi, who reported in an email to the researcher and former Air Force scientist, Robert Collins, that Trump was for disclosure and against disinformation.

Yet, we really don't know what Trump thinks about the subject, despite his apparent interest and past talk about conspiracy theories.

These conspiracy theories are often outlined in the *National Enquirer* newspaper which supported Trump during the election.

One of the reasons that we know so little is that Trump has not been confronted by the media or the public. The UFO community, whose job it is to advocate for disclosure, has a lot of opinions about what American leaders should do about UFOs, but not enough American reporters step up and demand explanations.

Trump would have been asked what his opinion was regarding the UFO topic, but the way he ran his campaign prevented reporters, like Daymond Steer, at the *Conway Daily Sun*, from asking.

Steer has brought up the UFO topic with most candidates, including Hillary in 2008, but was unable to do so with Trump, who did not run a traditional campaign in New Hampshire.

The normal political campaign spends 6 months to a year in New Hampshire in an attempt to win and gain momentum as New Hampshire is the second state to vote for the party candidates.

Everyone gets a bus and travels from town to town asking people in town halls what they think then trying to sell those voters on the candidates. Every candidate meets with editorial boards of small town newspapers in the state in hopes that they will do a positive article describing a particular candidate's platform and qualifications.

Trump did not do this. Trump really didn't care what anyone thought. He believed he had the answer to everything and had no need to go into a town hall or listen to people on the street. If you don't believe this, just remember that Trump said he knew more about Isis than military generals.

The way Trump operated in New Hampshire (and in every other state) was to fly in an hour before a speech in his Boeing 757 and like in the case of New Hampshire, fly back to New York after the event.

Therefore, Trump never appeared in the *Conway Daily Sun* newsroom where he would have faced the question on the UFO topic.

Now that Trump is in the White House, it is apparent that nothing has changed. Trump had done exactly that the 13 presidents before him (who had to deal with the issue) did. He could have said when he arrived, "Look at what I found. I told you the system was rigged."

He did not. For whatever reason, despite Pandolfi's claim that Trump is pro-disclosure, he did not drain the swamp on the UFO issue. But who knows, he may yet do it. Time will tell.

What we do know is, if Trump does, he will expose a world that is diametrically opposed to his own worldview; Trump and many of the aliens (in as much as we can predict their beliefs) have nothing in common.

This would indicate to me that disclosure is a road he will not go down.

Here is a comparison of the two worldviews.

Outer Space

Trump - Trump's few statements on space have made no reference to UFOs or the search for extraterrestrial life. He has made some speeches on space, and he has expressed support for manned exploration of the solar system, rather than having satellites flying around, studying things like weather.

This position has also been adopted by Republicans in Congress who have slowed progress and funding in this area for years.

There will, therefore, probably be a cutback in NASA's Earth science programs. "I will free NASA from the restriction of serving primarily as a logistics agency for low-Earth orbit activity," Trump told a Sanford, Florida audience in October.

Trump made one major speech on space in the final days of the campaign in Florida where he promised jobs and big things in space. It is evident from the speech that he was reading from a teleprompter, so the speech was probably written for him and designed to get votes. In his final Florida speeches, Trump proposed deep space manned missions, jobs, and an effort to compete with Russia and China who were very active in space.

Speaking off the cuff as he often does, his promotion of space and NASA is a little less promotional. One example was the time on the campaign trail when he told a 10-year-old that fixing potholes was a more pressing problem than anything NASA-related.

The man behind Trump's campaign space position was probably Robert Walker, who was the former chairman of the U.S. House Committee on Science, Space and Technology, and former chairman of the Commission on the Future of the U.S. Aerospace Industry. He was brought in to the Trump campaign to serve as the campaign's space policy advisor.

In an interview after Trump's victory, Walker wrote in an article he co-authored on the cutbacks in store for SLS – NASA Earth science program. NASA "has been largely reduced to a logistics agency concentrating on space station resupply and politically correct environmental monitoring," wrote Walker.

Aliens - Experiencers who have reported on the messages they received during their encounters report as one of the key messages the protection of the Earth. 39% of experiencers reported that they received an environmental message. Therefore, it would appear that the aliens would favor low-earth satellites monitoring the environment. As to deep space missions, I don't think the aliens would care. They know we aren't going very far away for a very long time.

Nuclear Weapons

Trump - He has supported a nuclear proliferation policy stating that he thought more countries should have nuclear weapons such as Japan, South Korea, and maybe even Saudi Arabia. This, reasoned Trump, would make the cost of America defending the world less costly (Trump has now denied ever saying this).

In a story by MSNBC's Joe Scarborough, he stated that while Trump was speaking with a "foreign policy expert," he repeatedly asked, "why can't we use nuclear weapons."

In a debate hosted by Chris Matthews March 31, 2016, Trump hypothesized about using nuclear weapons, "Somebody hits us within ISIS—you wouldn't fight back with a nuke?... why are we making them? Why do we make them?"

He added that the possible use of nuclear weapons would include Europe which is a big place, "Europe is a big place. I'm not going to take cards off the table. We have nuclear capability. Now, our capability is going down rapidly because of what we're doing. It's in bad shape."

Speaking to Mark Halperin at CBS, Trump expanded on nuclear weapons and Isis, "At a minimum, I want them to think maybe we would use it, OK?"

Aliens - One of the key concerns of the aliens appears to be nuclear weapons. They seemed to have appeared in mass number after we detonated the atomic bombs in 1945. Most of the early contactees spoke of messages they were getting from the aliens to stop the nuclear tests.

UFOs have been seen over nuclear weapons areas on bases and at main storage sites such as the Manzano Weapons storage area, outside of Kirkland Air Force Base. They have shut down and turned on nuclear weapons in both the United States and Russia.

Others have gotten images that may be related to nuclear weapons. Emily Trim, an eight-year-old, and one of the 62 school children that witnessed a UFO land on the edge of the playground at the Ariel school in Rhodesia in 1994, spoke about the messages she received through the eyes of the being. They were all related to the good and bad uses of technology and how humans could do better.

> *Telepathic images started going across my face ... communication through the eyes ... that's all I can really describe it as. It was just image after image after image. One of the other girls standing beside me, she got more communication about the environment, and, for me, mine was more technology uses and [inaudible] uses of technology.*

Trim did not remember any of the specific images except the last image which was a big explosion. The 1994 experience, and a second dramatic encounter with the being three years ago in Hamilton, Ontario, Canada, has left her shaken.

Following the second encounter, Trim suddenly was drawn to paint and has done 100 images that have alien symbols and messages from the aliens.

Oneness

Trump - The Trump model of the world is the materialistic Darwinist evolutionary model represented by a dog eat dog capitalist economic theory. It is a model where things are not one and connected but separate random objects in time and space. It is a model dominated by brutal, cold and insensitive competition as opposed to cooperation. It is a rape, pillage, and steal model, where the one with the most toys, when he/she dies, is considered the winner.

The Trump world is one of America first. Whereas Hillary's message was "stronger together," Trump's message was stronger apart, as when he encouraged the European Union to break up into separate countries. The Trump world is one that would be better off without alliances such as the United Nations or NATO.

The model by Trump in his America first foreign policy speech extended from individuals to countries:

> *My foreign policy will always put the interests of the American people and American security above all else. It has to be first. Has to be. That will be the foundation of every single decision that I will make.*

As opposed to the Clinton campaign slogan of stronger together, the Trump model is one where America uses every tactic at its disposal to win. The Mexicans, Chinese, Canadians, and other countries become competitors trying to steal American jobs.

Trade deals designed to work together with other countries have to be ripped up or renegotiated to get a better deal for America. Military alliances are no more if America has to pay. The new rule becomes an isolationist model where everyone is separate and must fend for themselves.

The Trump world is one of the blacks versus the police, brave Americans versus evil Arabs, and hard-working capitalists versus lazy economy destroying socialists.

It is the world where race becomes a critical separating factor. Thus, he picks as his political strategist, Stephen Bannon, who was called a "champion of racial division" by the Senate Minority leader. Most significantly it is the world the new law of the land enables children in a Middle School in Royal Oak, Michigan to chant "build the wall...build the wall" as their Latinos classmates cry and are forced to listen.

The Trump world is a world of perceived separation where it is me versus you, perceived good versus bad, rich versus poor, able versus disabled, strong versus weak. The successful enjoy, and the unsuccessful suffer.

Even his campaign was operated on a principle of separation. Hillary, the media, and Republican leaders all became opponents who were trying to attack and destroy Trump.

In the end, the whole country was dragged into the separation view of the country. The two political parties resorted to winning based on the evils of the opposition. Family members became pitted against each other, and the whole country is now in a pre-Syria condition. The only thing that differs in the United States is that the two opposing groups have not started killing each other as they are doing in Syria.

Aliens - There are many indications from experiencers, who are the closest connection we have to the beings, that "oneness" is a key principle they would like us to learn. 54% of the 2,500 experiencers who answered the FREE survey, reported that the felt "at one with the Universe" during their ET encounter. 54% of the 1054 people who answered the question stated ETs "gave a message of Love or of Oneness."

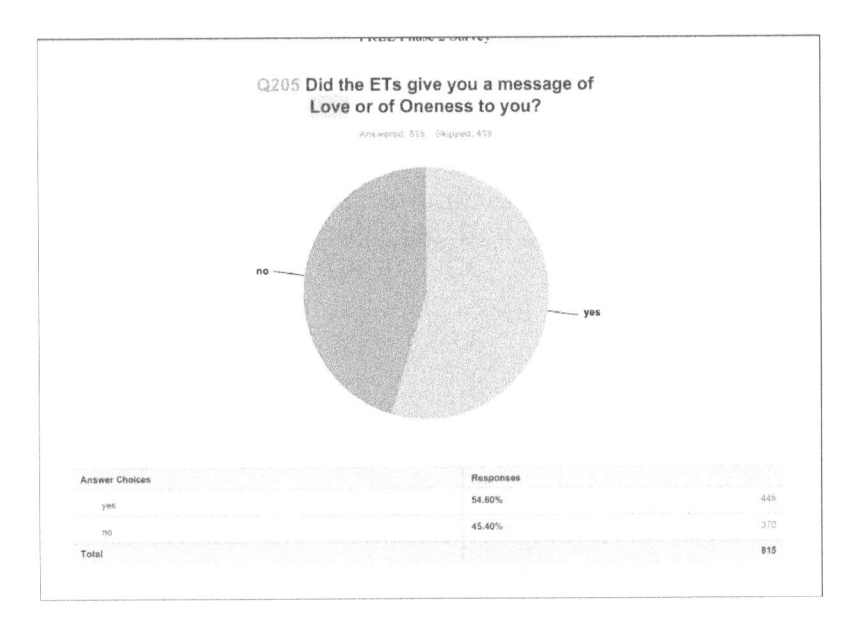

Q205 Did the ETs give you a message of Love or of Oneness to you?

Answered: 815 Skipped: 419

Answer Choices	Responses	
yes	54.60%	445
no	45.40%	370
Total		815

This oneness message, as it relates to UFOs, was also popularized by President Ronald Reagan and Mikhail Gorbachev during their meeting in November 1985.

The message (that Reagan put out almost a half dozen times) of the one world government sends chills up the spine of most Americans. It may be one of the main roadblocks to American government disclosure as selling the idea that Americans are not really special, but "all God's children" as Reagan put it. Likewise, getting the rest of the world to believe that America will be special among equals would be an equally hard sell.

The conversation was found in the Memorandum of conversations found in NSA files stated:

> *He said that previous to the General Secretary's remarks, he had been telling Foreign Minister Shevardnadze (who was sitting to the President's right) that if the people of the world were to find out that there was some alien life form that was going to attack the Earth approaching on Halley's Comet, then that knowledge would unite all the peoples of the world.*
>
> *Further, the President observed that General Secretary Gorbachev had cited a Biblical quotation, and the President is also alluding to the Bible, pointed out that Acts 16 refers to the fact that "we are all of one blood regardless of where we live on the Earth," and we should never forget that.*

It is also a message that was given by Kennedy when he said, "In the final analysis the most basic common link is that we all inhabit this small planet. We all breathe the same air, we all cherish our children's future, and we are all mortal." Many of the experiencers have also relayed a message of oneness from the aliens.

- George Adamski, who was the first person in November 1952 to be public about talking to an alien spoke about the oneness message he had been given by his alien visitors, "Always, you are One, you are All, as a centralized point of being, Undying, unchanging – and the Consciousness, Cause, and the Action – evolving, transmuting a form to a unified state of awareness."
- Sherry Wilde, author of the book *The Forgotten Promise*, about her life of experiences with a being she knows as Da, states that at the age of five, Da started teaching her three key lessons that she was to learn. She would be tested about them every time she was with them. The first and most important lesson was "We are one with our creator."
- Gene Roddenberry, creator of Star Trek, channeled Tom, a spokesman for The Council of Nine. Tom stated, "But we would say to you, yes, we are in connection with one that is higher, but in totality together we are one, as all the universe is one...."
- Bret Oldham, the author of his lifelong alien encounter in a book called *Children of the Grays*, asked the alien in control of

his abduction about God and was told, "We are one with the One, who is all."

The alien model also seems to be closely aligned with the world of quantum physics, a scientific paradigm that has replaced the old Newtonian physics model as closer to reality. Within this new model, we see non-locality rather than local causation. We see oneness versus separation. There appears to be a fundamental unity of a holographic universe first proposed by physicist David Bohm as the implicate order. Cells in the body communicating on a non-local level, and brain memories appear also to exhibit non-locality and oneness.

Material Possessions

Trump - In Trump's worldview, money and possessions are the measurements of happiness and achievement. Trump defends and plans to extend the worldview where it is justifiable for the eight richest people to have more than the bottom 50%, or for the ten richest people in America to gain 16 billion dollars in the first seven days of the Trump administration.

It is a worldview where Trump lives in a 30,000-square-foot $100 million-dollar apartment while 66 million refugees wander the world with no residence or country to call home.

Aliens - Based on the stories told by experiencers who have encountered the aliens and have been on their ships, the aliens don't appear to have anything of physical value. There are no reports of aliens with gold or jewelry.

Political System

Trump - The Trump political worldview is a strictly competitive amd capitalist model. It is a Darwinist paradigm where survival of the fittest is the rule. The strong become rich, and the weak perish. Trump's political system is one with few or if possible, no regulations or accountability. He accuses Obama of wire-tapping his office and then when asked to show the proof, he claims that that is not what he meant.

Aliens - A description of the alien political system would closely be reflective of an Israeli kibbutz, or a Hutterite Colony. The aliens work in what researchers describe as a hive environment. Each being on the ship has a job which works to achieve the task at hand. There does not seem to be a class structure. It closely resembles the ideological communist underlying philosophy, "From each according to his ability, to each according to his needs."

The aliens are without a doubt left wing socialists or ideological communists. They have been described by many as existing in a hive type social structure where there is no hierarky except by job. Everyone simply does their job. There are no reports of any material possessions. There are no descriptions of aliens with gold jewelry, designer clothes. There is no fancy furniture. Everything on the ship appears to be functional to the job they are doing.

Ecology

Trump - Trump is against laws to protect the environment as he thinks the regulations hurt business. The idea is related to the materialistic model that the Earth is to be used as a resource.

Despite this, Trump and two of his children signed a letter that was placed in the New York Times by a large group of business leaders in the eve of the Copenhagen Climate Summit in December 2009. The letter stated, "If we fail to act now, it is scientifically irrefutable that there will be catastrophic and irreversible consequences for humanity and our planet."

Trump has threatened to abolish the Environmental Protection Agency or at least start by cutting 50% of the staff. He has fast tracked two new pipelines, removing the White House webpage on climate change, and outlines plans to exploit untapped shale, oil and natural gas reserves on federal land and revive the U.S. coal industry.

Trump has openly claimed that global warming is a conspiracy started by China to slow down American business. He defends the use of asbestos arguing that the move to ban it "was led by the mob because it was often mob-related companies that would do the asbestos removal."[181]

Wind turbines promoted by those who feel that the environmental situation is bad, are described by Trump as "expensive," "doesn't work well," "detrimental to tourism," and they "kill all your birds. All your birds, killed."

Aliens - By far, the environment is the biggest difference in the beliefs between Donald Trump and the aliens.

The FREE survey of people who claimed to have encountered the intelligence behind the UFO phenomena asserts that the environment is a key concern. 1034 people answered the following question, "Did the ETs give you an environmental message regarding Earth?" 39% stated yes. [182]

1207 experiencers responded to a survey question about how their concern with environmental matters had changed because of their contact experience. 79% said it had increased strongly or somewhat.

There are scores of experiencers who report some catastrophe or change that is coming to the Earth, and most relate it to the environment. Experiencers also report that they are being trained for something. Of the 1134 people who answered 30% replied yes to the question, "Have you had contact with an ET in which you were asked to do something, or agree to do something, for them in the future?"

There are a couple, like Sherry Wilde, who have told me stories of a giant wave that will wash over the United States coming out of the Pacific. Experiencer, author, TV personality, and a host of the #1 radio talk show in Las Vegas told me that the vision she had experienced was an event where she could smell and taste in a real-time vision of the future where there were dead bodies everywhere. She felt that the number of dead totalled a billion and that the event appeared to be a flood. The aliens gave her a message saying, "This is what it may take for you people to get the message."

Sex

Even when it appears there is a connection there is not.

Trump - Trump has an great interest in sex for self-gratification.

Aliens - Aliens (greys) are reported without sex organs and their interest appears to be connected to reproducing hybrids, perhaps to seed another planet.

The Sole Commonality

Strangely, the only minor similarities between Trump and the aliens have to do with habits and not beliefs. The two common items are food and sleep.

Trump does not seem to be interested in high dining. He apparently eats a lot of fast food believing that eating is only a necessity and minimal he spends minimal time doing it.

Likewise, the aliens also do not appear to have an interest in food. In fact, there are almost no reports of them eating. The lack of eating reports indicates that they might not even be flesh and blood creatures.

Trump claims that he only sleeps a few hours a night, and this has a parallel with aliens from reports which tend to indicate they don't sleep at all. There are no known reports that I have heard.

The two similarities may not mean much because stories of aliens not eating or sleeping, also go along with reports that they can change from one form of being to another instantly, and that they do not seem to age. These examples would indicate that they may not actually be ETs but etheric beings that can take on apparent physical bodies.

OTHER BOOKS ON ITSALLCONNECTED PUBLISHING

GRANT CAMERON - MANAGING MAGIC

GRANT CAMERON - INSPIRED: THE PARANORMAL WORLD OF CREATIVITY

GRANT CAMERON - ALIEN BEDTIME STORIES

GRANT CAMERON - THE CLINTON UFO STORYBOOK

NANCY TREMAINE - SYMBIOSIS

DESTA BARNABE – MIRRORING WORLDS

Itsallconnected contact information:
Itsallconnected Publishing
445 Hudson Street
Winnipeg, Manitoba
Canada R3T OR1

If you wish to be added to my personal mailing list or be informed of new information, please visit me at my website: www.feeltheshift.ca or write to me at barnabed@mymts.net

Index

18 U.S. Code § 798, 4
1997 CIA study, 30
1997 CIA UFO study, 33
Adamski, George, 36, 37, 54, 56, 57, 58, 329
AFFA, 41, 68
AFOSI, 70, 89, 90, 93, 95, 98, 115
Alexander, John, 109, 110, 113, 247, 248, 306, 313
Alien Autopsy, 135, 136
Andrew, Lucille, 46
Andrews, John, 245
Angleton, James, 128
APRO, 64, 92, 93
Area 51, 5, 8, 9, 10, 50, 120, 122, 123, 128, 156, 157, 158, 169, 170, 171, 191, 192, 196, 197, 203, 207, 241, 246, 248, 279
Arnold, Kenneth, 48
Arroyo, Martina, 156
Ashcroft, John, 45
Bamford, James, 151
Barker, Gray, 58
Barnes, Thornton, 157
Barrow, Robert, 58, 80
Barry, Robert, 65, 87
Bassett, Steven, 161, 172, 173, 259
Battelle, 20, 184
Bay, Michael, 81
Bennewitz, Paul, 93, 95, 206, 207, 240
Berliner, Don, 129, 134
Best Possible World Hypothesis, 261, 264
Bigalow, Bob, 20, 113, 286
Bigelow, Bob, 19
Bird Code, 138, 139
Bledsoe, Chris, 283, 313
Blue Book, 12, 21, 50, 54, 55, 58, 64, 67, 68, 88, 100, 177, 242
Blum, Howard, 64, 108, 109, 110, 111, 112, 113, 114, 286, 314
Blum, Ralph and Judy, 64
Bohm, David, 43, 330

Boniardi, Adrian, 266
Brandon, Chase, 152, 153, 154, 155, 280, 307, 310, 311
Brazil, Varginha, 30
Brookings, 184, 339
Brookings Institute, 31, 32
Brookings, Institute, 20, 26
Bruni, Georgina, 62
Burton, Dan, 24
Bush, George H., 74, 75, 124, 126
Bush, George W., 19, 45
Bush, Vannevar, 52, 241, 318, 319
Byrd, Robert, 246
Cacciopo, Anthony, 88
Cage, Nicholas, 74
Canadian Embassy, Washington, 51, 52, 241, 318, 319
Cantwheel, Thomas, 130, 137, 140
Carey, Thomas, 230
Carter, Jimmy, 19, 64, 73, 74, 75, 76, 77, 78, 79, 80, 81, 82, 83, 84, 98, 99, 105, 242, 265, 276
CAUS, 76, 98, 114
Center for American Progress, 168
Center for UFO Studies, 45
Central Intelligence Agency, 45
Chapman, Kenneth, 78
Cheney, Dick, 29, 167
Chereze, Marco Eli, 30
Chop. Al, 58, 59
Clinton, Bill, 10, 24, 34, 35
Clinton, Hillary, 2, 4, 16, 27, 45, 158, 167, 168, 171, 172, 173, 178, 180, 181, 185, 189, 190, 195
Close Encounters of the Third Kind, 81, 82, 83, 84, 85, 91, 339
Coast to Coast AM, 24, 152, 153, 154
Cohen, William, 35
Coleman, Bill, 67, 69, 70, 71, 88, 104, 105, 106, 122
Collins, Bob, 138
Collins, Robert, 90, 103, 104, 114, 117, 121, 126, 127, 133, 244, 250, 254, 306, 307, 323

Collins, Robert, 103
Collins. Robert, 117
Collyns, Napier, 142
Condon, Edward, 78
Condor, 114, 121, 122
Conrad, Mike, 49
Cooper, Tim, 128, 129, 139, 143
Cooper, Timothy, 298, 299
Corso, Philip, 140, 163
Cox, Billy, 7, 69, 155, 339
Cronkite, Walter, 63
Cryptos Conundrum, 152, 310
Cutler, Robert, 107
D'Amato, Dick, 246, 247
Daschle, Tom, 168
Davidson, Leon, 53, 54, 178
Davis, Ronald L., 96
DeLonge, Tom, 2, 23, 31, 44, 113, 164, 178, 186, 187, 189, 190, 191, 192, 195, 196, 197, 198, 199, 200, 201, 202, 203, 204, 205, 206, 207, 208, 209, 211, 212, 213, 214, 216, 218, 219, 220, 222, 223, 224, 228, 229, 230, 231, 233, 236, 246, 260, 276, 282, 286, 297, 298, 299, 312
Disney, 59, 60, 61, 62, 136
Doty, Charles, 89
Doty, Edward, 88
Doty, Richard, 88, 89, 93, 99, 115, 116, 118, 121, 138, 145, 309
du Tertre, Nancy, 247
Dulles, Allen, 54, 140
Durant, Frederick, 63
Edwards, Ernest, 93
Einstein, Albert, 37
Eisenhower Library, 5
Eisenhower, Dwight, 5, 45, 59
Emenegger, Bob, 11, 12, 13, 61, 65, 66, 67, 69, 70, 71, 72, 84, 85, 88, 91, 100, 104, 105, 118
Executive Order, 20, 45, 46, 64, 75, 76, 112
Falcon, 94, 95, 101, 114, 121, 122, 241, 299
FEMA, 248
Firmage, Joe, 135, 142
Fitts, Catherine Austin, 141, 142
Flanagan, William, 82
Flying Saucer Review, 82

FOIA, 75, 76, 102, 103, 115, 171, 245
Ford, Gerald, 19, 74
Foundation for Research into Extraterrestrial Experiences, 22, 23, 220
Fournet, Dewey, 54, 59
FREE, 328
Friedman, Stanton, 61, 95, 101, 102, 103, 106, 107, 122, 129, 130, 134, 240, 241, 248
Frosch, Robert, 78, 79
Gannon, John, 309
Gates, Robert, 127, 241, 298, 306, 307, 308
Gersten, Peter, 28, 76, 98, 339
Gibbons, Jack, 36, 311, 339
Ginna, Bob, 50
Goldwater, Barry, 105
Good, Tim, 125
Good, Timothy, 103, 123, 124
Gorbachev, Mikhail, 108, 126, 237, 328, 329
Graff, Dale, 88, 301
Graham, Lee, 115
Graham, Robbie, 53, 58
Gramley, Allene, 46, 47
Green, Kit, 72, 76, 89, 286, 306, 309
Greene, Clarence, 58, 59
Greer, Steven, 24, 27, 29, 34, 35, 133, 141, 144, 169, 195, 203, 204, 205, 208, 213, 214, 216, 228, 237, 238, 244, 245, 246, 297, 298, 339
Gregory, George T., 58
Haines, Gerald K., 30, 129
Halperin, Mark, 325
Hancock, Herbie, 156
Hellyer, Paul, 248
Helms, Richard, 298
Hennessey, Barry, 115, 146
Hersh, Seymour, 108
Holloman Air Force Base, 11, 66, 84
Holt, Turner, 46
Hoover, J. Edgar, 60
Howe, Linda, 116, 117
Howe, Linda Moulton, 53
Howe. Linda, 117
Hull, Cordell, 47
Hull, Turner, 47

Hurley, William, 115
Hynek, J. Allen, 70, 72, 80, 104, 105, 106, 242
Institute for Defense Analysis, 35
Joel, Billy, 156
John MacArthur Foundation, 70
Johnson, Lyndon, 75
Jones, C.B. Scott, 115
Jones, Cecil B., 36
Keel, John, 58
Kennedy, John, 27, 329
Kerby, Michael, 115, 116
Keyhoe, Major Donald, 22, 23, 26, 51, 52, 55, 276, 277, 318, 319, 339
Keyworth, George, 108
Kimball, Ward, 59, 60, 61, 135, 136
Kimmel, Jimmy, 33, 158
King, Larry, 73, 74
Kirkland AFB, 93, 94, 98, 113, 240
Kissinger, Henry, 39, 307
Knapp, George, 9, 10, 122, 197, 198, 203, 206, 211, 223
Komarek, Ed, 148, 312
Kupperman, Robert, 248
L.A. Study, 81
Lazar, Bob, 9, 10, 122, 123, 157, 199
Lear, John, 9, 10, 117, 122, 199, 242, 243
Levenda, Peter, 206, 207, 209, 212, 239, 246
Lockheed Skunkworks, 133, 259
Lundahl, Arthur, 68, 302, 304, 305
MacArthur Foundation, 12, 70
Maccabee, Bruce, 76, 114, 124
MacLaine, Shirley, 73, 74, 156, 157
Maloney, Don, 135, 136
Maloney, Mike, 61, 62
Manzano Nuclear Weapons Storage Facility, 93
Marcel, Jesse Jr, 246
Marchetti, Victor, 15, 339
Marilyn Monroe Document, 128
McCasland, Neil Gen., 204, 230, 233
McClendon, Sarah, 34
McConnell, Hal, 113
McCurry, Mike, 169
Menger, Howard, 58
Miller, Will, 298
Mitchell, Edgar, 24, 312

MJ-12, 27, 75, 94, 95, 96, 100, 102, 103, 107, 109, 112, 115, 116, 117, 120, 128, 130, 239, 240, 241, 242, 243, 244, 245, 246, 247, 248, 249, 309
Moore, Bill, 89, 91, 92, 93, 94, 95, 96, 97, 98, 99, 100, 101, 102, 103, 104, 106, 107, 112, 113, 115, 116, 117, 118, 120, 121, 122, 126, 145, 197, 208, 240, 241, 242, 245, 248, 286, 288, 297, 298, 299, 304, 306, 307, 311, 316
Mr.Q, 87
NASA, 11, 20, 25, 68, 77, 78, 79, 80, 84, 91, 112, 124, 196, 201, 211, 246
National Science Foundation, 77
Nellis AFB, 115
New York Times, 13, 100, 108, 168, 286
NICAP, 51, 53, 69
Nixon, Richard, 39, 45
NORAD, 38
Norton Air Force Base, 12, 65, 69, 105, 118
NPIC, 124
Obama, Barack, 20, 26, 33, 151, 154, 156, 157, 160, 161, 167, 168, 169, 173, 174, 182, 183, 184, 185, 189, 253, 261, 264, 265, 269, 270, 271, 278, 282, 299
O'Brien, Christopher, 225, 227
Oeschler, Bob, 124, 243
Oldham, Bret, 329
Page, Thornton, 63
Pandolfi, Ron, 113, 126, 127, 128, 131, 132, 145, 146, 260, 263, 282, 283, 309, 311, 312
Pandolfi, Ronald, 22
Paradigm Research Group, 161, 173
Perkins, David, 225, 226
Petersen, John, 133, 141, 298
Peterson, Hans, 56
Peterson, John, 141
Pilkington, Mark, 145, 279
Pillsbury, Mike, 256, 260, 263
Pitts, Bill, 80
Podesta, John, 19, 27, 164, 165, 166, 167, 168, 169, 170, 171, 172, 173,

174, 175, 176, 178, 179, 180, 181, 182, 183, 184, 185, 186, 187, 189, 190, 191, 192, 195, 203, 230, 233, 264, 280, 339
Poston, Gretchen, 82
POTUS Briefing, 148
Powell, Jody, 76
Pratt, Bob, 55, 95, 96, 97, 276
Presidential Daily Briefing, 168
Press, Frank, 78, 81
Prince Philip, 82
Project Aquarius, 94, 95, 96, 109, 307
Puthoff, Hal, 108, 113, 286, 306, 309
Quayle, Dan, 124
Randles, Jenny, 103
Reagan Ronald, 328
Reagan, Ronald, 7, 8, 29, 30, 45, 103, 104, 108, 112, 144, 177, 237
Rich, Ben, 133, 245, 281
Rivas, Ray, 66
Robarge, David, 157
Rockefeller, Laurance, 36, 311
Roddenberry, Gene, 329
Rojas, Alexandro, 230, 239, 248
Rolling Stone Magazine, 197, 260
Roosevelt, Franklin, 45, 46
Roosevelt, Theodore, 15
Rose, Charles, 33
Rositzke, Harry, 301, 306, 307
Roswell, 5, 21, 22, 45, 47, 94, 96, 98, 100, 101, 140, 151, 152, 153, 154, 155, 241, 242, 243, 246, 247, 249, 280, 299
Rouse, Russell, 59
Ruppelt, Edward, 50, 54, 55, 59
Samford, John, 56
Sandler, Allan, 11, 12, 61, 65, 66, 67, 69, 70, 71, 72, 85, 91
Santana, Carlos, 156
Santilli, Ray, 135
Schulhauser, Garnet, 43
Scott, Robert, 106
Scully, Dana, 169
Scully, Frank, 50
Seamans, Robert, 66
Seligman, Michael, 122
Semivan, Jim, 258, 259, 260, 298, 312, 313
Serling, Rod, 71

Serpo, 89, 120, 144, 145, 306, 309
Shandera, Jamie, 95, 102, 103, 104, 106, 107, 116, 122, 138, 139, 240, 241, 245, 248, 299, 306, 307, 311
Shartle, Paul, 65, 66, 70, 71, 118
Skunkworks, 196, 207, 220, 229, 281
Smith, Dan, 127, 128, 163, 264, 282, 297, 298
Smith, Marcia, 74
Smith, Walter B., 140
Smith, Wilbert, 23, 35, 38, 51, 52
Solandt, Omand, 51, 52, 318
Spiegel, Lee, 155
Spielberg, Leah, 85
Spielberg, Steven, 81, 82, 83, 84, 85, 91, 190, 191, 192
SRI, 77, 108, 109, 221, 286
St. Catherine's Island, 265
Stafford, Thomas, 124
Stanford, Ray, 28
Steer, Daymond, 158, 180
Steinman, Bill, 50
Straub, Chris, 128, 130, 131, 257
Strieber, Whitley, 116, 118, 246
Stringfield, Len, 86, 87, 100, 114, 119
Stubblebine, Albert, 113
Tapper, Jake, 171
Terry, 265
The Council of Nine, 329
The Day the Earth Stood Still, 90
The Flying Saucer - Movie, 48
Tomorrowland, 136
Truman Harry S, 33
Truman Library, 5
Truman, Harry S., 45
Trump, Donald, 4, 22, 41, 45, 141, 143, 161, 163, 164, 255, 256, 259, 261, 263, 264, 266, 267, 268, 277, 278, 322, 323, 324, 325, 326, 327, 330, 331, 332, 333
Twinning, Nathan, 107
UAP, 1
UFO Cover up?...Live, 121
UFO Cover-up Live, 89
UFO Cover-up?... Live, 71
UFO Cover-up?...Live, 7
UFO Working Group, 108, 110, 111, 112, 113, 114, 243, 306, 314, 315

UFOs: Friend, Foe, or Fantasy?, 63
UFOs: It has Begun, 91
Vallee, Jacques, 71, 72, 80, 104, 105, 106, 112, 286, 301, 306
Vance, 265
Vandenberg AFB, 68
Victorian, Armen, 110
Walker, Eric, 28, 35, 37, 286
Washington Post, 13, 100, 165, 169, 173, 193
Webre, Alfred, 77
Weinbrenner, George, 67, 70
WikiLeaks, 164, 165, 172, 173, 176, 183, 186, 187, 190, 192, 202, 203, 280

Wilde, Sherry, 332
Wilson, Tom, 244
Wolamin, Barbara, 47
Wood, Bob, 130, 134, 135, 139, 144
Wood, Robert, 113
Wood, Ryan, 130, 139, 144
Woolsey, James, 133, 142, 310
Woolsey, Kames, 141
Wright Patterson AFB, 204, 232
Wurfel, Walter, 73
X-Files, 169
Youngblood, Jennifer, 155
Zanuck, Darryl, 53
Zechel, Todd, 76
Zeissig, Kurt, 69

Endnotes

[1] Alien Zoo, http://archive.alienzoo.com/filmandtv/mikefarrellcoverup.html
[2] http://www.nicap.org/papers/brookings.pdf
[3] UFO Evidence, "Conversations with Donald Keyhoe," http://www.ufoevidence.org/documents/doc1999.htm
[4] Ibid.
[5] Wilbert Smith interview with the *Sudbury Star*.
[6] Dr. Steven Greer's interview on Coast to Coast with Art Bell, August 8/9, 2004
[7] Victor Marchetti, "How the CIA Views the UFO Phenomena." Second Look, Vol. 1, No. 7, May '79
[8] Michael, Donald N., ed. *Proposed Studies on the Implications of Peaceful Space Activities for Human Affairs* by the Brookings Institution to the 87th U.S. Congress, report No. 242. Washington, D.C.: National Aeronautics and Space Administration (1961). Page 225
[9] Peter Gersten "Official Disclosure; A Practical impossibility" Alien Zoo 07/10/2000
[10] Interview of Dr. Eric Walker by Henry Azadehdel, August 18, 1990.
[11] It is rare that Ufologists agree on anything. However, when it comes to abductions all the top researchers agree on one point. Nothing can be done to stop abduction. Joe Montaldo, head of ICAR which has 7,000 contactees, stated "We have found no way to stop a contact." Elaine Douglass, one of the editors for the Journal of Abduction Research stated "The planet is being coerced…they have absolutely no control.
[12] Bernard Haisch, Ph.D., Black Special Access Programs
[13] Michael, Donald N., ed. *Proposed Studies on the Implications of Peaceful Space Activities for Human Affairs* by the Brookings Institution to the 87th U.S. Congress, report No. 242. Washington, D.C.: National Aeronautics and Space Administration (1961).
[14] Alexander, Victoria, "The Impact of UFOs and Their Occupants on Religion" report produced for the Bigelow Foundation 1994
[15] Greer, Steven, "Understanding UFO Secrecy" http://extraterrestrial-life.net/Understanding_UFO_secrecy.htm
[16] Memo – Wilbert Smith to the Controller of Telecommunications: Department of Transport, November 21, 1950.
[17] Letter – C.B. Scott Jones to dr. Jack Gibbons, 10/17/94
[18] http://www.presidentialufo.com/dwight-d-eisenhower/472-eisenhower-and-his-alien-contacts-part-1
[19] John Podesta, "John Podesta Remarks at Princeton University," March 2004, https://www.americanprogress.org/issues/general/news/2004/03/10/638/john-podesta-remarks-at-princeton-university/
[20] Interview with Arnold's daughter Kim done by James Fox for his movie "710."
[21] Robbie Graham and Matthew Alford, "Close Encounters with the Pentagon," http://www.presidentialufo.com/disney-ufo-connection/267-close-encounters-with-the-pentagon
[22] Letter – Wilbert Smith to Gordon Cox, January 3, 1951.
[23] Letter – Wilbert Smith to Major Donald Keyhoe, November 24, 1950.) Copy of

letter from Wilbert Smith files at the University of Ottawa Archives.)
[24] Memo – Wilbert Smith to Dr. Omond Solandt, November 24, 1950. (From Smith files.)
[25] Telephone Interview – Dr. Omond Solandt by Dr. Armen Victorian, June 8, 1991.
[26] In the November 1950, Top-Secret memo from Wilbert Smith to the Deputy Minister of the Department of Transport Smith reported that he had been informed through classified channels that "a small group headed by Dr. Vannevar Bush was looking into the modus operandi of the saucers."
[27] Letter - Gordon E. Cox to Wilbert Smith, January 6, 1951 (written on Canadian Embassy stationary, and found in the Wilbert Smith files) Also see Letter, Wilbert Smith to Gordon Cox, January 3, 1951.
[28] Ibid.
[29] Phil Coppens, "A lone chemist's quest to expose the UFO cover-up," http://www.philipcoppens.com/davidson.html
[30] http://www.presidentialufo.com/dwight-d-eisenhower/472-eisenhower-and-his-alien-contacts-part-152
[31] Ibid.
[32] Edward Ruppelt, "The Report on Unidentified Flying Objects," Page 87.
[33] UFO Evidence, "Conversations with Donald Keyhoe," http://www.ufoevidence.org/documents/doc1999.htm
[34] Video segment describing Adamski Kennedy meeting, https://www.youtube.com/watch?v=9ZcGnuuV23g#t=226
[35] Lou Zinsstag & Timothy Good, "George Adamski: The Untold Story," page 154
[36] Nicholas Redfern, "The FBI Files," page 305.
[37] Ibid.
[38] Alex Constantine, "Mind Control and UFOs," http://www.beyondweird.com/ufos/Bruce_Walton_The_Underground_Nazi_Invasion_27.html
[39] Robbie Graham and Matthew Alford , "Close Encounters with the Pentagon."
[40] Robert Barrow, "UFO Revisited," 1976, http://www.nicap.org/ufochop1.htm
[41] Mark Pilkington, Mirage Men," page 282.
[42] Grant Cameron, http://www.presidentialufo.com/jimmy-carter/93-jimmy-carter-ufo
[43] For the full story told by Marcia Smith to Danny Sheehan go to http://presidentialufo.com/jimmy-carter/98-the-marcia-smith-story-the-presidents-ufo-study
[44] Alfred Webre, "Carter White House Extraterrestrial Communication Study," http://human-science-research.blogspot.ca/2005/05/carter-white-house-extraterrestrial.html
[45] Disclosure Project, "Carter White House Denied UFO Info," http://www.ufoevidence.org/documents/doc944.htm
[46] Robbie Graham and Matthew Alford , "Close Encounters with the Pentagon," http://www.presidentialufo.com/disney-ufo-connection/267-close-encounters-with-the-pentagon
[47] Close Encounters promotional interview, available at: http://www.youtube.com/watch?v=BACQX-WzWeA
[48] John Baxter, "Steven Spielberg," HarperCollins 1996, page 109.
[49] In a 2007 interview Graff denied Kellerstrass's claims and doesn't know why he

would have made up such a thing. He did admit to working for Kellerstrass.

[50] David Rudiak, "Cpt. Lawrence H. Dyvad and Major Edward A. Doty," http://roswellproof.homestead.com/Dyvad1951.html

[51] Robert M. Collins & Richard C. Doty, "Exempt from Disclosure," Peregrine Communications, 2005, page 71.

[52] Robert Collins, "Exempt from Disclosure," Peregrine Communications, page 71.

[53] Bill Moore and Jamie Shandera, "The MJ-12 Documents: An Analytical Report Pre-Publication Draft July 1990 pages 29-30.

[54] Ibid page 42.

[55] CIA publishes its history, nearly 13 million pages of documents online" http://www.cnn.com/2017/01/17/politics/cia-documents-online/index.html

[56] Alien Zoo, http://archive.alienzoo.com/filmandtv/mikefarrellcoverup.html

[57] This is according to researcher Armen Victorian, http://ufoupdateslist.com/1997/sep/m14-004.shtml

[58] Tim Good, "Alien Liaison," Century Publishing 1991, page 199

[59] Ibid page 108.

[60] Ed Komarek, "Ron Enters Navy and Source A's Arena," http://www.ufodigest.com/news/0309/arena2.php

[61] " CIA publishes its history, nearly 13 million pages of documents online" http://www.cnn.com/2017/01/17/politics/cia-documents-online/index.html

[62] "CEO Quits Job Over UFO Views" *San Francisco Gate*, January 9, 1999 https://www.google.com/amp/www.sfgate.com/bayarea/amp/CEO-Quits-Job-Over-UFO-Views-Advances-in-2952834.php

[63] Greg Bishop, "Project Beta," Paraview , 2005, page 210.

[64] Robert C. Collins & Richard Doty," Exempt from Disclosure," Peregrine Publications, 2005, page 110.

[65] Ibid. One man, and one man alone appears to occupy the best possible position to probe into the facts, fantasies, and fallacies behind the real-life "X-Files" of UFOs, alien visitors, spies, lies, and polygraph tape.

[66] Catherine Fitts, "The $64 Question: What's Up With the Black Budget?" http://www.scoop.co.nz/stories/HL0209/S00126.htm

[67] Mark Pilkington, "The Mirage Men" Skyhorse Publishing, 2010, Page 278

[68] Gary Bekkum, "UFO Meeting at the CIA," http://www.starpod.us/2013/04/24/ufo-meeting-at-cia/#.WIuQOY-cHIU

[69] Ed Komarek, "Ron Enters Navy and Source A's Arena," http://www.ufodigest.com/news/0309/arena2.php

[70] RAM UNIVERSAL GRAVONICS, Potus Briefing; Executive Summary," 2009

[71] Ed Komarek, "ibid

[72] Gordon Novel, "Ram Universal Gravonics: Executive Summary, 2009

[73] Gordon Novel interview by Alan Steinfeld - New Realities - 2 June 2010, https://www.youtube.com/watch?v=AbKaWuwDkuk

[74] Grant Cameron, "Did Obama Fumble the UFO Cover-up?" http://www.presidentialufo.com/articles-a-papers/418-did-obama-fumble-the-ufo-cover-up

[75] Linda Howe, "Breaking — Why John Burroughs's Medical Records Are "Classified", http://redpillreports.com/red-pill-reports/breaking-why-john-burroughss-medical-records-are-classified/

[76] Alejandro Rojas, "Analysis of another Obama alien comment," http://www.openminds.tv/analysis-of-another-obama-alien-comment/36498

[77] John Podesta, "John Podesta Remarks at Princeton University," March 10, 2004, https://www.americanprogress.org/issues/general/news/2004/03/10/638/john-podesta-remarks-at-princeton-university/

[78] Martha Joynt Kumar, "Before the Oath: How George W. Bush and Barack Obama Managed a Transfer of Power" page 110

[79] Peter Baker, "For Hillary, John Podesta is a Right Hand with a Punch," February 15, 2015, http://www.nytimes.com/2015/02/16/us/politics/for-hillary-clinton-john-podesta-brings-a-right-hand-with-punch.html?_r=0

[80] Sirius Disclosure, "The Story behind Dr. Greer's Obama Briefing," February 15, 2015

[81] Grant Cameron, "John Podesta : Clinton's X-Files Man," http://www.presidentialufo.com/old_site/john_podesta.htm

[82] *Washington Post,* September 30, 1998.

[83] Knox College Commencement Address --John Podesta -- White House Deputy Chief of Staff, June 6, 1998, http://departments.knox.edu/newsarchive/news_events/releases_1997-98/Podesta_Commencement.html

[84] Ibid.

[85] John Podesta, 2002 press conference organized by the Coalition for Freedom of Information, Washington Press Club

[86] David Twichell, "Global Implications of the UFO Reality," page 11.

[87] Hearing before the Subcommittee on Science, Technology, and Space of the Committee on Commerce, Science, and Transportation United States Senate, One Hundred and Seventh Congress, Second Session, May 22, 2002.

[88] Bob Fish to John Podesta, "Subject: Leslie Kean book comment,"   2015-03-05 21:11

[89] Leslie Kean to John Podesta, "Subject: Re: Leslie Kean book - DSP program," 2015-03-07 18:28.

[90] Bob Fish to John Podesta, "Subject: Leslie Kean book - Blue Book ," 2015-03-06 18:10.

[91] Davidson to Podesta, 2015-11-13.

[92] Podesta to Davidson, 2015-11-13.

[93] https://Wiki-Leaks.org/podesta-emails/emailid/47438

[94] Coast To Coast AM interview of Tom DeLonge by George Knapp, March 27, 2016.

[95] Email, Tom DeLonge to John Podesta, 2015-10-26.

[96] https://Wiki-Leaks.org/podesta-emails/emailid/4804

[97] Daniel Krebs, "Tom DeLonge on Podesta Emails: 'Wiki-Leaks Messed Some Important Stuff Up' http://www.rollingstone.com/music/news/tom-DeLonge-comments-on-leaked-podesta-emails-about-ufos-w446276

[98] DeLonge interview with George Knapp March 27, 2016, Coast to Coast AM.

[99] Patrick Doyle, "Inside Tom DeLonge's UFO Obsession, Blink-182 Turmoil," http://www.rollingstone.com/music/news/inside-tom-DeLonges-ufo-obsession-blink-182-turmoil-20160427

[100] Tom DeLonge, Coast to Coast AM, December 18, 2011.

[101] Kerry Cassidy and Bill Ryan , "Flying into the Sun with John Lear: A video

interview with John Lear, Las Vegas, August 2006.
[102] Lisa Eckhart, "Blink 182's Tom DeLonge Has a Conspiracy Theory Website," http://www.deathandtaxesmag.com/127533/blink-182s-tom-DeLonge-has-a-conspiracy-theory-website/
[103] Tom DeLonge, Coast to Coast AM, December 18, 2011.
[104] Adrienne Jeffries, "Is Tom DeLonge for Real About this UFO Stuff? Motherboard Investigates," http://motherboard.vice.com/read/is-tom-DeLonge-for-real-about-this-ufo-stuff-motherboard-investigates
[105] Tom DeLonge, on Coast to Coast AM, December 18, 2011.
[106] Tom DeLonge, Coast to Coast AM, December 18, 2011.
[107] Ibid
[108] Steven Greer, "Cory Goode Deceived? Milabs, William Tompkins, Tom DeLonge and Gaia TV," https://www.youtube.com/watch?v=2TrWUsnhjuo
[109] March 27, 2016, Coast to Coast AM.
[110] DeLonge interview with George Knapp March 27, 2016, Coast to Coast AM
[111] "Corey Goode Deceived? MILABs, William Tompkins, Tom Delong, and Gaia TV - Dr. Steven Greer," https://www.youtube.com/watch?v=2TrWUsnhjuo
[112] Testimony of Dr. Carol Rosin, December 2000, http://www.bibliotecapleyades.net/exopolitica/esp_exopolitics_ZCab.htm
[113] March 27, 2016, Coast to Coast AM.
[114] Ibid.
[115] Ken Kress: Central Intelligence Agency Studies in Intelligence Vol 21, No. 4 Winter 1977 – Source: The CIA Star Gate Collection Files.
[116] David Jacobs on Abduction – Video Camera, http://aliencases.conforums.com/index.cgi?board=abduction&action=print&num=1192706634
[117] March 27, 2016, Coast to Coast AM.
[118] Articles, and a link to Robert Hastings book and documentary on the subject of UFOs and nukes can be found at his website http://www.ufohastings.com/
[119] From Robert Hastings website, http://www.ufohastings.com/
[120] "Bovine serum albumin (BSA) can replace patient serum as a protein source in an in vitro fertilization (IVF) program." https://www.ncbi.nlm.nih.gov/pubmed/2794734
[121] "Bovine Spongiform Encephalopathy (BSE) Questions and Answers" http://www.fda.gov/BiologicsBloodVaccines/SafetyAvailability/ucm111482.htm
[122] Podcast UFO, "Chris O'Brien, Experiencer, UFOs, Cattle Mutilations More, 11-23-2016," https://www.youtube.com/watch?v=x-EDF_XNOvg
[123] Christopher O'Brien, "Secrets of the Mysterious Valley," page 429.
[124] UFO Podcast interview with Chris O'Brien, November 24, 2016, https://www.youtube.com/watch?v=x-EDF_XNOvg
[125] Taylor gave one of the most popular TED talks of all times. To read about the right left barin aspect of her talk read "A brain scientist discovered Nirvana–or inner peace–in the right side of the brain." at https://daringtolivefully.com/jill-bolte-taylor
[126] Sirius Disclosure Interview with U.S. Marine Corporal Jonathan Van Weygandt: https://youtu.be/G2m_-6Wep7k
[127] An earlier director of Skunk Works Ben Rich also stated non-local consciousness was the key when asked how UFOs got here after a lecture in March 1993.
[128] Alejandro Rojas, "Hillary campaign manager held UFO meeting with USAF

generals, rock star and top secret aircraft developer,"
http://www.openminds.tv/hillary-campaign-manager-held-ufo-meeting-with-usaf-generals-rock-star-and-top-secret-aircraft-developer/38698

[129] Email, DeLonge to Podesta, February 22, 2016.
[130] Email, Tom DeLonge to John Podesta, January 25, 2016.
[131] Email, DeLonge to Podesta September 24, 2015.
[132] Email, Steve Sebelius to George Knapp, February 13, 2016.
[133] Email, George Knapp to Tom DeLonge February 13, 2016.
[134] Dr. Michael Salla, Was UN Secretary General Abducted by Aliens in 1989 to Prevent ET Disclosure? http://exopolitics.org/was-un-secretary-general-abducted-by-aliens-in-1989-to-prevent-et-disclosure/
[135] http://www.huffingtonpost.com/alejandro-rojas/majestic-12-is-this-legen_b_5447618.html
[136] http://kevinrandle.blogspot.ca/2014/06/mj-12-beginning.html
[137] Good, Timothy, Above Top Secret: The Worldwide UFO Cover-up, Sidgwick & Jackson, London, 1987, p. 359.
[138] Ann Eller, Dragon in the Sky: Prophecy from the Stars," p. 26-27.
[139] Tim Good, "Alien Liaison/Alien Contact." Alien Liaison/Alien Contact.
[140] Dr. Steven Greer & Ret. Commander Willard Miller : Insight Into New Energy - (February 8th, 2013), https://www.youtube.com/watch?v=XdoHAeaTc2A.
[141] Peter Levenda interview with Jason McClelland, December 1, 2016.
[142] http://www.bibliotecapleyades.net/sociopolitica/sociopol_greer09.htm
[143] John Alexander Interview with Nancy du Tertre June 15, 2013 http://hotleadscoldcases.podomatic.com/
[144] June 13, 2013 Nancy du Tertre Interview with John Alexander
[145] Gus Russo, "The Real X-Files - Is Uncle Sam a Closet UFOlogist?" http://www.realityuncovered.net/ufology/articles/realxfiles.php
[146] Gary Bekkum, "The Government Exorcist: GOD, Dan, IT, CIA and Ron Pandolfi," http://www.starpod.us/2010/12/27/the-government-exorcist-god-dan-it-cia-and-ron-pandolfi/#.WIOhzZKly00
[147] Gary Bekkum, "Dan Smith and the Best Possible World, Part one," http://www.starpod.us/2012/10/12/dan-smith-interview-part-one/#.WIPG3pKly00
[148] Maureen Dowd, "We're Not alone," *New York Times*, June 25, 1997.
[149] Dan Smith post, *Open Minds Forum*, January 25, 2017.
[150] Tom DeLonge, https://www.instagram.com/p/BG79EYeLuwv/
[151] Dan Smith, *Open Minds Forum*, February 23, 2017.
[152] *Open Minds Forum*, http://openmindsforum.forumotion.com/t251p650-hello-cy-omf-ii-part-2
[153] Dan Smith, *Open Minds Forum*, http://openmindsforum.forumotion.com/t251p675-hello-cy-omf-ii-part-2
[154] Ibid.
[155] Dan Smith, *Open Minds Forum*, February 23, 2017.
[156] *Open Minds Forum*, http://openmindsforum.forumotion.com/t251p650-hello-cy-omf-ii-part-2
[157] Dan Smith, *Open Minds Forum*, http://openmindsforum.forumotion.com/t251p675-hello-cy-omf-ii-part-2
[158] Ibid.
[159] Jim Semivan, foreword to the Paperback Edition of Tom DeLonge's book "Sekret

Machines: Chasing Shadows."
[160] UFO Evidence, "Conversations with Donald Keyhoe," http://www.ufoevidence.org/documents/doc1999.htm
[161] Reinerio Hernandez, J.D., M.C.P., "Contact with Non Human Intelligence and the Quantum Hologram Theory of Consciousness:" http://www.experiencer.org/ Toward an Integration of the Contact Modalities
[162] Ray Williams, "Why We Love Bad News More Than Good News, " https://www.psychologytoday.com/blog/wired-success/201411/why-we-love-bad-news-more-good-news
[163] Mark Pilkington, Mirage Men," page 296.
[164] Mark Pilkington, Mirage Men," page 280-283
[165] Bill Moore, "The MJ-12 Documents: An Analytical Report." Never published
[166] http://necrometrics.com/20c5m.htm
[167] http://necrometrics.com/20c5m.htm
[168] Some will claim that Moore was working for the government, but that is not accurate. It would be more accurate to say that he worked with the government, and that he exchanged reporting on other UFO researchers, and passing at one document which was used in a counterintelligence effort against businessman/researcher Paul Bennewitz, in exchange for information about how the government managed the UFO program. There is no evidence he was ever paid for what he did.
[169] After he quit the UFO field Bill Moore admitted that he may have been used and that the information he received may not have been true. At the same time he told me in a letter that the government secret was way beyond anyone's ability to unravel. He basically said, with ego intact, that he had tried to get to the bottom of what the government was doing, and because he couldn't do it, no one else had a chance of doing it.
[170] New York Times, "Air Force Order on 'Saucers' Cited' February 28th 1960.
[171] W. Todd Zechel, "The CIA's Most Secret UFO Counterintelligence Project: The Condon Committee," http://www.paradigmresearchgroup.org/article-zechel-1.html
[172] Gary Bekkum, "The Falcon and the Core UFO Story" http://www.starpod.org/news/1201181.htm
[173] Steven Greer and John DeCamp, "Why Was Former CIA Director William Colby Assassinated?" https://archive.org/details/WhyWasFormerCiaDirectorWilliamColbyAssassinated
[174] Gus Russo, "The Real X-Files - Is Uncle Sam a Closet UFOlogist?" http://www.realityuncovered.net/ufology/articles/realxfiles.php
[175] Ryan Dube, "Christopher "Kit" Green," http://www.realityuncovered.net/ufology/articles/kitgreen.php
[176] Billy Cox, "Brandon's Roswell claims new to Gates," http://devoid.blogs.heraldtribune.com/13566/brandons-roswell-claims-new-to-gates/
[177] Others at the website realityuncovered.net claimed they had evidence fingering five people at the source of Serpo including Christopher Green. Dr. Harold Puthoff, and Richard Doty.
[178] NGO Study Center, "Supranational society: Masterlist of 1,300 NGOs and the top 400 people in them," https://isgp-studies.com/ngo-list-foundations-and-think-tanks-worldwide
[179] Håkan Blomqvist´s blog, September 12, 2015
[180] Howard Blum, "Out there: the government's secret quest for extraterrestrials,"

page 211
[181] Ibid
[182] FREE Survey Phase 2 results, Question 226, http://et.websitesbyjim.com/wp-content/uploads/2016/08/Phase-2-Questions-1-257.pdf

CPSIA information can be obtained
at www.ICGtesting.com
Printed in the USA
FSHW022108070219
55557FS